T

Tabloid Century

The Popular Press in Britain, 1896 to the present

Adrian Bingham and Martin Conboy

Peter Lang Oxford

Peter Lang Ltd
International Academic Publishers
52 St Giles, Oxford, OX1 3LU
United Kingdom

www.peterlang.com

A catalogue record for this book is available from the British Library

Library of Congress Control Number: 2015933539

ISBN 978-1-906165-32-1 (print)
ISBN 978-3-0353-0700-9 (eBook)

Printed in the United Kingdom

Contents

vi

Preface

The popular newspaper was one of the most successful products of the twentieth century. After the launch of the *Daily Mail* in 1896, the habit of regular newspaper reading gradually spread so that by the early 1950s around 85 per cent of the population saw a paper every day and the market was effectively saturated. The British public consumed more newspapers per head than any other nation, and the leading London titles, such as the *Daily Mirror*, the *Daily Express* and the *News of the World*, achieved some of the biggest circulations in the world. Although readership levels declined in the second half of the century as competition from other media forms, particularly television, intensified, newspapers retained much of their political and cultural power, and they shaped British society in countless ways. They provided millions of people with one of their main windows on the world. This book examines how the popular press represented Britain to its readers, not only narrating major public events such as wars, political campaigns and coronations, but also describing and defining personal and social identities such as gender, sexuality, class and race. This mixture of public and private, serious and trivial, lies at the heart of the tabloid model and helps to explain its popularity and resilience.

There are, of course, plenty of histories of the press, but most of them focus on the production of newspapers – on the owners, editors, reporters and printers who wrote, packaged or paid for the news – rather than on their content. Those that do examine content tend to look at specific journalistic genres, such as war reporting, or limit their focus to particular titles or periods. This book sets out some of the broad patterns of continuity and change in popular newspaper content over the twentieth century in the belief that understanding the political and social impact of the press requires an awareness of this wider context. We hope that it will be of value both to readers interested in the press's past, and also to those wanting to learn more about the trajectories that have led to the high-profile controversies and debates of recent years. Such expansiveness inevitably means much has had to be omitted or passed over quickly. We have generally focused our attention on the market-leading national newspapers, and on dailies more than Sundays. Some important types of content, such as sports reporting or crime news, receive little coverage, and we have not been able to explore national or regional variation in the detail we would have liked. We hope that the payback for such selectivity is a breadth rarely found in other volumes.

This book attempts another difficult balancing act. We have tried to pitch our writing some way between the chatty reminiscences found in many Fleet Street memoirs, and the dense and self-referential writing of much of the academic literature. We have tried to synthesise the scholarly work in a serious but accessible way, adding plenty of colour from the tabloids themselves. For those interested in delving more deeply, we have included references to the best work in the field.

This book has taken longer to write than we had anticipated, and we'd like to thank everyone at Peter Lang, especially Lucy Melville, for her patience. The Departments of History and Journalism Studies at the University of Sheffield have provided pleasant and friendly working environments, and the events hosted by our Centre for the Study of Journalism and History have brought plenty of intellectual stimulation from many scholars working in this area. On a personal note, Adrian would like to thank Felicity, Anna and Thea for all their love, support and smiles, and Martin has benefitted as always from the dynamic patience of Lara and Simone.

Introduction: The Rise of the Tabloid

On 1 January 1901 the readers of the New York *World* woke up to find that their newspaper had shrunk. Some thought it was a hoax, but it was actually an experiment – and a sign of the future. Joseph Pulitzer, the *World*'s owner and one of the leading figures in American journalism, had invited Alfred Harmsworth, a thirty-five year-old Anglo-Irish businessman who had made his name in Britain by launching the *Daily Mail* five years earlier, to take control of his paper on what contemporaries regarded as the first day of the twentieth century. Harmsworth decided to take the opportunity to test his ideas about how journalism could be transformed for the modern age. He reduced the newspaper pages to half their usual broadsheet size, and told reporters to boil down stories to no more than 250 words. The front page declared the paper was 'The Daily Time-Saver', providing 'All the News in Sixty Seconds'. Harmsworth told readers that 'by my system of condensed or tabloid journalism hundreds of working hours can be saved each year'. The term 'tabloid', a contraction of 'tablet' and 'alkaloid', had been copyrighted by the pharmaceutical company Burroughs Wellcome and Co. in 1884 to advertise compressed medicines in the form of small tablets. It now provided the perfect metaphor for Harmsworth's paper, conveying the combination of reduced dimensions with speed and power. The *World* was sold out by 9 in the morning and extra editions were printed as curious readers flocked to see 'the 20th Century newspaper'. Professional journalists were sceptical, and the experiment would not be soon repeated. The world was not yet ready for the 'tabloid', and its punchy, digested journalism, but it was a powerful marker of things to come.[1]

The tabloid that eventually dominated twentieth-century British journalism would combine many of the innovations of Harmsworth's *World*, including its size and emphasis on concise writing, with a number of other populist elements: chatty, vernacular language, a visual style based on bold black headlines and eye-catching images, and content driven by the insistent pursuit of sensation and scandal. It emerged from an extended process of editorial experimentation and consumer testing over several decades. Harmsworth's *Daily Mail*, Britain's first morning daily newspaper aimed squarely at the mass market, was full of brightly written human-interest stories, but it retained a broadsheet format and a respectably conservative visual appearance. In 1903, Harmsworth tried something different, launching the *Daily Mirror* in the half-broadsheet size, and using more illustration, but its conventional language and tone marked it out as a publication aimed at a (lower) middle-class readership. It was not until the *Mirror* underwent an editorial reinvention in the mid-1930s, drawing inspiration from the brash, populist approach of American city papers such as the New York *Illustrated Daily News*, that it adopted a recognisably tabloid style. For all its subsequent popularity – the *Mirror's* circulation steadily rose and it became Britain's best-selling paper in 1949 – its main rivals, the *Express*, the *Mail* and the *Herald*, all stuck to their broadsheet format. It was only with the introduction of an even more brazenly sensational title, Rupert Murdoch's *Sun*, in 1969, that a wave of tabloidisation occurred. By the end of the 1970s, the popular market had fully converted to the tabloid model. Indeed, so appealing was the new format that by 2004, the most stolidly traditional paper of all, *The Times*, had adopted it, even if it preferred to describe itself as a 'compact' to underline its stylistic distance from the tabloid 'red-tops'.

This book explores how the tabloids reported the century that they dominated. We employ a broad definition of the term 'tabloid' to include all the papers that embraced the populism, accessibility and brevity of Harmsworth's *World*, whatever the size of their pages or their typographical style. Before examining the tabloids' content, though, we offer a brief overview of the editorial strategies, commercial pressures and audience expectations that did so much to shape it. This Introduction starts by outlining the deep cultural roots of the tabloids, before turning to the three waves of editorial innovation – at the turn of the twentieth century, and then during the 1930s and the 1970s – that led to the triumph of the tabloid model.

The cultural roots of the tabloid

The popular dynamic which is at the heart of tabloid journalism preceded the emergence of tabloid newspapers or even popular mass newspapers. With the development of printing in Western Europe from the fifteenth century, a range of newssheets and political pamphlets was targeted at the landowning and commercial classes. The market for these relatively expensive offerings was limited, however, and printers seeking to make money turned to chapbooks and printed ballad broadsheets which were distributed on a wider scale. Cuckolds, scolding wives, terrifying monsters, freaks of nature, saints and kings, great heroes in battle, villains, murderers and moral exemplars were all common fare. These characters took their place within narrative structures which provided a great deal of continuity with the established patterns of popular culture. Printed ballads, in particular, could generate profit for both printer and hawker by combining entertainment with a commentary on topical events. They have been described as 'a kind of musical journalism, the forerunner of the modern prose newspapers, and a continuation of the folk tradition of minstrelsy'.[2]

Early popular printed materials, like the modern tabloid, sought to make themselves accessible and, where possible, visually appealing. At a time when literacy rates were low, they were designed to be sung or read out loud to groups of listeners. Throughout the sixteenth and seventeenth centuries, there was a great deal of continuity between popular printed material and the characteristics of the spoken language of the ordinary people. Cheap woodcut illustrations were often included to attract those with limited or no reading ability. These ephemeral printed ballads and almanacs, sold on the streets and at markets, provided a carefully reworked version of everyday life. They claimed the allegiance of the people commercially and even politically.[3]

Until the early nineteenth century, regular periodical print publications, such as newspapers and magazines, were largely restricted to the wealthier classes, not least because their price was inflated by the various duties and taxes imposed by a state fearful of the circulation of popular literature. These included a stamp duty imposed on every page, thereby encouraging the production of densely packed broadsheets, as well as advertising and paper duties. The poor had to make do with more ephemeral literature. It was only in the Napoleonic period that weekly newspapers targeted readers outside the traditional circles of political and commercial elites, as publishers and editors such as Thomas Wooler, William Cobbett and Richard Carlile engaged in a critique of political corruption and the plight of the rural poor. They constituted highly successful attempts at addressing the common people, representing them and their concerns in a direct vernacular aimed at constructing a tangible, effective and radical political community. These papers, cheap, popular and politically radical, were swept away by the passing of the draconian Six Acts in 1819 but they left their mark in the fabric of the popular periodicals which followed. William Benbow, who had been an agent for Cobbett, set up the *Rambler's Magazine* in 1822, which published material in the French libertine tradition, illustrating the sexual depravity of the aristocracy and clergy. John Cleave's *Weekly Police Gazette* from 1834 was a short-lived but influential indication of how the sensationalism of the courts could provide scandal and entertainment for working-class readers. Both sexual and criminal sensationalism could stake claims for radical intent in that they exposed the wrongdoings and corruption of the establishment.

The radical tradition, which reemerged in the 1830s, found that its clear political goals were often compromised by the desire for the sensational which had become established within the popular press. The radical publisher Henry Hetherington introduced a periodical broadsheet entitled *Twopenny Dispatch* which provided a diet of 'Fun and frolic', 'Police intelligence', 'Murders, Rapes, Suicides, Burnings, Maimings, Theatricals, Races, Pugilism' – in effect, everything which tickled the popular public's fancy. But the more seriously committed, class-oriented newspaper had not disappeared from the streets. The Chartist *Northern Star* was published successfully between 1837 and 1852 with a circulation rising to half a million. Identifiably a newspaper rather than a political pamphlet, it helped to focus and sustain the Chartist community by providing information about the movement, fund-raising and supporting petitions to Parliament. Using a didactic rhetoric which claimed to speak on behalf of the working-class readership and assist in the improvement of their lot, it drew upon and extended the political traditions of the open-air political meeting.[4]

In the middle of the nineteenth century, changes to Britain's economic, political and cultural environment created new commercial opportunities for publishers. Greater prosperity increased the spending power of many ordinary families, while the emergence of a range of new technologies, including the train, the telegraph, steam printing and the rotating cylinder press, enabled news to be collected, printed and circulated far more efficiently than ever before. Over the same period, the state gradually lifted the heavy burden it had imposed on the market. Advertising duty was halved in 1833, and abolished in 1853; paper duty was halved in 1836 and abolished in 1861, and stamp duty was reduced by three-quarters in 1836 and abolished in 1855. A new wave of publishers emerged who drew on earlier radical rhetoric but diluted it with entertainment to appeal to the tastes of advertisers and less directly political readers. Sunday newspapers targeted working-class families looking for reading material on their day of leisure. They combined the vernacular and the sensational with aspects of popular theatre and fictional narratives, enlivened with copious woodcut and engraved illustrations. The best known and most commercially successful of these papers were *Lloyd's Illustrated London Newspaper* (1842, subsequently renamed *Lloyd's Weekly News*), the *News of the World* (1843) and *Reynolds's Weekly Newspaper* (1850). From this point on, any newspaper aiming at a popular audience had to design a market-orientated mode of address to its readers: entertaining them, informing them but most of all appealing to them in a language that represented their everyday experiences.

By the final decades of the century, the commercial possibilities of mass publishing were moving beyond the Sunday market into weekly magazines and then daily newspapers. One of the most influential and successful experiments was George Newnes's penny weekly *Tit-Bits*, launched in 1881, and soon reaching a circulation of around 700,000 copies. The magazine provided brief articles on a wide range of subjects designed for easy reading – dismissed by condescending contemporaries as 'snippet-journalism' – and sought to develop what has been identified as a 'sympathetic intimacy', a direct, personal and informal form of address which became central to the popular market. Alfred Harmsworth himself was an early contributor, and his first entry into the world of publishing, in June 1888 at the age of 22, was to launch an imitator, *Answers to Correspondents*. *Answers* supplied intriguing and unusual nuggets of information in response to readers' questions, and was soon a resounding success: within four years it was selling over a million copies a week. The magazine's profitability enabled Harmsworth to set up a company, Amalgamated Press, to launch other titles, including the pictorial magazine *Comic Cuts*, and the women's weekly, *Home Chat*.[5]

National and local daily evening newspapers also started to develop brighter, more accessible and less politically dominated content – an approach that the critic Matthew Arnold famously described in 1888 as the 'new journalism' – for a broader readership. Its most famous proponent was W. T. Stead, who from 1883 was the editor of the *Pall Mall Gazette*, a London evening paper. Stead introduced into the British market innovative American techniques in interviewing, cross-head layout and aggressive self-promotion. His most striking editorial strategy, though, was to run sensational campaigns, most notoriously the 'Maiden Tribute of Modern Babylon' series of 1885 investigating child prostitution, which ended with Stead in prison for procuring a thirteen-year-old girl. Other titles, such as T. P. O'Connor's *Star*, followed suit, providing sensational daily journalism with a radical edge, and covering stories such as the 'Jack the Ripper' murders with a grim relish.

This new and vibrant style of journalism changed the relationship between newspaper and reader. Newspapers cultivated the impression of a close bond with their readers, assisted by sub-editors ensuring a more consistent 'voice' across the publication and journalists adopting a more personalised tone. The popular press in Britain had, by the late nineteenth century, shifted from representing the collective interests of working people as a way of enabling political change to expressing those interests within market-orientated imperatives. They sought to appeal to the tastes of ordinary readers, report on their pastimes and entertainments, and voice their frustrations and complaints, with a more individualistic, rather than class-based, form of address. For all the focus on a 'new journalism', though, newspapers and magazines retained many of the longer traditions of popular print culture which had already proved their commercial worth.

The emergence of the modern popular daily press

Having amassed a considerable fortune, as well as a wealth of experience, in eight years of publishing popular magazines, Alfred Harmsworth in May 1896 transformed the newspaper business with the launch of the *Daily Mail*. Harmsworth applied the populist techniques previously found in the Sunday and evening press, weekly magazines, and American journalism, to the more traditional and conventional, but more high profile and culturally significant, morning newspaper market. Hamilton Fyfe, a trusted contributor, recalled that 'the Chief' wanted his new paper to 'touch life at every point': 'He saw that very few people wanted politics, while a very large number wanted to be entertained, diverted, relieved a little while from the pressure or tedium of their everyday affairs.' Like Stead, Harmsworth sought to create news as well as reporting it by launching campaigns on a wide range of issues – from the type of bread that people ate to the hats they wore – generating controversy and publicising his papers in the process. He also reached out explicitly to female readers, a previously neglected newspaper audience, by ensuring that the *Mail* provided the kinds of material that had been successful in women's publications – features on fashion and domestic life, serialised fiction, and a gossip column. At the same time, he understood that the morning daily market had particular requirements and expectations, so he ensured that the *Mail* had a 'respectable' appearance in terms of typography and illustration. He accepted the convention of placing advertisements, rather than news, on the front page. Harmsworth wanted to the *Mail* to be popular, but not vulgar, and he disapproved of the use of slang and Americanisms.[6]

As significant as the *Mail's* editorial template was the business model that it developed, in which high levels of investment in staff, technology and publicity were matched by large revenues from mass readership and lucrative advertising. Harmsworth changed the economic basis of the daily press by placing much greater emphasis on the competition for circulation, printing 'certified' figures detailing the exact numbers sold every month. With retailing and consumer industries developing rapidly, and branding increasingly significant, advertising space was becoming ever more valuable, especially where large audiences could be delivered. The *Mail*'s advertising department began to expand the space allocated to display advertising, especially for the products of major drapers and department stores. This illustrated advertising gradually came to occupy a central place in newspaper finances; indeed one advertising historian argues that these pioneering operations in the *Mail* 'effectively ushered in the industrialization of the press'. Here was a powerful extra incentive to chase the mass circulation: the greater the number of readers that could be promised to advertisers, the more expensive was each inch of space. Circulation managers chartered trains and devised elaborate delivery systems to ensure that newspapers produced in London circulated as widely as possible throughout Britain. The task was considerable easier when there were multiple production sites and in 1900 the *Mail* opened a printing plant in Manchester that produced an edition for northern England and Scotland. The *Mail* was the first paper to become a truly national, rather than metropolitan, operation.[7]

The *Daily Mail* was a commercial triumph, soon reaching a circulation of a million copies a day – well beyond any previous daily newspaper. Harmsworth's revolution ushered in the tabloid century, where developments in the popular newspaper began to drive the practices of the entire press and beyond that, the media in general. The very scale of his success left other proprietors little choice but to adapt their newspapers to match or improve upon his template. Inevitably others took up the challenge.

Harmsworth's main rival was Arthur Pearson, a year younger than the *Mail* proprietor and with a striking similar career trajectory. He worked as a manager at *Tit-Bits* before launching a popular magazine, *Pearson's Weekly*, and a successful publication for women, *Home Notes*. In 1900, he joined Harmsworth in the newspaper market by launching the *Daily Express*. He imported American techniques, most notably by placing news – rather than advertising – on the front pages to encourage street sales, and introducing banner headlines to underline this immediate visual appeal. The paper's Americanisms and abbreviated writing style were both reinforced by the hiring of several American journalists, notably Ralph Blumenfeld, who served as editor from 1904 to 1932. Although relatively successful at first, it was not until the Canadian businessman Lord Beaverbrook bought the *Express* in 1916 that it began seriously to rival the other daily popular newspapers. Beaverbrook had strong political opinions and launched numerous campaigns – the famous 'Red Crusader' appeared on the masthead in 1933 – but it was his considerable investment in a first-class news service, bright design, and enticing serialisations, combined with the optimistic, aspirational tone that he encouraged, that enabled the *Express* to catch and then surpass the increasingly gloomy *Mail* in the late 1920s and early 1930s.[8]

Before the First World War, the *Mail's* main rival was, remarkably, another paper established by Alfred Harmsworth: the *Daily Mirror*. The *Mirror* was launched in 1903 as a daily newspaper specifically for women. Encouraged by the success of a similar paper in France, *La Fronde*, and hopeful of securing lucrative advertising revenue, Harmsworth established the *Mirror* with an all-female staff under the original editor of the *Mail's* women's columns, Mary Howarth. The paper was a spectacular failure, eventually losing him £100,000. Complacent after a string of successes, Harmsworth had skimped on the essential preparatory work and market research. Misreading the demands of his audience, the *Mirror's* mixture of crime and human-interest stories, fashion advice, and domestic articles did not hit the right note for a 'high class' journal for 'ladies'.

Harmsworth retrieved the situation with another of his commercial masterstrokes: turning the *Mirror* into an illustrated paper. Although woodcut illustrations had featured prominently in weekly magazines and newspapers during the nineteenth century, daily papers generally remained visually austere, and had found it difficult to take advantage of the emergence of photography. In 1890 one notable London illustrated weekly, the *Graphic*, run by the artist and entrepreneur William Luson Thomas, launched a spin-off publication, the *Daily Graphic*, which the following year printed the first half-tone newspaper photograph, featuring George Lambert, a Liberal parliamentary candidate. The *Daily Graphic's* printing technology could only produce 10,000 illustrated copies an hour, however, and the paper's editorial team demonstrated little flair in appealing to the emerging mass market. Harmsworth spotted an opportunity to take advantage of new techniques enabling the rapid rotary printing of half-tone photographs to launch a modern, illustrated paper that would be aimed at both sexes but would have a different appeal to the *Mail*. The *Daily Illustrated Mirror*, as the paper briefly became, demoted politics and the public sphere even further than had the *Mail* and the *Express*, in favour of human-interest stories and feature articles. Its main appeal rested on its pioneering photography, however, which at certain dramatic moments – such as when it famously secured pictures of the recently deceased Edward VII – enabled it to reach circulations exceeding the *Mail*. But its unusual tabloid format and its partiality to pictures of glamorous society women allowed it to be stereotyped by traditionalist critics as more of a fashion magazine than a newspaper, a 'lowbrow', 'feminine' publication not to be taken seriously. Such condescension did not prevent others recognising the commercial opportunities, however, and in 1908 Edward Hulton launched a rival, the *Daily Sketch*.[9]

In little more than a decade from the birth of the *Mail* in 1896, therefore, a number of imitators and rivals had been launched and a flourishing popular daily newspaper market had emerged. These newspapers were the most potent symbols of the commercialised mass culture that was to characterise the twentieth century, and their owners became wealthy figures with a powerful public profile. Alfred Harmsworth was ennobled in 1905 as Lord Northcliffe (the name he will be given hereafter in this text), and his brother Harold, who oversaw the financial operation of Associated Newspapers and would inherit the papers on Northcliffe's death in 1922, soon became Lord Rothermere. In this new market, high circulations, and thus high profits, could only be maintained by concentrating on a popular formula. Alternative editorial strategies, reminiscent of the older radical press, were hard to sustain, as the *Daily Herald* discovered.

The *Herald* had started as a strike sheet founded by print workers in 1911, and the following year George Lansbury, a prominent Christian socialist and Ben Tillett, a trade union leader, transformed it into a daily newspaper with capital of only £300. The *Herald* was dedicated to expounding the workers' perspective against the 'dope' peddled by the capitalist press, but with a lack of resources and investment, and a left-wing stance and relatively low readership that did little to entice advertisers, it struggled to compete. During the First World War it barely managed to survive as a weekly, broadly maintaining an anti-war stance, before relaunching as a daily in 1919. The editorial team refused, however, to dilute its political beliefs or compromise with the populism that characterised the daily market. Human-interest stories and racy crime and divorce reports were regarded as unwelcome distractions that merely obscured from the worker the need for collective political action. Ernest Bevin, a trade union leader involved in the running of the *Herald*, insisted in 1919 that 'Labour's press must be a real educational factor, provoking thought and stimulating ideas'; it should not 'be full of the caprices of princes, the lubricities of courts and the sensationalism produced by display of the sordid.' The Trades Union Congress (TUC) formally invested in the paper in 1922, but its political purity and relative lack of resources ensured that it could not compete with rivals such as the *Mail* and *Express*. By the end of 1926 it was still only receiving 20 per cent of its revenue from advertising, compared to more than 50 per cent brought in by the market leaders.[10]

Finally, in 1929, the TUC accepted that it could not buck the market, and sold half of its stake to J. S. Elias's Odhams Press, the commercially successful publishers of the weekly magazine *John Bull* and the popular Sunday paper, the *People*. The terms of the sale ensured that the *Herald* remained committed to the TUC line in its political and industrial news, but Elias was given a free hand to develop the rest of the paper. The transformation when it was relaunched in March 1930 was spectacular. News values were reoriented, human interest entered the columns, and the amount of space given over to photographs, features, and advertising increased dramatically. Far more attention was now paid to the women's market. The reinvention of the *Herald* was the clearest sign yet of the triumph of the Northcliffe revolution. It was no longer possible to sustain the nineteenth-century model of popular political journalism amidst the cutthroat competition of the twentieth century.

The birth of the modern tabloid

The relaunch of the *Herald* kicked off one of the fiercest periods of competition the British media have ever seen. The *Mail* and its rivals had originally targeted the lower middle classes, while picking up readers in other social classes too. The *Herald* was aimed squarely at the (unionised) working classes, but it had only been able to scratch the surface of this expanding audience. By the early 1930s, as other markets became saturated, the working class provided the main growth area. The battle to entice the previously uncommitted into the habit of daily newspaper readership saw every trick in the editorial and commercial books being used. There was an intensive use of door-to-door canvassers, offering free gifts, such as the collected works of Charles Dickens, for subscribers, along with competitions and free insurance. It was estimated in June 1933 that the four main papers were spending between £50,000 and £60,000 a week – some £3.5 million pounds today – on buying readers. At the same time, editors made their papers as bright, accessible and appealing to as wide a readership as possible. The result was the most spectacular circulation growth in the history of the popular press, and the emergence of the modern tabloid format, providing the template for the journalism of the rest of the century.[11]

The Odhams *Daily Herald* soon demonstrated the potential of the working-class market. Within weeks of its relaunch it broke through the 1-million circulation barrier and in 1933, it became the first daily newspaper to sell 2 million copies. The *Herald*'s success forced its competitors to respond. The *Daily Chronicle* and the *Daily News*, two liberal dailies which had always struggled to keep up with their right-wing rivals, merged in 1930 to form the *News Chronicle*. In August 1933, both the *Express* and the *Mail* introduced significant redesigns. The *Express*'s redesign – overseen by Arthur Christiansen, a journalist of technical genius who would edit the paper for almost twenty-four years – was particularly influential in Fleet Street. Christiansen devoted himself to making the *Express* more readable. He gave the paper cleaner print, better spacing, bolder headlines, and concise cross-headings to break up the page into more accessible sections.

Photographs became bigger and more numerous, and were integrated into the editorial in more inventive ways. Under Christiansen, newspapers started to break free of the tyranny of the column that had defined their appearance for over two hundred years, and moved towards a more fluid and visually appealing 'jigsaw' design. This dynamic, attractive and well-resourced paper soon matched and surpassed the *Herald*'s circulation, and was market leader from the mid-1930s until 1949.[12]

The most significant and commercially influential relaunch of all, though, occurred at the *Daily Mirror*. After the First World War, the *Mirror* gradually fell behind its rivals. As other papers started integrating photographs into their pages, much of the *Mirror*'s original appeal was lost, and it lacked a distinctive editorial personality to set it apart from the other popular dailies on the right. By 1934, its circulation had slumped to 720,000, barely a third of the *Daily Express*. Its core audience was now middle-class women in the south of England, and it lagged far behind all its main rivals in working-class households. It was at this low point that personnel changes brought an infusion of new ideas and, eventually, a new direction for the *Mirror*. At the centre of the reinvention was Harry Guy Bartholomew – 'Bart' – who became editorial director in 1934, having joined the paper as a cartoonist thirty years earlier. The son of a clerk, and with no more than an elementary education, Bartholomew relied on his visual flair and technical expertise to rise in journalism. Self-conscious about his lack of articulacy, he harboured a deep-seated suspicion of social elites and detested pretension and snobbery. He immediately sought to make significant shifts in the style and content of the *Mirror*, and in this process he was supported by Cecil King, Northcliffe's nephew and a key member of the paper's board of directors.[13]

Bartholomew took the advice of the American advertising agency J. Walter Thompson, and drew up a new editorial template heavily influenced by successful American tabloids such as the New York *Daily News*. The new format included the liberal use of heavy black type and bold block headlines; the writing became more colloquial, the pursuit of sensation more pronounced, and the sexual content more explicit. Further momentum was given to these editorial changes by a raft of new appointments in 1935, including Basil Nicholson, who moved from a career in advertising, the young Welsh journalist Hugh Cudlipp, who joined as Nicholson's assistant in the features department, and William Connor, a former copywriter for J. Walter Thompson, who became the star columnist 'Cassandra'. The result was a new style of paper in the British daily market: a brash populist tabloid aimed directly at a working-class audience, updating and refreshing Northcliffe's popular newspaper model with the insights of American commerce and the democratic instincts of a reform-minded editorial team. If papers like the *Mail* and the *Express* had aimed to be 'popular not vulgar', the *Mirror* now portrayed itself as 'vulgar but honest'. The paper's sales started to rise dramatically.[14]

By the outbreak of the Second World War, the *Mirror* had developed a distinctive left-of-centre appeal, seeking to articulate a working-class political perspective that, in contrast to the *Herald*, was not tied to the institutions of the labour movement. The *Mirror* was patriotic and pro-monarchy, but railed against the complacency of the ruling elites and the conformities and rigidities of British society. It offered a prominent platform for the working-class voice by the extensive use of letters in columns such as 'Viewpoint' and 'Live Letters', while also providing some earthy replies to correspondence through the voice of the so-called 'Old Codgers'. Yet while politics was taken seriously, it never dominated as it did in the *Herald* or even the *News Chronicle*, and the editorial team retained a keen eye for the sensational, bizarre and curious. Sport, film and popular entertainments were covered extensively, while the sentimental streak in working-class culture was catered for with romantic and heart-warming tales, and pictures of babies and animals. The *Mirror*'s skilfully balanced tabloid miscellany catered for almost all tastes.

The *Mirror*'s patriotic but class-conscious editorial strategy was perfectly attuned to the climate of the 'People's War', and it became a valued mouthpiece for popular frustration at the inefficiencies and peculiarities of officialdom (see Chapter 1). The *Mirror* was widely seen as the forces' paper: a survey of newspaper consumption in autumn 1941 found that no fewer than 30 per cent of military men were regular readers. Wartime newsprint rationing prevented a quicker circulation growth, but in 1949 the *Mirror* overtook the *Express* as Britain's most popular paper. By 1951, it was selling over 4.5 million copies a day, about 350,000 more than the *Express*, and more than *Mail* (2.2 million) and the *Herald* (2.1 million) combined. In 1967, the *Mirror* reached the unmatched, and now unmatchable, daily circulation of 5.25 million sales. It had become the most influential expression of British popular print culture.[15]

The *Mirror*'s success did not, however, immediately lead to a wave of tabloidisation. The *Express*, the *Mail*, the *Herald* and the *News Chronicle* all preferred to retain the broadsheet format that was perceived to convey greater seriousness and respectability. Only the lacklustre *Daily Sketch*, constantly struggling along with a circulation of around 1 million, shared the tabloid format. The *Mirror* remained in a category of its own, a noisy eruption of mass culture that was admired and loathed in equal measure. Conscious of the condescension it received, it frequently explained and justified it approach, notably in 1949 when the editor, Sylvester Bolam, penned a famous definition of 'public service sensationalism':

> The *Mirror* is a sensational newspaper. We make no apology for that. We believe in the sensational presentation of news and views, especially important news and views, as a necessary and valuable public service in these days of mass readership and democratic responsibility ... Sensationalism does not mean distorting the truth. It means the vivid and dramatic presentation of events so as to give them a forceful impact on the mind of the reader. It means big headlines, vigorous writing, simplification into familiar everyday language, and the wide use of illustration by cartoon and photograph.

For Bolam, sensationalism was a democratic imperative, providing the only way to inform a mass readership and enable it to participate in the public sphere. 'Every great problem facing us,' he argued, 'will only be understood by the ordinary man busy with his daily tasks if he is hit hard and hit often with the facts.' Sensational treatment, he concluded 'is the answer, whatever the sober and "superior" readers of some other journals may prefer.'[16]

Such protestations did little to assuage the many critics of tabloid journalism, and there was a widespread belief in Fleet Street that it was futile to compete with the *Mirror* on its own terms. In 1963, for example, Beaverbrook asked one of his executives to explain why the *Mirror* was outperforming the *Express*. The reply made no attempt to disguise the disdain for the tabloid rival:

The *Daily Mirror* is easier to read. It doesn't take a lot of effort on behalf of the youngsters to look at the *Daily Mirror* in the bus or the train early in the morning and enjoy the humour of the *Daily Mirror*. It appeals to busy housewives who will not be bothered to read more serious newspapers. It has also been described as a handbag newspaper, for typists and other females can stick it in their handbags to read during their lunch break and this is valuable because they can improvise items of gossip.

The executive emphasised that it was his strongly held view 'that it would be a mistake for us to go after the *Daily Mirror* and compete for their readers in the D and E classes'.[17]

Indeed, secure that there was no downmarket challenger, and desirous of the respect they believed they deserved, Cudlipp and King in the 1960s sought to push the *Mirror* gently upmarket. Believing that its working-class audience was becoming better educated and more affluent, in 1962 the *Mirror* introduced 'Mirrorscope', 'two pages of serious and informed comment on the night's late news'. This editorial strategy was reinforced in 1964 when Mirror Group Newspapers sought to relaunch the *Daily Herald*, which it had bought three years earlier, as *The Sun*. The sociologist Mark Abrams, commissioned to investigate the 'newspaper readership of tomorrow', and thereby provide data for the relaunch, emphasised the blurring of class distinctions since the war. 'Some working-class families have incomes as high as some white-collar families,' he reported, 'and there is little to choose between their styles of living and the goods and services they consume.' Seeking to reach this audience, the new *Sun* made a significant play of its modernity, aspirationalism and classlessness. It was a resounding failure, and within four years, IPC, as the Mirror Group had become, was looking to get rid of it. They saw little danger in selling it to the young Australian entrepreneur, Rupert Murdoch.

The tabloid unleashed

By the end of the 1960s the tabloid had demonstrated its commercial value, but it was a model that few others seemed inclined to develop. Rupert Murdoch and Larry Lamb, the first editor of the relaunched *Sun*, overturned the status quo. By demonstrating so powerfully the appeal of an updated tabloid, they altered the basic assumptions of the market, and tabloidisation quickly came to be seen as essential for survival. Not only did existing titles change their format, new papers entered the fray, and in the bitter competition for readers, the desire to move gradually upmarket soon seemed hopelessly outdated.

Murdoch and Lamb's central insight was that the *Mirror* was losing touch with its market and failing to refresh its now rather tired formula. While Abrams's identification of rising affluence and education was entirely reasonable, he didn't fully appreciate how the inexorable rise of television was altering the wider media environment. With ITV's launch of the thirty-minute *News at Ten* in 1967, and BBC's subsequent lengthening of its *Nine O' Clock News* bulletin, broadcast news services were expanding rapidly. The BBC and ITV duopoly provided a considerable amount of respectable, entertaining 'middlebrow' content. The gaps for the press were either in the provision of greater detail and analysis, or by offering more outspoken, disreputable, and intrusive content. At the same time, a more youth-focused, consumerist and permissive pop culture had emerged which mainstream outlets, including the *Mirror*, were failing to cater for. Class identities remained resilient, but they were expressed in different forms. There were opportunities for a paper which could tap into this younger, less socially deferential, working-class audience.[18]

Murdoch and Lamb grasped the opportunity with considerable commercial shrewdness. The relaunched *Sun* was remarkably open in its borrowings from the *Mirror*. The paper's slogan was 'Forward with the People', which had been adopted by the *Mirror* in 1945 and only recently dropped. 'It is not original', the *Sun* admitted, 'But we make no apology for it. Because that is what we believe in'. Robert Connor, the son of the *Mirror*'s star columnist, 'Cassandra', was given a column brazenly entitled 'Son of Cassandra'. The letters column was entitled 'Liveliest Letters', to outdo the *Mirror*'s 'Live Letters'; even the *Mirror*'s popular cartoon, 'Garth', was copied with the *Sun*'s version featuring a female protagonist, 'Scarth'. There was, however, an evident difference in tone, too, most obvious in the treatment of sex. With topless models included from the second issue – if not initially on page 3 – and major serialisations of Jacqueline Susann's 'bonkbuster' novel *The Love Machine* and Jane Garrity's sex guide, *The Sensuous Woman*, the *Sun* identified itself as a sexually permissive, hedonistic paper, at least within the parameters of the heterosexual 'family newspaper' genre. At the end of the first week, the paper produced a statement of its core beliefs, and it emphasised that it was 'For youth, for change and always for the people':

> The permissive society is not an opinion. It is a fact. People who pretend that yesterday's standards are today's, let alone tomorrow's, are living a lie. The *Sun* believes that any man – from the Archbishop of Canterbury to Mick Jagger – is entitled to put forward his own moral code. And people are entitled to accept it or to reject it.[19]

These worthy declarations were not necessarily honoured of course, any more than its other pledges that it was 'strongly opposed to capital punishment', 'for entering Europe', and concerned about the 'colour problem' (*'The Sun* is for building bridges, not walls'). When combined with its risqué content, though, they helped to position the paper in the readers' minds as fresh and up-to-date. It was thoroughly modern, too, in its attitude to television, embracing it far more energetically than other papers, and recognising it as an important source of celebrity stories and gossip. The inclusion of a detailed weekend television guide helped to make the *Sun*'s Saturday edition its best-selling one of the week. The *Sun* also demonstrated the value of television advertising, publicising the paper from the start with a series of cheeky commercials that deliberately sought to bait the television authorities (the paper was banned from including references to Sir Thomas Crapper and the River Piddle). Lamb noted that 'We bought books, commissioned series, dreamed up offers and competitions, all with an eye on their suitability for television promotion'. Drawing on Rupert Murdoch's expertise, the *Sun* was able to exploit the opportunities provided by different media forms.[20]

The results were spectacular. Within a year the paper was selling over 1.5 million copies a day, more than twice the circulation inherited from the IPC's broadsheet *Sun*. By autumn 1974, it had overtaken the *Express*, and its 3.5 million daily sales were double the *Mail*'s. The seemingly inexorable rise continued until 1978, when it overtook the *Mirror* as the nation's bestselling paper, and briefly reached circulation figures of 4 million in an otherwise declining market. The potential of the tabloid model could no longer be doubted.[21]

Other papers inevitably responded. When Vere Harmsworth succeeded his father, Esmond, the second Viscount Rothermere, as chairman of Associated Newspapers in 1970, he was determined to revive the *Daily Mail* after decades of relative underperformance, and was clear that decisive action was required. He hired a talented new editor, David English, and in 1971 merged the paper with the *Daily Sketch* in a new tabloid format. 'In years to come', the *Mail*'s first tabloid issue declared confidently, 'the old broadsheet papers will look as dated as Victorian playbills.' Vere Harmsworth was clear that 'the size was a great advantage in every possible way', because 'with a tabloid, the whole page can be given a tremendous impact, and you get twice the number of pages for the same total of newsprint.' The *Mail*, under English and his successor Paul Dacre, became renowned for the 'tremendous impact' it made with a rather different form of tabloid journalism from the *Sun*'s working-class populism. It used its pages to articulate and dramatise the moral and cultural preoccupations of the respectable middle classes, defending marriage and 'family values' against the threats of 'permissiveness' and moral 'relativism', arguing for a tax and welfare system that rewarded hard work and saving, and robustly criticising 'scroungers' and 'immigrants' who took advantage of the system. It did this much more dynamically than the *Daily Express*, which had lost its way since the death of its driving force, Lord Beaverbrook, in 1964. The *Express* went tabloid in 1977, in an attempt to stem the steady decline in its circulation which had seen the loss of some 1.5 million daily sales in the previous ten years. The shift had a limited impact, though, and in the mid-1980s, it finally fell behind its long-term mid-market rival, the *Mail*.[22]

The success of the *Sun* also suggested to some that there was more space in the working-class market. In 1978 Victor Matthews, who the previous year had led Trafalgar House's take-over of the faltering Beaverbrook Newspapers, decided to launch the *Daily Star* as a downmarket stablemate for the *Express*. The *Star* aped the *Sun* as blatantly as the *Sun* had copied the *Mirror* nine years earlier. The *Star*'s editors Derek Jameson and Peter Grimsditch were open in their intention to outdo Murdoch's paper for titillation: 'Sex sells – that goes for pictures and words. So the *Star* will have its daily quota. Bigger and better than anyone else'. Instead of 'page 3 girls', then, the paper offered full-colour topless 'Starbirds'. The opening issue also promised an 'easy-to-find TV guide, the best in newspapers'. Like the *Sun*, the *Star* lavishly advertised itself on television. If the content was unoriginal, the paper did have two selling points which concerned Murdoch: a cover price (6p) that was a penny lower than the *Sun*, and a production centre in Manchester, which, the paper claimed, allowed it to provide an 'unbeatable late news and sports service for readers in the North and Midlands.'[23]

The *Star* was never able to threaten the better-resourced *Sun*, but its entrance into the market did lead to a circulation war that rivalled in intensity that of the early 1930s: the result, in the 1980s, was the emergence of an increasingly aggressive, outspoken and jingoistic journalism accompanied by a rash of £1 million bingo contests and celebrity exclusives. In this pitiless contest, the *Sun*'s abrasive editor Kelvin MacKenzie emerged as champion. In the Thatcherite 1980s, with its celebration of bold opinion, no-holds barred competition, profit-seeking and flag-waving patriotism, the tabloid had truly found its moment. With the breaking of the unions and the move out of Fleet Street from 1986, moreover, the profitability of the tabloid model increased still further.

Few realised how brief this moment would be. By the late-1980s, Rupert Murdoch's attention was increasingly focused on satellite television, while the rapid spread of the internet, mobile phones and computer technology from the 1990s started to overwhelm consumers with media content. While newspaper circulations started on a steady, and seemingly unstoppable, decline, tabloid instincts and insights were applied to other media forms and young men and women stopped picking up the newspaper habit. The reputation of the tabloids was also severely damaged by revelations about phone hacking and the payment of officials that led to the closure of the *News of the World*, the holding of the Leveson inquiry and the conviction of former *Sun* editor Andy Coulson. By 2014, daily newspaper circulations were less than half the level of the 1950s. The tabloid century, ushered in by a triumphant Alfred Harmsworth, in 1901, was coming to an ignominious end.

If the tabloids' power is starting to slip away, however, their political and cultural significance across the twentieth century can hardly be denied.

This is not, of course, to suggest that the press were able to determine the opinions of a passive and uncritical public. Readers could ignore, resist or misunderstand newspaper content, and their views on most subjects were shaped by a variety of sources. Most people did not trust the tabloids to the same extent as the BBC or the elite press, and they often remained suspicious of the reliability and accuracy of the more outrageous or unlikely stories. The tabloids' emphasis on entertainment ensured that they were often treated as a bit of fun. Consumers also tended to choose newspapers that matched their own political inclinations: there was always an extent to which newspapers were preaching to the converted. Nevertheless, the longer-term, cumulative influence of the tabloid representation of the world should not be underestimated. The influence of the press rested not on its short-term power to convince readers of the merits of specific individuals, parties or policies, but rather on a more subtle process of framing of issues in particular ways, helping to set the agenda for public and private debate, and enabling certain types of people and institutions to dominate discussion, while marginalising others. The press mattered, too, because politicians, policymakers, officials, campaign groups and other media professionals thought they mattered. Many of the key participants in public life were acutely concerned about how they or their institutions were covered by the press, and often shaped their behaviour or policies accordingly. For all the increasing power of television, tabloids were unconstrained by requirements of impartiality and were noisier, more opinionated, intrusive, and persistent. Their huge circulations seemed to give them authority in representing key swathes of public opinion, and they played a crucial role in setting the tone of popular culture. They were a daily reference point that was difficult to ignore, and it was a serious risk for anyone in public life to take them on, because they usually had the last word.

The cumulative influence of the popular press is best appreciated by taking a long view. This book is therefore based on six broad thematic chapters which explore how the tabloids reported, and thereby shaped, this dramatic century. The first three chapters focus on the coverage of key public events, institutions and people: the wars that Britain fought, the political debates that shaped the nation's internal development, and the individuals that topped its social and status hierarchies, namely the royal family and popular cultural celebrities. The second three chapters explore the personal and social identities that structured tabloid content and the world-views of readers: gender and sexuality, class, race and nationality. The diversity of this material precludes the drawing of simple conclusions – indeed, perhaps the main conclusion to draw is that tabloid culture is more complex and nuanced than many have given it credit for. Those making the familiar criticisms of popular newspapers – that their journalism is crude, reactionary and hypocritical, that they pander to majority opinion and stigmatise minorities and minority tastes, that their desire for profit drives a materialistic and individualistic ethos – will all find plenty of evidence here. At the same time, popular newspapers should not be measured against an abstract, ideal standard, but against the culture of which they were a part. Viewed in this way, we can find instances when tabloids were progressive and generous, when they provided a powerful voice for ordinary people against elitism and vested interests, and when they challenged the entrenched majority view. They offered a platform for a wide range of voices and contributors. Love them or loathe them, we need to take the tabloids seriously and understand how they contributed to the unfolding of British life over the last century.

War

War provides the most dramatic, intense and urgent news stories of all. It imperils the lives of citizens and the security of nations; after the dropping of atomic bombs on Hiroshima and Nagasaki in 1945, it seemed to threaten the very existence of the human race. Because of the stakes involved, though, wars are also the hardest stories to cover. Information becomes a priceless commodity, which the state scrutinises, manages, restricts and distorts. Reporters operate in dangerous and uncertain conditions, facing the deeply entrenched suspicion and hostility of military authorities whose default position is secrecy. Journalism is never more inaccurate, deceptive and dubious than during wartime.

The popular press has frequently been accused of retailing a toxic mixture of belligerence, jingoism and myopia in their coverage of international affairs and military conflict. Critics of the *Daily Mail* argued that by irresponsibly stoking anti-German sentiment, the paper actually helped to create the conditions which enabled conflict to break out in 1914. 'Next to the Kaiser,' wrote the esteemed liberal editor and journalist A. G. Gardiner, 'Lord Northcliffe has done more than any other living man to bring about the war.' Similar charges had been levelled at Hearst and Pulitzer's newspapers in the United States in the run-up to the Spanish-American war of 1898. War reporters are commonly portrayed as state lackeys, slavishly following the official agenda rather than informing readers about the grim realities of war. The soldier-poets of the Great War lambasted the press for its preoccupation with military heroism and glory while millions were dying in atrocious conditions in the trenches; the *Sun*'s bombastic coverage of the Falklands War was seen by some as reducing the conflict to little more than vicarious entertainment for an audience eager for Britain to reassert itself on the world stage once more. Tabloids are charged with underpinning a militaristic culture that has fomented war, imperialism and military interventionism.[1]

If jingoism has been a striking feature of the British popular press, the overall picture is more complex than critics often allow. The default position of the popular press during wartime was certainly to try to unite the national community around a patriotic vision of resolution, togetherness and virtue – in opposition to a demonised and caricatured enemy, whether 'Huns', 'Japs' or 'Argies' – while also offering unflagging support for the bravery and gallantry of the troops on the front lines. During the First and Second World Wars, and the first Iraq war, most papers adopted this line. The Suez and Second Iraq conflicts, by contrast proved far more controversial, and papers on the left took up a position of principled opposition, while seeking to avoid suggestions of a lack of patriotism. Even during the more consensual wars, moreover, most tabloids sought to maintain sufficient critical distance to attack ineffectual leadership, and stand up for troops against bureaucracy. During the First World War, for example, the *Daily Mail* proved to be a ferocious critic of the Prime Minister, Henry Asquith, and his War Minister, Lord Kitchener, while during the Second World War, Churchill's government was so exasperated by the *Daily Mirror*'s coverage that it considered closing it down.

State-imposed censorship regimes, and the culture of secrecy in the military, also left the press with little choice but to hide some of the more brutal truths of the war from the public. During the First World War, the press made heavy use of the official rhetoric of honour, glory and imperial greatness, but it did not – and could not – disguise the entirety of the catastrophe that was unfolding. 'The 'high diction' of 1914 did not withstand the bloodshed of the trenches, and the language surrounding the Second World War was far more measured and pragmatic. As the war came to the British mainland with the Blitz, moreover, it was harder to hide the realities of the conflict. After 1945, the press did not downplay the awesome power of the atomic bomb, and frequently speculated about the damage to civilian areas in the event of a nuclear war. For the more remote and less immediately threatening wars of the later twentieth century – particularly the conflicts in Falklands, Iraq and Afghanistan – the tabloids' reporting did tend to lapse into a jingoistic, rather uncritical, style, but even then, there were some notable exceptions, and scepticism about engagements in the Middle East inevitably grew as the military operations dragged on and became ever more costly.

Rather than stereotyping tabloids as invariably being crudely bellicose, it is more accurate to see them as conforming to – or, less charitably, being imprisoned within – the underlying logic of Britain's 'warfare state'. If there was sometimes disagreement about particular interventions, there was almost unanimous support for Britain as a strong nation with an international role, fulfilling the role bequeathed by its glorious history. Journalists were consistently seduced by the danger and glamour of military endeavour, and they fed a public fascination with the technologies and strategies of war. Newspapers devoted their resources to narrating the twists and turns of diplomatic crises and to recording the cut and thrust of the military campaigns, rather than asking deeper questions about the seeds of conflict and the underlying tensions of the international system. Leader-writers and columnists adopted a pragmatic outlook on world affairs, and portrayed peace campaigners as being hopelessly idealistic and unworldly; correspondents at the front-lines tried to live up to the esteemed tradition of war reporting. For all its horror, wars sold papers, and the risks and rewards of covering them were prized more highly than recording the painstaking search for peace.[2]

Empire, patriotism and the First World War

The tabloid template was forged in an imperialistic nation in which British greatness was rarely questioned and Britain's right to rule broad swathes of the globe was widely accepted. Pledging allegiance to the empire seemed to be a natural part of appealing to the national reading community. Northcliffe's first editorial as a newspaper proprietor, having taken over the *Evening News* in 1894, set out his ambition to 'preach the gospel of loyalty to the Empire'. The *Daily Mail*, founded two years later, took this policy a step further. Its editorial team believed that public interest in empire was 'one of the greatest forces' for the new mass press to exploit, and it sought to double the amount of space newspapers typically devoted to recording colonial events and the courageous exploits of British pioneers. This policy bore fruit very quickly. Patriotic coverage of the Second Boer War (1899–1902), penned by reporters such as G. W. Steevens and Edgar Wallace (later famous as a novelist), enabled the *Mail* to become the first daily paper to break the one-million circulation barrier. The *Daily Express*, launched during the conflict, in April 1900, was similarly insistent about its loyalty to the nation. Its first editorial declared: 'Our policy is patriotism; our party is the British Empire.' The *Express*'s belief in empire only became more resolute when it was taken over by Lord Beaverbrook, a Canadian, in 1916. Beaverbrook was adamant that 'the cause of Empire is the greatest issue in public life', and he famously told the Royal Commission on the Press in 1948 that it was the mainspring of his newspaper 'propaganda' efforts. Liberal papers such as the *Daily News* were more critical of Britain's imperial ambitions, and from 1912 the *Daily Herald* gave space to pacifist views, but these papers could not fully counter the noisy patriotism of their right-wing competitors.[3]

In the two decades before the outbreak of the First World War, imperial engagements in places such as Sudan, South Africa and Nigeria enabled the popular press to provide numerous stories describing British heroism and manliness in exotic locations. One of the best ways for reporters to counter the military's scepticism about their presence was to polish the reputation of the officers and admire the pluck and bravery of the troops. Celebratory dispatches turned figures such as Herbert Kitchener and Robert Baden-Powell into national celebrities. 'When Shall Their Glory Fade? History's Most Heroic Defence Ends in Triumph' declared the *Express*'s front-page after the relief of the siege of Mafeking in May 1900. The paper highlighted the 'indomitable spirit, and the unconquerable pluck' of Baden-Powell, who had overseen Mafeking's defence, and described the 'very orgie [sic] of rejoiceful patriotism' with which London greeted the news of the garrison's safety. 'The number of sentimental young women who sleep with a photograph of the heroic Baden-Powell under their pillows is legion,' noted the *Express* approvingly, adding that 'one hero-worshipping damsel' put fresh flowers by his picture every day. Yet such triumphs revealed more than admirable leadership; in a society saturated by racial thinking, they seemed to demonstrate the continued fitness of the British people in an increasingly competitive world. 'Men, and women, and children have shown so bravely the characteristic British quality of bull-dog pertinacity', wrote an *Express* editorial. 'We can only thank God for Mafeking, as a perpetual memorial of the courage and strength of our race.' Such sentiments were frequently voiced by popular papers, which helped to spread and consolidate this form of Social Darwinism. As the historian Glenn Wilkinson has noted, war was portrayed by newspapers not as a catastrophe to be avoided but as 'beneficial and desirable to the societies engaged in it' because it staved off degeneracy and decline.[4]

There was, nevertheless, a darker side to this form of reporting. The press investment in military achievement and national greatness provoked anxiety as well as triumphalism. The press accordingly gave voice to growing concerns that the dominant international position Britain had enjoyed during the mid-Victorian period was coming to an end, and that military and economic competition was intensifying. For all the perceived heroism of Baden-Powell and others, the Boer War was a lengthy and gruelling conflict which demonstrated how difficult it was for Britain to impose its will throughout its empire. The popular press did not disguise the setbacks or the level of casualties; by the end of the conflict moreover, the *Daily News*, a popular liberal paper, had joined in the criticism of what the Liberal leader Henry Campbell-Bannerman denounced as the 'methods of barbarism' used by the British military against the Boer peoples (including gathering families into inhospitable 'concentration camps'). The high proportion of men rejected for military service fed fears of 'degeneration', and the *Mail* and other papers took up the popular cry of 'National Efficiency', demanding that social problems be tackled so that the British people did not lose their vigour and virility.

The travails of the Boer War, combined with the greater diplomatic assertiveness of Germany, Japan and the United States, also generated considerable momentum for the campaign to strengthen Britain's armed forces. 'This is our hour of preparation', wrote Northcliffe in 1900, 'tomorrow may be the day of world conflict.' The same year, the *Daily Express* declared that

'Our navy is unsound, and it is largely a paper figment dangled before the eyes of the people'; pre-emptively disarming accusations of irresponsible sensationalism, the paper added that 'Our articles are alarmist: they are meant to be alarmist.' Throughout the Edwardian period the right-wing press lent their considerable weight to the prominent and well-organised movement for greater military strength and preparedness, led by pressure groups such as the Navy League and the National Service League.[5]

The *Mail* focused, in particular, on the growing threat posed by Kaiser Wilhelm's Germany. In spring 1906 the *Mail* commissioned and lavishly serialised popular author William Le Queux's *Invasion of 1910*, documenting the consequences of a German incursion into Britain. The series was a sensational collision of commerce and polemic. Le Queux had carefully researched military strategy, but the route of the invasion was determined by towns where the *Mail* hoped to increase its circulation. In London, the series was advertised by the alarming sight of men in Prussian-blue army uniforms and spiked helmets marching down Oxford Street wearing *Daily Mail* sandwich boards. The serialisation was a great success, and, with such publicity, the novel eventually sold over one million copies. But Northcliffe was not content with fictional warnings of the German menace. In 1909 he commissioned the socialist journalist Robert Blatchford to visit Germany and assess its diplomatic aspirations. The resulting articles were suitably inflammatory, declaring that Germany was preparing to undermine the British Empire and 'force German dictatorship upon the whole of Europe'. Reprinted as a penny pamphlet, the articles sold some 1.6 million copies. The warnings continued to flow until 1914. Indeed, so consistent had been paper's anti-Germanism that when war finally broke out the *Mail* styled itself as 'the paper that foretold the war' and proudly published a selection of its 'scaremongerings' as a sixpenny pamphlet.[6]

The popular press entered the conflict with Germany in 1914 with a combination of self-confident patriotism, Christian faith and a professional determination to rally the nation around the war effort. It was certain both of the rightness of the British cause and of the suitability of the 'official rhetoric' of the war: the language of honour, glory, heroism, and sacrifice that expressed traditional martial and patriotic values. On the day before war was finally announced, the *Mail* told its readers that 'Our duty is to go forward into this valley of the shadow of death with courage and faith – with courage to suffer, and faith in God and our country'. 'On us of this generation has come the sharpest trial that has ever befallen our race,' the paper continued: 'We have to uphold the honour of England by demeanour and deed.' 'England Expects That Every Man Will Do His Duty' ran a streamer headline on the front page of the *Express* on 5 August. '[T]he nation accepts the challenge of an arrogant foe, and with confident courage commits its cause to God.' The war was presented as an opportunity to demonstrate the valour and virtue of individuals and the nation as a whole. If 'England had grown fat and slothful with prosperity', the *Express* declared, '... Germany's threat has called to life again the England of Henry V, the England of Drake ... the England of Nelson.' Female readers were equally expected to relish the opportunity to serve the nation. The *Express* ran 'The Diary of a Soldier's Wife', which professed to share the national sense of duty: 'It is a wonderful time for us to live through – and to come through with laurels. I, for one, am truly thankful, and there must be many a soldier's wife who feels the same.' Such patriotic resolution did not generate overconfidence. The press repeatedly underlined the magnitude of the task – the lament of Sir Edward Grey, the Foreign Secretary, that war would be 'the greatest catastrophe' ever to befall Europe, was widely publicised – and it is very difficult to find any of the 'over by Christmas' triumphalism of popular memory. Calmness was the order of the day: 'let us bear our part with equanimity', wrote the *Mirror*, 'without silly flag-waving, food-flustering, gaping and idling, and useless clamour in the streets.'[7]

In the early months of the war, the censorship regime was so tight that the press was forced to feed off scraps. The British Expeditionary force was sent to France without any accompanying reporters, and a newly instituted War Press Bureau scrutinised newspaper content with a stern gaze. The War Minister, Lord Kitchener, gave orders that reporters found in the field were to be arrested. The press was expected to rely upon the official dispatches penned by Colonel Ernest Swinton, an officer in the Royal Engineers who wrote under the name 'Eyewitness' (he was soon dubbed 'Eyewash'). With such limited scope for independent reporting, the popular press devoted much of its space to stories that emphasised the savagery and brutality of the German war machine as it moved through Belgium and France. Only two days after war had been declared, the *Mail* was claiming that German troops in Belgium had 'disgraced themselves by unpardonable atrocities'. A week later the *Express* argued that 'Germany's conduct of the war has been characterised by a barbarism which would make a South American revolutionary blush with shame'. German soldiers, it seemed, were being encouraged by their leaders to flout all the rules of civilised warfare. The destruction at Louvain, the *Mail* reported in September 1914, was 'almost incredible in its wickedness':

> [men were] remorselessly shot down by the guards. They drove the women and children into the fields, perpetrating upon them atrocities which cannot be detailed in cold print. They then bombarded the city and destroyed the best part of it in a few hours ... Germans have been systematically taught by their military to be ruthless to the weak. The Kaiser, a single word from whom would have stopped this riot of savagery, has, on the contrary, done his best to kindle the lowest passions of his men.[8]

Although the 'atrocity stories' of the early months of the war were not entirely without foundation, there can be little doubt that the press colluded with the military authorities to publicise and sensationalise the events in Belgium. The British armed forces were, after all, reliant on volunteers, and such stories offered a direct challenge to the masculinity of the men back home: military service was not just the defence of an abstract 'King and Country', but protection of innocent women and children. These messages were hammered home by the use of fonts and pictures larger than any previously used in national newspapers. The bombardment of Rheims prompted the first ever full-page photograph in the *Mail* on 22 September 1914, with the paper portraying the town's cathedral in all its magnificence before its destruction.[9]

If German soldiers demonstrated mechanical brutality and an insatiable lust for destruction, the British troops were models of patience, bravery and valour. Reporters soon developed the ability to transpose almost any series of events into a glorious narrative. Philip Gibbs's report for the *Daily Chronicle* on 3 September was headlined both 'German Army Closing in on Paris' and 'Wonderful Story of British Heroism'. A substantial concession of territory was rewritten into 'the most heroic story which may be read by any man now living'. The Allies were 'always retiring before an overpowering and irresistible enemy, but never in actual retreat, never fighting a rearguard action with their backs to the foe, but always face forward, yielding every mile with stubborn and sublime gallantry'. Even children could see through the optimism of the coverage. Jim Flowers, an engineer's son born in 1905, would later recall his headmaster reading aloud rosy dispatches from the *Daily Chronicle*: 'It struck me that if ever the British had to go backwards they wouldn't say it was a retreat, it was a strategic withdrawal so that they could swallow up the enemy later on.' It was unsurprising that the troops at the front lines resented such reporting, believing that it glorified the conflict, or, at best, prevented civilians from understanding the realities of the war. They preferred to seek consolation in the grim humour of the trench newspapers. In his war memoir *Good-Bye to All That*, Robert Graves observed that returning soldiers were often disturbed that 'civilians talked a foreign language; and it was newspaper language.' The denizens of Fleet Street accordingly became prime targets for the bitter soldier-poets.[10]

Yet if editors and journalists were generally prepared to accept that they had a duty to restrict or put a positive gloss on their reporting, they did not lose their critical faculties. The press's preoccupation with military strength and efficiency ensured it demanded greater dynamism and urgency in the prosecution of the war. For Northcliffe's *Daily Mail*, in particular, this became an almost all-consuming duty. At a time of party political truce, the press, in its self-appointed role as representative of the people, became the main voice of opposition to Asquith's administration.

By the end of 1914, Northcliffe's restlessness was fed by his growing conviction that the strict censorship regime was serving only to hide failures in the management of the war effort. 'What the newspapers feel very strongly,' wrote Northcliffe to Lord Murray of Elibank, the former Liberal chief whip, 'is that, against their will, they are made to be part and parcel of a foolish conspiracy to hide bad news. English people do not mind bad news.' Drawing both on the experiences of his visits to the front, and on private sources of information from his many correspondents, Northcliffe became increasingly convinced that several men in leading positions were not up to their job – including Asquith, Kitchener, and Winston Churchill, the First Lord of the Admiralty.[11]

The episode that crystallised this concern, and which saw Northcliffe putting both his and the *Mail*'s reputation on the line, was the 'shells crisis' of May 1915. Northcliffe had received letters from the front claiming that British military operations were being undermined by the lack of the right kind of shell, and after the Allies failed to capitalise on an initial breakthrough at Neuve Chapelle due to a lack of munitions, these criticisms began to be publicly aired. On 15 May 1915, *The Times* (also owned by Northcliffe at this time) published a telegram from its respected military correspondent, Lieutenant-Colonel Charles à Court Repington, highlighting the problem, and Northcliffe decided to go on the offensive. After some critical editorials, the *Mail* on 21 May published an incendiary piece personally written by Northcliffe and headlined 'The Tragedy of the Shells: Lord Kitchener's Grave Error'. Northcliffe pinned the blame for the shells scandal directly onto Kitchener:

> Lord Kitchener has starved the army in France of high-explosive shells. The admitted fact is that Lord Kitchener ordered the wrong kind of shell ... He persisted in sending shrapnel – a useless weapon in trench warfare ... The kind of shell our poor soldiers have had has caused the death of thousands of them.

Such a direct, and grave, public attack on a widely esteemed figure at a time of national crisis was shocking, and generated fury among many of Northcliffe's critics. Members of the London Stock Exchange burned copies of both the *Times* and the *Mail*, and anxious advertisers cancelled contracts. Thousands of readers stopped buying the papers. Northcliffe, though, was undaunted: at this point he was concerned not with circulation, but with what he perceived as his national duty. It was clear even to Northcliffe's opponents, moreover, that there were problems with Britain's munitions supply. Northcliffe was soon vindicated. By the end of the month, the Liberal Government had fallen, to be replaced by a Coalition administration. Asquith remained as Prime Minister, and Kitchener stayed in post, but Lloyd George, whom Northcliffe admired, was appointed as Minister of Munitions to address the supply problems. There were also changes in the censorship regime. From mid-1915, a system of official accreditation was established, with a small number of correspondents attached to British forces on the Western Front, in the Middle East, and at Gallipoli. These reporters were still heavily restricted, but there was now some more variation in the coverage of the war.[12]

These changes were not enough to stem the criticism from the *Mail*. When Northcliffe read a devastating report by the Australian journalist Keith Murdoch (father of Rupert) on the failures of the Dardanelles operation, the *Mail* went on the offensive once again. The paper accused the government of using censorship to hide mistakes:

> Unless the British public takes the matter into its own hands and insists upon the dismissal of inefficient bunglers among the politicians and at the War Office, we shall lose the support of our Allies, the enthusiasm of the Dominions; we shall waste the magnificent efforts of our soldiers and sailors; and, eventually, we shall lose the war.

The *Mail* adopted a typical tabloid crusading pose, contrasting its fearless truth telling with the 'Hide-the-Truth' newspapers which 'have chloroformed the masses into the belief that everything is going well with us.' And while Asquith and Kitchener remained in power, the attacks continued. The *Mail* argued, for example, that the existing cabinet of 23 was unwieldy and inefficient: a more focused 'war cabinet' would be more decisive. The paper repeatedly pushed the government to end the 'recruiting muddle' and introduce conscription to ensure that Britain had the necessary manpower to take on the German military. It also showed its support for the 'magnificent men' at the front by demanding that they be properly equipped: during 1915 and 1916 there were numerous calls for more machine guns and shrapnel helmets. Convinced that the nation's leaders were dangerously lethargic, the *Mail* passionately believed in its duty to awaken the public to the need for a more strategic and interventionist government.[13]

Over the course of 1916, the tide seemed to turn in the *Mail*'s direction. The Military Service Act of January 1916 introduced conscription for unmarried men aged 19 to 40, and this scheme was gradually extended. The *Mail*'s chief enemies were also dispatched. Kitchener's death at sea in July 1916 was greeted by Northcliffe with barely concealed relief, while by the end of the year, Asquith was losing his authority. Once again, the *Mail* pressed home the attack, attacking the 'limpets' that were clinging onto power:

> A moment in our struggle for existence has now been reached when Government by some 23 men who can never make up their minds has become a danger to the Empire ... The notorious characteristic of our 'Government' of 23 is indecision ... It just waits till the Press and the Germans have done something which forces it to decide in a hurry – and too late.

Behind the scenes, Northcliffe and Lord Beaverbrook, the new owner of the *Daily Express*, assisted the manoeuvres of those conspiring to replace Asquith as Prime Minister. Asquith eventually stepped down and was replaced by the far more dynamic Lloyd George. These dramatic events did much to enhance the myths of the 'press barons' wielding political power, and many now saw Northcliffe as the power behind the throne. The *Mail's* harassment of wartime governments was, as the historian Niall Ferguson has noted, 'quite extraordinary', and at times 'Britain seemed to be heading for a Press Government'.[14]

If a Press Government never quite arrived, Lloyd George was shrewd enough to bring the press barons into his administration, rather than having them rail against it. In 1917 Northcliffe was appointed head of the war mission to the United States, before becoming Head of Propaganda in Enemy Countries. Lord Rothermere, Northcliffe's brother and since 1914 the proprietor of the *Daily Mirror*, became Air Minister, while Beaverbrook was appointed Minister of Information. While these appointments encouraged troublesome papers to throw themselves behind the government, there was widespread concern at the power being accumulated by the press barons. Austen Chamberlain, a leading Conservative MP, accused Lloyd George in the House of Commons of creating an 'atmosphere of suspicion and distrust' by allowing his government 'to become so intimately associated' with 'great newspaper proprietors'. Lloyd George's cynical use of patronage would have damaging long-term effects on his reputation.[15]

The troops at the front remained insulated from the criticism levelled at those running the war, however, and the descriptions of the fighting continued to be couched in a patriotic and sanitised language of determined optimism. The newspaper reports on the first day of the battle of the Somme in July 1916 – the single worst day in the history of the British army, when almost 60,000 casualties were sustained – were all similar in their avoidance of the grim realities of the trench slaughter, their downplaying of the terror of the soldiers involved, and their refusal to recognise the strategic failure of the assault. Beach Thomas, the *Mail*'s main correspondent in France, was sure that 'we have beaten the Germans by greater dash in the infantry and vastly superior weight in munitions', and praised the unfailing pluck of the men going over the top: 'The 'Up-and-at-'em' spirit was strong in our Army this summer morning.' The *Mirror* was similarly positive: 'Our splendid men will not hear of any doubt or difficulty! They mean to win through (they add) very quickly too. Never has such a buoyant spirit been observable all along the front'. The *Daily Express*'s reporter claimed to have heard 'men declare that they were getting fed up with life in the trenches, and would welcome a fight at close quarters.' He concluded that the 'day's operations' were 'entirely satisfactory to ourselves and our allies.' The 'toll of blood' may have been 'fairly heavy', but it was 'by no means excessive, having regard to the magnitude of the day's operations'.[16]

As the losses mounted and the failures of the Gallipoli and Somme offensives demonstrated the difficulty of finding a way out of the bloody stalemate, this self-confident patriotism was severely tested. Philip Gibbs, the *Daily Chronicle*'s war correspondent, was soon writing in a markedly more bitter vein: 'If any man were to draw the picture of those things or to tell them more nakedly than I have told them ... no man or woman would dare to speak again of war's "glory", or of "the splendour of war", or any of those old lying phrases which hide the dreadful truth.' By the end of 1917 the *Daily News* feared that the traditional certainties were collapsing: 'The spirit of the nation is darkening. Its solidarity is crumbling. We began this war with a splendid faith in our aims and with a unity of moral purpose that was priceless ... but our faith has grown dim.' Despite the growing exhaustion and the questioning, though, the silences and the sanitisation continued. If morale was sagging, it had to be sustained. In December 1917, Lloyd George heard Philip Gibbs privately describe 'what the war in the West really means'. As he told C. P. Scott, the editor of the *Manchester Guardian*, the following morning, 'If people really knew, the war would be stopped tomorrow. But of course they don't know and can't know. The correspondents don't write and the censorship would not pass the truth.'[17]

Eventual victory in November 1918 seemed to vindicate the press's support of Lloyd George and the Allied commanders. Grief at the cost of the conflict mingled with the exhausted relief that it was finally over. 'The wraiths of the heroic slain will march with their comrades when they come home', declared the *Express*. Forgiveness of the 'Hun' was far more difficult. The *Mail*'s insatiable determination to intensify the war effort now transmuted into a passionate desire to see a punitive peace imposed on the Germans. During the election campaign that was launched shortly after the signing of the armistice, the *Mail* encouraged candidates to pledge that the Kaiser be tried, that the nation receive 'full indemnity from Germany', and that the authorities secure the 'expulsion of Huns' from Britain. The *Mail*'s determination on these points seems to have hardened Lloyd George's own stance on peace-making; and after a decisive victory for his Coalition government, the Prime Minister went to Paris the following year conscious that wide sections of the public wanted to see Germany made to pay for the unprecedented bloodshed of the Great War. But Lloyd George rejected any suggestions that Northcliffe have an official role in the peace-making process, and in April 1919 decisively turned against the 'press baron' for presuming to interfere in the diplomatic negotiations and 'sowing dissension between great Allies.' With his reputation threatened by his close relations with newspaper proprietors, the Prime Minister now cast them adrift.[18]

The dangerous legacies of the Great War

The celebration of the peace enabled a final flowering of the traditional imperialistic and patriotic rhetoric that had characterised the popular press since the Victorian period. The nation was exhorted to prove itself worthy of the 'heroic slain' and the public were encouraged to 'pay tribute to the gallant Dominion troops who so readily responded to the Empire's call and won renown on many a hard-fought field'. 'Kitchener's men', the original volunteers, remained secure in their status as 'the pick of the nation's manhood'. After the signing of the Versailles peace treaty on 7 May 1919, the *Express* rejoiced 'What a great day it is!'

> [T] he greatest grandeur of England is now and here ... No man ... should ever forget that he is in some sense set apart in the eyes of history both from those who came before 1914 and those who come after, because he was privileged to serve his country in her greatest need and speed her to her greatest glory.

The valiant exploits of the 'war generation' were celebrated by regular serialisations of their autobiographies and journals in the Sunday papers. Those who missed out on wartime service admitted 'a little envy of those who had the years to prove their manhood'.[19]

This rhetoric did not long survive the disappointments of the peace – economic dislocation soon put paid to electoral promises of a land 'fit for heroes' – and the gradual recognition of the full scale of the horror and brutality of the war. The *Herald*, relaunched as a daily in March 1919, highlighted the political and social realities obscured by the appeal to patriotism and military valour, pointing out that wartime sacrifice and service did not guarantee lasting security or even recognition for working men. It argued that the war had been a fundamental betrayal of working-class interests, a time when the 'peace and happiness of the world' had been allowed to fall into the 'murderous hands of a few cynical old men'. The Versailles treaty was denounced as 'a dangerous peace' that would 'make new wars inevitable'; its aim was simply 'to make the world safe for Plutocracy'. Will Dyson's eerily prescient cartoon 'Peace and Future Cannon Fodder', published in the *Herald* in May 1919, portrayed a child representing the '1940' class weeping at the treaty. This sense of disillusionment gradually spread beyond the pages of the *Herald* into the liberal press. An editorial in the *Daily News* in November 1922 scathingly observed how 'ex-soldiers – the men who won the war – sell matches from door to door; their children huddle in the rat-infested slums', while politicians 'patter platitudes about patriotism and about the "prestige" of a country in which such things are done.' The war and its legacy were becoming a cause of serious political division.[20] During the late-1920s, a wave of bitter and anti-heroic memoirs by former soldiers such as Robert Graves and Siegfried Sassoon fundamentally altered the popular understanding of the war. It was at this point that the right-wing popular press started to rework and reassess its traditional jingoism. In these years, indeed, it reflected, and contributed to, the wider social reaction against militarism. The *Sunday Express*, for example, prominently serialised Erich Remarque's anti-war novel, *All Quiet on the Western Front*. The serialisation seemed to tap straight into the popular desire for a different sort of war literature. Despite being a serious novel written by a largely unknown German author, the paper's circulation manager informed Beaverbrook in September 1929 that it was 'a winner and the best single thing for circulation that the *Sunday Express* has ever done'.[21]

As the global mood darkened in the early 1930s, with the onset of economic depression, the rise of fascism and the outbreak of war between China and Japan, resignation and bitterness were far more evident in Britain than jingoism and militarism. As it became obvious that the Great War had not been 'the war to end all war', it was easier to portray the conflict as a futile tragedy; the elevated language of 1914 was badly tarnished. In February 1932 the *Express*, contemplated the 'war weariness of the human race', because 'civilians have learned that in modern warfare no one wins'. When the paper produced a photographic history of the First World War the following year, warfare was portrayed as the 'crucifixion of youth' rather than as the testing ground of manliness. 'There is no glamour left in war after turning these pages' noted an editorial, while George Lansbury, leader of the Labour Party, announced that it was 'the best anti-war document I have ever seen.' Accounts of the war increasingly focused on the strategic mistakes that had contributed to the slaughter of the trenches. A *Daily Mirror* editorial discussing Lloyd George's memoirs in 1934 described the 'ghastly failure of the higher command', whose tactics consisted in 'continually and vociferously demanding "more men" to hurl into deathtraps.' 'What has been done,' the paper asked, 'to get some brains into the Army ...?' The sort of unthinking militarism and conservatism that was now widely regarded as having triumphed during the First World War was satirised in

David Low's 'Colonel Blimp' cartoons, which appeared regularly in the *Evening Standard* from 1934. ('If I wanted to attack the officer class very successfully,' complained Captain Frederick Bellenger, a Labour MP, in the Commons in 1942, 'I would employ the methods adopted by David Low in his cartoons of "Colonel Blimp"').[22]

The main exception to this anti-militarist trend was the *Daily Mail*, whose proprietor, Lord Rothermere, was attracted by the national regeneration supposedly offered by fascist movements abroad, and who briefly supported Oswald Mosley's British Union of Fascists (see Chapter 2). Rothermere also maintained the *Mail*'s preoccupation with Britain's military preparedness, and in 1935 the paper established and publicised a National League of Airmen, to encourage 'a rapid advancement in our air force strength'. Rothermere was, however, deeply committed to avoiding the outbreak of another conflict, not least because his two elder sons had been killed during the Great War. With this rather confused and idiosyncratic position, it is little surprise that the *Mail*'s circulation stagnated in these years.[23]

Whereas the popular press had contributed to the momentum to war in the years before 1914, in the late 1930s Fleet Street largely fell in behind the National Government's policy of appeasement. With the advent of the bomber, whose destructive impact was dramatically demonstrated during the Spanish Civil war, papers knew that their readers faced the terrifying prospect of being on the front lines. The failure of the Versailles treaties to secure lasting peace left little reason to believe in the effectiveness of a future war. When Hitler remilitarised the Rhineland in March 1936, the *Mirror* could do little more than voice its disgust with the old rhetoric, and pray that war could be avoided:

> Who will be caught again by lying twaddle about war to end war, and about our sacred honour and our solemn oath? The futile pacts and obsolete treaties may lie in pieces wherever Hitler or anybody else has thrown them. Better flimsy fragments of imbecile documents on the ground than millions of rotting bodies of young men.[24]

The *Express*, which overtook the *Mail* and the *Herald* to be the most widely circulating paper in the second half of 1930s, became the leading popular cheerleader of appeasement – to the extent that critics suggested that its optimistic appraisal of the diplomatic situation was driven by advertisers desperate for consumers to keep spending. Chamberlain's agreement with Hitler at Munich in October was enthusiastically celebrated ('Praise be to God and Mr Chamberlain. I find no sacrilege, no bathos, in coupling these two names,' gushed the influential columnist Godfrey Winn in the *Sunday Express*), and as late as 7 August 1939 the *Express* confidently predicted on its front page that there would be 'No War This Year'. Even after the Molotov-Ribbentrop pact between Germany and the Soviet Union signalled that conflict was imminent, the paper declared that 'the position is not critical yet'. If the rest of the press was not quite so determinedly positive, most papers maintained the belief that it was possible to negotiate with Hitler. There was, in any case, also a widespread determination to avoid inflaming the delicate diplomatic situation. These tendencies were reinforced by the aggressive information management policies of the Chamberlain administration. Ministers and officials cynically manipulated lobby briefings and put pressure on editors to support the government's appeasement policy. There was, as the historian Stephen Koss has noted, an 'epidemic of self-restraint' in Fleet Street.[25]

The *Mirror* and the *Sunday Pictorial*, in the early years of their tabloid reinvention, were among the few major titles to challenge the thinking underlying appeasement. By the second half of 1938, the *Mirror* had dropped its earlier support for concessions to Hitler, and was calling on the public to heed the warnings of Winston Churchill. The paper was confident that ordinary people were prepared to stand up to Hitler: in a poll of its readers shortly before the Munich Agreement, more than 70 per cent declared themselves 'ready to fight if Germany insists on a warlike solution to the Sudeten crisis'. Yet the *Mirror*'s language, best exemplified by the paper's star columnist Cassandra, was markedly different from the elevated rhetoric of national glory, imperial manliness and Christian piety that had been so widely used in 1914. War, declared Cassandra, 'may be lawful but it is also obscene, murderous, bestial, profoundly evil, and in general a thoroughly Satanic procedure. So if we are going to war let us remember that God is on neither side and to invoke his name is, in my view, blasphemy unbounded.' Cassandra's justifications for supporting the war effort were unapologetically pragmatic. 'When the triggers start going off I'll do some shooting myself to save my skin,' he noted with grim humour. More broadly, though, he was adamant that 'the rulers of Germany' – he was careful not to demonise the ordinary German citizens – 'are the biggest bunch of gangsters that ever clubbed a man to death'. 'I'll not be in it for love, for money, for glory or for honour,' he concluded, 'but because the most detestable regime since the days of Attila the Hun wants to carve up our way of life to fit its own evil purpose.' Through columns like these, Cassandra was able to articulate for his working-class audience a persuasive form of the 'temperate masculinity' – which combined elements of inter-war anti-heroism with traditional soldierly qualities – that the historian Sonya Rose has argued was dominant during the Second World War.[26]

'Standing alone': The Second World War

When it became clear, in the final days of August 1939, that the outbreak of war was inevitable, the press defaulted to its standard role in times of crisis, namely reminding the nation of its glorious past and reassuring it of its ability in the present to withstand any external threat. The tone of the newspaper columns was markedly more muted and pragmatic than in 1914, because there could be no hiding the inevitable horror of the war to come. At the same time, the callous brutality of the Nazi regime, and the insatiability of its diplomatic demands, meant that justifying the war, and portraying it as a struggle of good against evil, was more straightforward than it had been twenty-five years earlier. The *Mirror* captured the national spirit of defiance by placing a photograph of a roaring lion on its front page and declaring its 'sure faith that, through endurance and courage, we can save the world from one of the most ruthless and desperate tyrannies that have ever threatened mankind'. Editorials and opinion pieces emphasised the determination, resolution, calmness and unity of the British people. 'Probably the greatest strength of Britain is its tenacity,' wrote the *Express*'s star columnist, Viscount Castlerosse. 'We may suffer, and suffer terribly. But we have a habit of seeing things through.' Conscious that the military leaders of the First World War had been vilified in recent years for their incompetence, an *Express* editorial emphasised that Viscount Gort, head of the British Expeditionary Force, was a different breed – no 'donkey' but 'a fighting man', nicknamed 'Tiger' and holder of the Victoria Cross: 'Much will be asked of British troops in the days to come. They will know that their commander asks nothing that he would not do himself.' The *Mirror* warned, though, that the public would not accept the mistakes of the past: 'In 1939 we cannot endure fools in high places as we did after 1914. The self-revealed blunderers must go.'[27]

The introduction of the Ministry of Information and the full apparatus of wartime censorship meant that the press, once again, operated under severe restrictions. Journalists broadly accepted these restrictions as being necessary, especially as the worst excesses of the Kitchener regime of 1914–15 were avoided. This was, however, a very different war which required a different sort of journalism. During the period of 'phoney war' until April 1940, there was relatively little to report, and before the Normandy landings of June 1944, Britain's direct military involvement consisted mainly of the war in the air, and operations in North Africa. At the same time, the advent of the bomber meant that the war came crashing into the homes and workplaces of ordinary people in mainland Britain. Unlike twenty years earlier, then, a considerable amount of the press coverage was focused not on the front lines, but on the destruction caused by the bombing of civilians. This was usually a more human and empathetic style of reporting – sometimes, indeed, undertaken by female journalists such as the *Express*'s Hilde Marchant – than the rather stilted heroic narratives penned by the official correspondents of 1914–18.

The popular press's most significant contribution was to articulate and entrench the mythology of the 'People's War', especially once Winston Churchill assumed the premiership after the fall of Chamberlain in May 1940. Churchill's speeches, and J. B. Priestley's 'Postscripts' for BBC radio, are rightly highlighted for constructing a vision of shared sacrifice and indomitable spirit, but the popular journalism of the *Express* and, in particular, the *Mirror* – then coming into its own as the 'Forces' paper' – was at least as important. The *Mirror's* earthy, direct, conversational columns, with their skilful blend of realism, sentimentality and grim humour, gave working-class readers an account of the war in their own language, rather than the language of the officer class. Ordinary voices also came through strongly in the letter columns, to which the paper gave more space and prominence than its rivals. The paper became a valuable forum for the sharing of questions, anxieties and grumbles – a repository of hopes as well as an outlet for frustrations. The opinion research organisation Mass-Observation concluded in 1942 that the *Mirror* was 'probably the biggest source of opinion forming' for men in the forces.[28]

The *Mirror* played a key role, for example, in recasting the military defeat and evacuation of Dunkirk in June 1940 into a symbol of British courage, endurance and togetherness. The troops of the British Expeditionary Force were celebrated as 'Gort's Unbreakables – "Unshaken, unbroken, unbeaten"' – or, in the words of one editorial, 'Bloody marvellous'. Two days before J. B. Priestley's famous BBC radio talk about Dunkirk, *Mirror* reporters were detailing 'How Little Ships Rescued the BEF'. Civilian sailors used '[e]verything that would move and float' to transport men away from danger in France: 'Open motor-boats, slick varnished motor-cruisers, hard-bitten tarred fishing boats, Thames barges and the "shilling trip around the lightship" pleasure boat of the peace-time beach': here was the visible manifestation of British ingenuity and unity, as ordinary men and women worked tirelessly to assist – and save – the national military machine. The back-page headline 'We'll Be Back' gave a stirring warning that the British troops would avenge their defeat in the future:

> All of them gave one backward glance to the beach which spoke volumes. 'We'll be back, Jerry,' they seemed to say ... I saw men at the last gasp. I saw men die, shattered and bloody. I saw men die ashore before we could get to them. But I saw no dejection, no fear – just a grim intensity, so grim it frightened me[29]

If Dunkirk exemplified ordinary British citizens selflessly rallying to the military cause, the press portrayed the response to the Blitz as a demonstration of British resilience and fortitude under the immense pressure of direct attack. Fear and distress were minimised in favour of descriptions of resolute bombing victims determinedly carrying on under pressure. 'They Took It, With Chins Up' was a typical *Mirror* headline: 'After the raid, these street residents rallied and helped each other as best they could. Their homes are wrecked, but not their morale. There's nothing of despair about them.' Herbert Mason's front-page photograph for the *Daily Mail* of St Paul's Cathedral rising unscathed from another night of German aerial bombardment became one of the iconic images of the war. Under the headline 'War's Greatest Picture', the report declared that the photograph 'symbolises the steadiness of London's stand against the enemy: the firmness of Right against Wrong.' The mythology of the 'Blitz spirit' was produced most powerfully and influentially in the daily columns of the popular press.[30]

As well as celebrating the public's bravery and grit during the Blitz, the press voiced the popular desire to repay the Germans in kind. In September 1940 the *Mirror* demanded a 'gloves off' approach, arguing that the bombing of Berlin was 'the only effective method available to us in self-defence'. 'Bomb for bomb and the same all round' was 'the only policy' on which 'our dauntless suffering people insist.' In modern conflicts, in which the lines between military and targets were fuzzy and blurred, the paper suggested that the traditional rules of warfare were obsolete. 'It is now "retaliate or go under". We are not dedicated to passive and polite martyrdom. We must hit back'. These sentiments seemed to be widely shared amidst the public, and in valorising the RAF, and particularly Bomber Command, as epitomising the most modern, dynamic and fearless aspects of Britishness, the press offered readers hope and consolation at a time when the outcome of the war seemed so uncertain. At the same time, British journalists continued to claim ethical superiority. 'Berliners are learning that their city is no more immune than is London from large-scale bombing, noted the *Daily Mail* in autumn 1940: 'The one difference is that our airmen select their targets and concentrate on objects of military value.' The intensification of the bombing of German cities after 1943 brought few moral qualms in a popular press fuelled by what the historian Mark Connelly has described as 'righteous anger': 'The significance of Dresden,' he concludes, 'and the haunting, accusing, sight of Germany's devastated cities, is a post-war imposition on British memory.' If reservations were expressed in some of the elite papers, popular journalists learnt to channel the twin desires for military retribution and moral certainty, briskly dismissing any potential tensions or contradictions.[31]

The newspaper coverage of the government and military authorities was less critical than it had been in the First World War, not least because Churchill seemed a more vigorous and inspiring war leader than Asquith. There was, moreover, no dominant figure in Fleet Street ready to take up Northcliffe's mantle as the voice of the press and public. Rothermere's health was failing, and he died in November 1940, while Beaverbrook was soon brought into his friend Churchill's administration as Minister of Aircraft Production. Nevertheless, newspapers consistently chivvied the government into fighting the war more urgently and efficiently. The *Express*, voicing the concerns of its proprietor, relentlessly focused on obstacles to industrial efficiency: the 'chief foundation of victory,' it declared, 'is arms production'. The *Mirror*, for its part, was insistent that its working class readers at home and in the Forces should not suffer due to official incompetence. The fall of Chamberlain in May 1940 was greeted with relief, but the *Mirror* urged that the remainder of the pre-war appeasers, the ineffectual 'Chamberlain gang', should be removed too. Tom Wintringham, a noted left-wing writer and journalist, demanded in his regular *Mirror* column that the war be run by leaders with an understanding of modern weaponry and military strategies, rather than by those rooted in traditional thinking: 'We need a clean sweep away from the old days of war. We need a war to win the war.' Editorials offered similar thoughts: 'Shall we never get rid of these boobies who cannot understand that anything may happen to those who will not be prepared in time for the new form of war?' The paper noted its distaste for the 'everlasting rot about valour and one Briton being the equal of a dozen Germans.'[32]

The columnist Cassandra was even more outspoken, attacking the timidity, inflexibility and pedantry of the military administration. The Dunkirk evacuation, he suggested, had exposed 'the political botchers who, guided only by supreme ignorance and stubborn selfishness, did nothing during the first eight months of the war.' A year later, he lamented that '[w]e are still not fully geared to fight. Our effort lacks punch ... [and] some of the Service Chiefs are still thinking along the lines of strategies that they were taught about a dozen years ago at Sandhurst, Cranwell, or Dartmouth.' By January 1942 he was adamant that 'Bungling and mismanagement of the Army are on a scale that cannot be concealed and is obvious to all'. Unlike most of his colleagues, the acerbic Cassandra was prepared to puncture the myth of unity embodied in the 'People's War'. Noting in September 1941 that stock values had risen by £6 million after the government's plan for renting the railways 'was divulged by somebody in the know', he surmised that 'the wide boys cleaned up nicely': 'The Ministry of Transport stated firmly that "no leakage could possibly have occurred." Just a curious coincidence. That's all.' Unwilling to accept the official line, Cassandra continued to point out how workers and ordinary soldiers were exploited and mistreated by those with power over them.[33]

Other papers attacked the government in the difficult early years of the war – the *Daily Herald* condemned 'ostrichism' in those overseeing both the war industries and the military strategy, while in March 1942, the *Express* led a high-profile campaign to open up a second front to assist the Soviet Union – but the *Mirror*'s criticism, rooted in a class-based appraisal of the amateurism of the political and military elites, significantly outdid its rivals in its directness and consistency, and increasingly riled Churchill and his cabinet. The *Mirror* and its sister paper, the *Sunday Pictorial*, received several warnings, both private and public. On 8 October 1940, Churchill told the House of Commons that the tone of 'certain organs of the Press' was 'so vicious and malignant' that it would be 'almost indecent if applied to the enemy'; similar points were made in letters to and meetings with Cecil King, the director of the paper. Churchill's patience finally snapped in March 1942 after the publication of an arresting cartoon drawn by Philip Zec, showing a wounded sailor clinging to a raft after his ship had sunk. The caption, penned by Cassandra, ran '"The price of petrol has been increased by one penny."- Official.' What Zec and Cassandra had intended as a warning to the public about wasting petrol was interpreted by the Cabinet as suggesting that seamen were risking their lives to bring ever-greater profits to the petrol businesses. The *Mirror* was given an official warning and was threatened with closure. This was no idle threat: in January 1941, the Communist-supporting publications the *Daily Worker* and *The Week* had been closed. In March 1942 the *Mirror* was the subject of a debate in the House of Commons where it was both attacked and defended with passion. Support for the *Mirror* in Parliament and Fleet Street encouraged the government to step back from the brink; Cassandra's decision to join the army provided a convenient way out for both sides, although the paper ultimately emerged the happier. Mass-Observation found that this warning from above served only to 'increase the proportion of people who feel favourably towards the *Daily Mirror*', and reinforced the popular notion that the paper was for 'us' against 'them'.[34]

The gradual turn of the tide of the war in favour of the Allies from 1943 eased the tensions between the government and the press, and enabled journalists to focus on the heroism of the troops rather than the weaknesses of leadership. 'We Are In!' celebrated the *Sunday Pictorial* after the Allies established a bridgehead in Sicily. The D-Day landings in June 1944 were presented as signalling the start of the final phase of the war. 'The third and last episode in the rebirth of Britain is now beginning' declared the *Express*. 'Today our honour asserts itself. It shouts louder than any other noise in the world.' For left-of-centre papers like the *Mirror* and the *Herald*, progress in the military arena was accompanied by a desire to look ahead to the reconstruction of politics and society. There was a determination that promises of a better future should not be betrayed as they had been in 1918. The *Mirror* gave considerable publicity to the Beveridge Report when it was released in December 1942. This blueprint for a post-war welfare state, covering everyone from 'Duke to Dustman', promised to 'Banish want', and provided a specific vision to rally around and campaign for. Shortly after the D-Day landings, a *Mirror* editorial entitled 'Votes for Heroes' was adamant that the troops were already looking beyond the military conflict to the political battles to come: 'These gallant men are fighting and they know what they are fighting for. Their first task is to rid the world of tyranny. Their second, no less important, is to create a "new world" in which men may live in peace and fairly shared prosperity'. Garry Allighan, in his regular Forces column, implored soldiers to register and not to leave themselves voteless, because the next election 'will be your opportunity to compel the politicians to give you "the better Britain" they now talk about'. Similar messages about the importance of political engagement were directed to female voters. The *Mirror* took every opportunity to emphasise the power of ordinary people, if only they would be prepared to use it.[35]

The final months of the war brought two stories of unprecedented magnitude that were immensely challenging for journalists to communicate to their popular audience. The first, from April to June 1945, was the discovery of the concentration camps and the gradual recognition of the full scale of the Holocaust. The conditions revealed in camps such as Belsen and Buchenwald were scarcely comprehensible and seemed to represent, as one shocked observer commented, 'the lowest point of degradation to which humanity has yet descended.' British newspapers had such a long tradition of demonising the enemy through the publication of sensationalised atrocity stories, from the gruesome accounts of German activities in Belgium in 1914 to the despairing tales of the Japanese incursions into Hong Kong in 1942, that it was difficult for papers to find the appropriate language to convey the entirely different scale of premeditated and calculated slaughter found in the camps. Newspapers gave space to what *Picture Post* described as '[h]orror stories that made the stories of Edgar Allan Poe read like fairy tales', with key perpetrators described as being inhuman in their cruelty ('The Beast of Belsen', the 'Mad Doctor') – but for the *Daily Express*, this was insufficient to bring home to readers the extent of what had happened. In order to educate the public, the *Express* held a free exhibition in Trafalgar Square of twenty-two photographs from the camps under the title 'Seeing is Believing'. The 'Horror Camp Pictures' were designed to provide 'a terrible and convincing exposure of German brutality'; some of them were also sent to other venues. Such reporting powerfully reinforced British hostility to the German people: 'A race which can produce so much foulness must itself be foul' argued one article in the *Mirror*.[36]

The second story almost incomprehensible story was the dropping of the atomic bomb on the Japanese cities of Hiroshima and Nagasaki in August 1945. The British press immediately recognised, as the *Express*'s front-page declared, that this was 'The Bomb That Has Changed The World'. The atomic explosion, argued the paper's editorial, had 'blotted out a whole universe of ideas'. 'Steeled as people have become to news of weapons of destruction, they can but gasp in wonder at this revelation of man's power over the forces of Nature'. Photographs of the mushroom cloud and the destruction on the ground were heavily restricted by the US military and were slow to filter out, but no one was in any doubt that this was 'the most fearful device of war yet produced'. The cataclysmic nature of the bomb was significantly reinforced by the *Express*'s front-page scoop, penned by the Australian journalist Wilfred Burchett, who was the first Allied reporter to enter Hiroshima unaccompanied by military minders. His famous report, published on 5 September 1945 and headlined 'The Atomic Plague – "I write this as a warning to the world"', infuriated the American authorities by drawing attention in dramatic terms to the radio-active fall-out from the bomb:

> people are still dying, mysteriously and horribly – people who were uninjured in the cataclysm – from an unknown something which I can only describe as the atomic plague ... They developed an acute sickness. Their gums began to bleed. And then they vomited blood. And finally they died. All these phenomena ... [Japanese scientists] told me, were due to the radioactivity released by the atomic bomb's explosion of the uranium atom

The evocative language of the 'plague' raised the terrifying prospect that modern science had manufactured a weapon whose after-effects were reminiscent of the medieval 'Black Death'. Burchett also emphasised the sheer extent of the physical destruction caused by the initial explosion. 'Hiroshima does not look like a bombed city,' he wrote, 'It looks as if a monster steamroller had passed over it and squashed it out of existence ... It makes a blitzed Pacific island seem like an Eden.' The American authorities reacted to this report both by targeting Burchett and by working to calm public fears about the fall-out; as a result, there was little immediate follow-up to it. Nevertheless, as the Second World War came to end, the press had ensured that the British public recognised that a civilised society might not be able to survive a third such conflict.[37]

Cold War, decolonisation and 'decline'

After 1945, the wars and military operations Britain was involved in were smaller in scope, less immediately threatening to the public at home, and in places less familiar to most readers: Korea, Suez, Falklands, Iraq, Afghanistan and the various outposts of the declining Empire. In the sphere of war reporting, in particular, the press also increasingly lost its pre-eminence to radio and then television. Dramatic on-the-spot broadcasts and film footage had an immediacy that newspapers found it hard to match. The broader processes of tabloidisation, too, led popular papers to focus more intently on domestic news and entertainment, generally leaving the detail of international events and foreign affairs to the elite press. Rather than providing detailed reporting and analysis, the popular press was more preoccupied with defending and bolstering a vision of Britain as a strong and united national community determined to be a major player in the world arena. In the Cold War world defined by the military and diplomatic standoff between the two global superpowers of the United States and the Soviet Union, it was difficult to pretend that Britain had the status it had enjoyed in the past. Nevertheless, the popular press, and particularly the right-wing papers, demanded that Britain seek to preserve, and live up to, the perceived 'greatness' of the recent past, using its 'special relationship' with the United States, its role as head of the Commonwealth, and its influence in Europe, to shape the international politics of the post-war period. The Suez debacle of 1956 damaged, but by no means destroyed, this world-view. By focusing so resolutely on British power and the opportunities for using it, the press made it harder for the public to come to terms with 'decline'; similarly, the emphasis on diplomacy with the United States, on the one hand, and the relations with the former Empire, on the other, marginalised coverage of the Continent and discouraged the view that Britain might have a place in the emerging project of European unification.

The resilience of the tabloid belief in British 'greatness' was evident in the demand for a British atomic bomb, despite the anxieties about its awesome power and the threat of nuclear Armageddon. The bomb was desired as a symbol of national virility; Britain was also regarded as having a special claim on it due to the significant contribution of British scientists to the Manhattan Project. After the destruction of Nagasaki, an *Express* editorial portrayed the weapon as a product of British genius: 'let us British take pride in our achievement. Let us now praise the famous British, a race incomparable in ingenuity, unparalleled in swiftness of hand and brain.' For the bulk of the popular press, possession of the bomb was, as Churchill would famously observe, 'the price we pay to sit at the top table'. In the late 1940s and early 1950s, the *Express*, in particular, repeatedly criticised the Labour government for its failure to produce an atomic bomb, observing in August 1950 that Britain had as a result been 'dwarfed and dwindled' by the United States and Soviet Union. Without a nuclear capability, Britain could not operate independently on the world stage, and it was left in the humiliating position of relying on the might of the United States: 'Britain's aim should not be to lean on American strength. But to be able to buttress that strength with sure and adequate striking power of her own.' When a British bomb was successfully tested in October 1952, the *Express* rejoiced that 'Overnight it has restored Britain to the status of a major Power' and that no longer was Britain 'a weakling standing naked between American and Russian atomic might'. The *Mirror* was similarly celebratory. 'Today Britain is Great Britain again' wrote correspondent Bill Greig. The successful test

> signalled the undisputed return of Britain to her historic position as one of the great world Powers ... Now the nations of Western Europe have lost any illusions they may have had that they can survive without Britain ... To the Commonwealth it means that the Mother Country is once more able to deter the enemies of her sister nations in any part of the world.[38]

In the period from the successful atomic test in October 1952 to the Suez humiliation at the end of 1956, the popular press portrayed Britain as a resurgent great power confidently bestriding the international stage. 'With a fleet of ... planes stationed at strategic points about the Empire, and with a good stock of Sir William Penney's bombs ready to load into them, Britain could keep the peace of the world' declared the *Express* in October 1953. Governments were encouraged to deal firmly with colonial resistance movements. After a report from Kenya headlined 'Babies Die In Mau Mau

Massacre', the *Express* argued that 'whatever steps' needed 'to hunt down and smash these foul and bestial murderers' would 'have the support of every decent-minded man in Britain.' Buoyed by the enthusiasm associated with the coronation and the dawning of the 'second Elizabethan age', newspapers encouraged the complacent belief that British ingenuity and creativity would enable the nation to punch above its weight and match its bigger rivals.[39]

The Suez crisis, prompted by President Nasser of Egypt suddenly nationalising the Anglo-French owned Suez Canal in July 1956, shattered these comfortable delusions. The affair challenged the whole tabloid model of war reporting that had been perfected in the first half of the century. For the first time since the emergence of the modern mass press, Fleet Street was not able to share the task of rallying a largely united readership behind a military conflict; instead it reflected and reinforced the deep divisions in the nation. The usual rhetoric about defending civilisation, democracy and agreed national borders was difficult to deploy when, in the eyes of many, Britain was a scheming aggressor, acting against the wishes of many of its allies and in contravention of international law. Newspapers divided over whether they prioritised the need to project national strength or the importance of preserving Britain's international reputation; combining the two did not seem possible, even for the crafty wordsmiths of Fleet Street.

The *Express*, the *Mail* and the *Sketch* adopted a belligerent position, generally accepting Prime Minister Eden's view that Nasser was a dangerous dictator who should not be appeased. Setting a template for all post-war international coverage, the crisis was presented through a Second World War lens. Under a front-page headline 'Hitler of the Nile', the *Daily Mail* insisted that 'Nasser must not get away with this', and called for a reoccupation of the canal zone. The right-wing press requested decisiveness and resolution from a premier who had been portrayed as weak – the *Daily Telegraph* had recently requested 'The Smack of Firm Government' – and celebrated the eventual Anglo-French intervention in Egypt as a welcome sign of the persistence of Britain's global authority. The *Sketch*'s headline perfectly captured the traditional tabloid fondness for demonstrations of national strength: 'It's *Great* Britain Again.'[40]

The *Mirror*, the *Herald* and the *News Chronicle*, by contrast, followed the *Guardian* and the *Observer* in the unusual and sensitive course of deliberately and explicitly campaigning against British foreign policy. The *Mirror*, in particular, used all its well-practised campaigning techniques to try to persuade readers of Eden's folly. A series of prominent editorials explained the 'folly for Britain to think of "going it alone" in the face of world opinion': 'Of course Britain and France could move troops into the Canal Zone. Even so, are we ready to police the entire Middle East? Where would military action end? Britain must stick to the policy of collective international action.' Political seriousness was combined with the tabloid penchant for presentational inventiveness. In mid-September, the paper surprised its readers with a headline in Latin, 'Si Sit Prudentia', which called on Eden to show in this crisis the prudence that was advised in his family motto. The *Mirror* took care to ensure that it could not be accused of encouraging disobedience amongst serving soldiers: 'This newspaper has taken no part and will take no part in inciting discontent among the troops. But in a democracy that must not mean that all criticism of the Government has to be stifled once shooting starts'. Instead the paper directed its attacks at the Prime Minister himself, with headlines insistently repeating that this was 'Eden's war' rather than one fought in the name of the British people. This press opposition, coming as it did from what Eden regarded as the usual left-wing suspects, was not enough to alter his determination to punish Nasser, but the humiliating British withdrawal, prompted by the immediate and severe diplomatic censure from the United States, enabled the critics to declare their reservations had been fully justified.[41]

For all the political bravery involved in these oppositional campaigns, and despite the vindication they received from the eventual outcome, they came to be viewed with some ambivalence in Fleet Street. The *Mirror* and the *Observer*, in particular, found that significant numbers of readers, and some advertisers, were dismayed by their apparent disloyalty and lack of patriotism. Both experienced a short-term loss of circulation, which was taken in Fleet Street to demonstrate the dangers of dissension at times of national crisis. '[T]he readers were all for bashing the Wogs', recalled Hugh Cudlipp in later years. The rhetoric of British greatness had such an entrenched cultural power that many readers, even in the *Mirror*'s audience, were keen to see the nation exercise its global authority. On the right, though, the Suez crisis brought home the decline in Britain's power that had been obscured by its atomic capability. By the late 1950s and into the 1960s, pride in Britain's nuclear weaponry was increasingly tempered by the growing recognition of how dependent Britain was upon the United States for the production and maintenance of its deterrent. The United States's cancellation in 1962 of the Skybolt system that the British government had been relying upon made it starkly apparent that the transatlantic relationship was a very one-sided one: a Cummings cartoon in the *Express* showed the US repeatedly pulling the chair from under Britain. In 1964, newspapers gave great publicity to Harold Wilson's admission that Britain relied on the United States for crucial aspects of the Polaris system. As the *Mirror*'s front-page put it, 'Premier shatters independent H-bomb myth'.[42]

During the 1960s and 1970s, the British press's coverage of foreign affairs was marked by an uncertainty of tone. Numerous commentators highlighted, and lamented, Britain's international decline and loss of prestige as decolonisation gathered pace and the economy struggled to keep up with its competitors. At the same time, the celebration of a strong national community was so central to the tabloid model that it was difficult for the press to give up the idea of British exceptionalism. Signs of British success were sought in the new popular culture (for example, the Beatles's 'invasion of America' in 1964), sport (the World Cup victory of 1966) or exploration (Sir Francis Chichester's solo circumnavigation of the globe in 1966). Many of the tensions surrounding national identity and great power status rose to the surface in the heated debates about whether or not to join the evolving European Community (see Chapter 6). By 1975, the whole spectrum of the press supported the 'Yes' campaign in the referendum on membership of Community: acceptance of decline was then sufficiently widespread that few believed that Britain could any longer stand alone as a leading power.

The Falklands War of 1982 provided a last hurrah for the old-fashioned language of patriotism and national greatness. Few tabloid readers would have known anything about the Falkland Islands before the Argentinian occupation, but for much of Fleet Street, just as much as for Mrs Thatcher, they quickly became a symbol of Britain's willingness to challenge 'decline' and stand up for the nation's place in the world. Kelvin McKenzie's *Sun* revelled in its first opportunity to report a British war, taking the traditional tabloid jingoism to an entirely new level, and refashioning it with elements of its sex and celebrity agenda. In contrast to previous decades, first-hand experience of conflict was in short supply in Fleet Street, and, egged on by the intense newspaper competition of the early 1980s and conscious that this was a remote campaign that would directly impinge on few of the target audience, the war sometimes seemed to become a savage spectator sport for a public seeking distraction from economic and social turmoil at home.

Resorting once again to the imagery of the Second World War, the right-wing tabloids ridiculed opponents of military action to regain the Falklands as craven appeasers. The *Express* labelled Lord Carrington, the Foreign Secretary, and John Nott, the Minister of Defence, as Thatcher's 'guilty men' for their failure to maintain Britain's military capabilities in the South Atlantic, while a Franklin cartoon in the *Sun* portrayed Carrington as a mouse, feeble in contrast to a Churchillian bulldog. The *Sun* insisted not just that 'the Argentine invaders must be sent packing', but that the recent cuts in the armed forces be reversed so that Britain could project its power in the world. 'If this adventure crumbles into debacle,' warned lead columnist Jon Akass, 'then there will be nothing left for us to do for the next 20 years except cringe'. While the right-wing tabloids adopted their usual belligerent position, the *Mirror* called for restraint and negotiations, repeating its Suez refrain that military action should only be the absolute last resort in the modern world. An editorial on 5 April observed that 'might isn't right' and suggested that Britain should pay to relocate the islanders: 'The Argentine occupation has humiliated the Government. But military revenge is not the way to wipe it out.' Keith Waterhouse shrewdly predicted the political dangers that lay ahead for the left, noting that there is nothing like 'patriotic hysteria' to make 'citizens forget their three million unemployed.' As in 1956, the divisions in Fleet Street eventually degenerated into bitter name-calling. After the sinking of the HMS *Sheffield*, the *Mirror* repeated its call for 'peace through diplomacy', only to be accused by the *Sun* of being a 'timorous, whining publication' doubtful that the British people had 'the stomach for the fight'. The *Mirror* responded that the *Sun* was a 'coarse and demented paper' that had 'fallen from the gutter to the sewer' in seeking to satisfy its 'bloodlust'.[43]

But if some of the rhetoric was familiar, there was a significant difference in tone from previous wars, especially in the *Sun's* coverage. Humour, sex and consumerism were added to the usual mixture of patriotism, heroism and armchair strategising. Over forty years earlier, Evelyn Waugh had satirised the way in which the popular press blurred the boundaries between war and entertainment, but the *Sun* now seemed determined to outdo the apparently preposterous speculations of *Scoop*. Instituting a daily series of 'Argy-Bargie' jokes, the *Sun* offered readers £5 for their contributions. Favourite puns were endlessly recycled. Having dismissed potential negotiations with the headline 'Stick It Up Your Junta', the paper then sold t-shirts emblazoned with the phrase. The *Sun* adopted its own missile by getting its reporter, Tony Shaw, to sign it and add the words 'Up Yours, Galtieri': 'The *Sun* – on behalf of all our millions of patriotic readers – has sponsored the missile by paying towards HMS Invincible's victory party once the war is over.' Attempting to improve the morale of 'our boys', the paper airlifted fifty gigantic 'page 3' pin-up pictures, each two feet high, so that at least one could be placed in every mess in the task force. The culmination of this coverage was the callous 'Gotcha' headline that introduced the report of the sinking of the Argentinian ship *Belgrano* on 4 May. The front-page was removed in later editions as an error of judgement, but not before it had circulated widely, and it came to symbolise the jingoism fostered by Fleet Street, and encouraged by the government. This was, as the journalist and author Robert Harris has noted, a 'comic-book exclamation' that described a 'fantasy war which bore no resemblance to reality.'[44]

This was a fantasy with important political implications. Underpinning the reporting was the belief that Britain would recover its greatness if, both individually and collectively, people stood up for themselves. Victory seemed to vindicate the Thatcherite belief in strong, uncompromising action on difficult issues – rather than the timid, consensual approach that had supposedly fostered British decline since 1945 – and the 'Iron Lady' received a considerable political boost that helped to propel her party to electoral success. 'We had almost lost track of our history, had almost given up the roots of our past', wrote the *Express* in its victory edition on 15 June 1982. 'But now we have fought again for what is ours, and the blood is up, the heart is strong ... We will be a better country for the testing experience we have been through'. The war legitimised the 'patriotic hysteria' that Waterhouse had feared; celebrating British military heroism was no longer hopelessly nostalgic, but modern and sexy. The *Sun* valorised the 'gallantry and sacrifice' of 'our boys', while offering readers the 'chance to show the world how proud you are of Britain's stand over the Falklands' by buying 'patriotic panties and shorts'. Even the *Mirror* could not hide its admiration for the Prime Minister's resolution: 'In the Falklands crisis she dared. And won'. Any reservations that the right-wing tabloids had about 'Maggie' were swept away, and, having tackled the 'enemies without', she was now given powerful backing to take on the 'enemies within'.[45]

Iraq, Afghanistan and the 'war on terror'

The fall of the Berlin Wall and the collapse of Communism left the United States unchallenged as the remaining global superpower, and provided a new set of foreign policy questions for the British press and political establishment to grapple with. The key decision was whether Britain should align itself with the United States as it sought to protect and consolidate its global reach, or whether it should pursue its interests in a European community that was moving to a closer political and economic union. The popular press was a powerful force orienting the British public across the Atlantic rather than over the Channel. Rupert Murdoch's commercial interests in the United States inevitably helped to ensure that the *Sun* and the *News of the World* tilted westwards, but the preference for America over Europe was deeply rooted. The popular press's articulation of British national identity – fixated on the Second World War as the country's finest hour, and based on a conception of Britain as an 'island nation' with a glorious imperial past – consistently worked against the sharing of sovereignty with European partners. As the celebrity agenda became ever more prominent within popular newspapers, the United States's cultural advantage over

Europe only widened: the British entertainment industries were preoccupied with American markets and trends, and the glamorous stars of New York and Hollywood got far more coverage than their equivalents in Paris or Berlin. The opening of the Channel Tunnel in 1994, and the cheap flights offered by operator such as EasyJet and Ryanair, enabled more Britons than ever to get to know Europe first-hand, but the British press continued to incubate a powerful Euroscepticism, which would be further inflamed the following decade by stories of immigration from Eastern Europe.

This cultural sympathy ensued that large sections of the British press remained consistent advocates of American foreign policy in the 1990s and 2000s. John Major's decision to support the American-led assault on Saddam Hussein's Iraq, following its invasion of Kuwait in August 1990, was widely supported, and Hussein himself became a monster for tabloid demonisation. 'Time to put the mad dog down' argued a typically pugnacious Richard Littlejohn in the *Sun*, adding that 'It should be unnecessary to point out that Saddam Hussein is barking mad.' The *Sun*'s coverage repeated the Falklands formula of belligerent patriotism, boyish admiration for military hardware, and sexualised humour. 'RAF pilots have been handed the task of slaying evil Saddam Hussein if war explodes – because they're the BEST in the world', it reported enthusiastically, before summarising the voice of the troops as 'We'll Kick Saddam's Ass'. The paper devoted a front page to a Union Jack for readers to display: 'Support Our Boys and Put this Flag in Your Window'. Women, meanwhile, were reduced to their traditional role of sustaining morale. 'Flash Your Knickers for Our Brave Boys', it suggested, encouraging female readers to send 'cheeky snaps' of themselves wearing their underwear. The other papers were more restrained, but similarly supportive of the war effort. The *Mirror*, the traditional critic of military adventurism, was adamant that 'Our future safety and prosperity depend on swift and total victory', even if it did provide space for long-serving columnist Paul Foot to argue that the operation was motivated by oil. 'Operation Desert Storm' was notable for the US military's tight control of journalists and its ability to seduce the Western media with information and imagery about its high-tech, 'precision' weaponry. 'It must count as the most brilliant air operation in the history of warfare,' gushed the *Sun*, casually blurring entertainment and reality with its headline 'The Terminators: Top Gun fliers celebrate bulls-eye strikes on Iraq', and reporting that Stealth bombers were so advanced that they were able to 'target the men's room or the ladies' room'. The war was soon chalked up as a success, with little attention paid to the collateral damage or the uncertain legacy left by the intervention.[46]

After the devastating attacks on New York's World Trade Centre on 11 September 2001 – the 'Day That Changed The World' declared the *Sun* the following morning – the British tabloids became preoccupied with the insidious threat posed by radical Islamic terrorism, led by Al-Qaeda. Osama Bin Laden (temporarily) replaced Saddam Hussein as the chief monster in tabloid demonology, and most popular journalists accepted and reinforced the militaristic rhetoric of the US President, George Bush. 'We Are At War' announced the *News of the World*'s front page. Tony Blair's decision to stand 'shoulder to shoulder' with the United States was widely, if not universally, welcomed by the tabloids, as were the initial NATO operations against the Taliban in Afghanistan. Yet as the 'War on Terror' expanded and new targets were sought, the consensus in Britain evaporated and foreign policy suddenly became one of the most divisive issues in British politics.[47]

The Iraq War of 2003 renewed all the divisions of Suez and the Falklands, with, if anything, even greater bitterness. While the *Sun* and the *Mail* accepted the Blair government's claim that the threat of Saddam Hussein's regime possessing weapons of mass destruction (WMD) justified military intervention, the *Mirror*, under the editorship of Piers Morgan, drew on its oppositional tradition to argue against the use of force. The tabloid inventiveness of 1956 was once again in evidence, although this time it was harnessed to a campaign led by social movements and extra-parliamentary protest groups, rather than through the traditional institutions of the Labour party and trade unions. Readers were invited to sign a petition against the war, which was taken not just to Downing Street but also to Capitol Hill in Washington; a 30-foot 'No War' banner was unfurled as George Bush landed in Azores for talks; and the *Mirror*'s 'No War' slogan was projected onto the Houses of Parliament. The *Mirror* also attempted to underline its argument that the invasion of Iraq was distracting attention from the genuine terror threat by organising a helicopter flight over the

Houses of Parliament and breaching the security of a nuclear power station. Despite the substantial and striking protests on the streets of London, attracting over a million people (and with *Mirror* banners conspicuously showing), the anti-war movement of 2003, as in 1956, failed to stop military intervention. The Blair government had enough support in Parliament and the press to ignore or outmanoeuvre the opposition. Morgan himself was later fired when photographs the *Mirror* had published of British soldiers allegedly abusing Iraqi prisoners were shown to have been faked.[48]

In the longer-term, however, the failures of the reconstruction efforts in both Iraq and Afghanistan, and the accusations that the British and American governments had misled their electorates in making the case for war, left a poisonous legacy. The ease with which officials had been able to plant stories, or persuade reporters on the flimsiest of evidence, left journalism as a whole tarnished, and reporters and columnists turned their ire and embarrassment on the Labour government. The *Sun* and *Mail* remained unfailing in their support for the 'heroes' on the ground – the former became a prominent champion of the 'Help for Heroes' veterans' charity from its launch in October 2007 – but became savagely critical of the political and strategic errors made above them, and keen to expose occasions when the armed forces were left without the proper kit and equipment. Right-wing papers thus spent the first decade of the twenty-first century pushing for greater military investment, just as they had a hundred years earlier. The *Mirror*, meanwhile, argued that its opposition to intervention had been vindicated, just as it had been in 1956. The widespread popular disillusionment with British military intervention led in 2013 to widespread opposition to operations in the Syrian civil war, despite the urging of Prime Minister David Cameron: 'Brits Say No To War' ran the *Sun*'s front page on 28 August 2013. The resurgence of support for a militarily strong and active Britain that the tabloids had done so much to foster since the early 1980s seemed finally to be fizzling out.[49]

The total wars of the first half of the twentieth century had seen the press involved as key partners in the mobilisation of the nation. In both the First and Second World Wars, the press largely fulfilled their self-appointed duties of uniting their readerships and helping to sustain civilian morale, while also voicing a public demand for a more intensive and effective prosecution of the war effort. After 1945, though, war became a focal point for deep-seated differences of opinion about Britain's international role. The *Mirror* consistently stood opposed to an interventionist foreign policy, and while it could do nothing to prevent military action, it did provide an opportunity for the jingoism of British popular culture to be questioned and challenged. The right-wing press, by contrast, was a vital support for Prime Ministers seeking to maintain Britain's global reach and to stand alongside the United States. Yet for all these differences, there remained an underlying tabloid consensus about Britain's exceptionalism and a pride in its military 'strength'. The press fed the belief that Britain's greatness was inextricably linked with its success and endurance in warfare, particularly during the Second World War, and enshrined Winston Churchill, with his 'bulldog spirit', in an unchallengeable position as the greatest Briton of all. The language of Dunkirk, the Blitz and 'standing alone' remains deeply entrenched in tabloid culture, as does the suspicion and misrepresentation of the political project that emerged from the ashes of the Second World War, the European Union. So much, and yet so little, had changed from the *Express*'s proud declaration in 1900 that 'our policy is patriotism'.

CHAPTER 2

Politics

The tabloid model is based on the assumption that most people are not very interested in the detail of Westminster politics. It emerged initially as a reaction to the intensely serious-minded political coverage of late-Victorian papers such as *The Times* and the *Manchester Guardian*, which reported public speeches and Parliamentary debates at great length, and sometimes verbatim, and made little attempt to summarise or analyse their content. Editorials were written from the perspective of an insider in the corridors of power, and offered carefully nuanced opinions on the machinations of party politics with the expectation that readers would be familiar with the complexities of subject at hand. Northcliffe recognised that this level of political content was not appropriate for a paper seeking a mass audience, like the *Daily Mail*. Before 1918, after all, every woman and around a third of men lacked the vote, and the party battles at Westminster often seemed a remote affair. 'Four leading articles, a page of Parliament and columns of speeches will NOT be found in the *Daily Mail* on 4 May', promised advertising posters before the first issue, and the pledge was kept. Other editors imitated the *Mail's* style and took it even further. The reduction in political content prompted criticism at the time and since, as commentators suggested that the press was undermining the public sphere and preventing people from properly understanding political life. Such attacks were easy to sustain. Popular newspapers did not usually provide enough information to enable readers to make independent judgements about the issues of the day or to comprehend the underlying structural issues that shaped political, social and economic developments. Yet in many respects tabloid newspapers were simply adapting their content to an audience whose education was often limited, and many of whom unsurprisingly viewed politics as an elite activity conducted by 'them' rather than 'us'.[1]

The reduction of political content led many observers to assume that politics was of little importance to popular newspapers. This was not the case. Politics remained a key component of the editorial package throughout the century, and it was often taken very seriously. As Larry Lamb, editor of the *Sun* in the 1970s, observed, 'Politics don't sell newspapers, but they cannot be sold without them'. Without some political content, tabloids would have been nothing more than entertainment sheets, and would have lost their privileged place in national life. But political coverage was more than commercial strategy. Owners and editors often had strong political views and were committed to expounding them to the public, in bright and accessible language. Tabloids may not have covered routine political developments, but certain issues – those deemed to be of supreme national importance, or those which impinged directly into the lives of the newspaper reading public – were reported extensively. Indeed, rather than being interested but essentially passive observers of political life, offering thoughtful commentaries from the sidelines, popular newspapers sought to seize the initiative and reorder the political agenda according to their own interests. They launched crusades which appealed over the heads of politicians directly to their readers; they harried, criticised, sneered and pestered with sufficient energy that politicians could no longer ignore them. At the heart of the criticism of popular newspapers was not, in fact, that they trivialised politics – politicians were perfectly accustomed to presenting their policies in populist language – but that they were a disruptive presence seeking to wrest control of the political agenda from the main parties, and were often disrespectful while doing so.[2]

Conservative voices predominated in the popular press across the century, but the balance and tone of support shifted considerably over time. We can identify four broad periods: two of stark right-wing ascendency, followed by a swing of the pendulum to more evenly contested eras, as editors became disillusioned with the direction of Conservatism and the Labour movement made greater efforts to win over media support. From the turn of the twentieth century to the 1930s, the market was dominated by overtly right-wing and imperialistic newspapers, such as the *Mail*, the *Express* and the *Mirror*, owned by outspoken and interventionist press barons, Lords Northcliffe, Rothermere, and Beaverbrook. From the 1930s, left-of-centre voices became more prominent and a more politically balanced press emerged. The *Mirror* reinvented itself as a centre-left tabloid, and the trade union-supporting *Daily Herald* became more commercially oriented and grew its circulation. These papers made an important contribution to mid-century reform and reconstruction. At the same time, Baldwin's 'Power without Responsibility' speech served to clip the wings of the 'press barons' and ensured that their ambitions were moderated.

During the 1970s, Rupert Murdoch's *Sun* led a shift to the right, and the severe imbalances of the early decades of the century returned. The tabloids played a significant role in the success of Margaret Thatcher's administration and the rise of a neoliberal political agenda, while also fostering a more aggressive and strident form of political journalism. The Labour Party – and particular the leaders Michael Foot and Neil Kinnock – were prime targets of this new aggression. After the traumatic defeat in the 1992 general election, the 'New Labour' project sought to detoxify the party brand and transform its media image. By capturing the middle ground and playing to traditional conservative themes such as fiscal rectitude and law-and-order, Tony Blair wooed right-wing papers disillusioned by John Major's divided and uncertain administration. Having won over the *Sun*, in 1997 Labour for the first time went into a general election with the support of the majority of the press. Labour's *rapprochement* with the right-wing press would prove difficult to sustain, and when the Conservatives finally chose an electable party leader in David Cameron, traditional allegiances reasserted themselves. After Blair's fall from grace, however, few politicians received the warm endorsement enjoyed by Thatcher during the 1980s; after the Parliamentary expenses scandal of 2009, and the compromises of the Coalition government elected in 2010, the dominant tabloid tone was a combination of cynicism and frustration.

Tabloid politics

Tabloid political journalism was based on four main strategies, all set out at the start of the century. The first was accessibility. Politics had to be discussed crisply and concisely, in terms that ordinary readers could understand. Northcliffe was well aware that many potential readers had received only a very limited education, and he continually reminded his journalists not to adopt a complex or dense prose style that such people would find difficult to follow. Kennedy Jones, Northcliffe's right-hand man in the early years of his newspaper career, told his staff to 'Make the news clear. Avoid technical terms or explain them. State who the persons are whose names are mentioned ... Don't forget that you are writing for the meanest intelligence'. Northcliffe warned his journalists that just because they were familiar with the complexities of public life, they should not assume that their readers were too. 'The Paper is constantly referring to "contingent guarantees" and the "Osborne judgement"', he complained to the *Mail*'s news editor in 1910. 'Nobody knows what these phrases mean, and they will not know until you have explained them twenty or thirty times'. He asked his journalists to try to step out of their own metropolitan bubble: 'The parochial Fleet Street view of the world explains the inability of the public to understand what the average newspaper is talking about'. Beaverbrook held similar views. 'Success never depended upon pandering to the public taste', he wrote to Beverley Baxter, the editor of the *Express*, in 1931. 'It has always been founded on simplicity'. Arthur Christiansen, who replaced Baxter as editor, likewise judged the *Express*'s content by considering whether it would interest ordinary provincial readers: 'Headlines, writing, thinking, phrasing, lay-out, recipes, fashion, all came under the ruthless test of whether they would be comprehensible to the people of Derby and Rhyl'. Christiansen sought to 'simplify news in such a way that it would be interesting to the permanent Secretary of the Foreign Office and to the charwoman'.[3]

The second strategy was to highlight – or, if necessary, to create – drama in political life. Political issues were rendered in stark terms, in black and white rather than shades of grey. Journalists constructed narratives full of 'crises', 'moments of decision' and 'turning points', using hyperbolic and sensational language. By running their own campaigns on particular issues – 'Anti-Waste', 'Empire Free Trade' and many others – newspapers could seek to make the political agenda more interesting to their audience, and generate stories and developments that fitted their news cycle better than the slow-moving world of Westminster. Even more strikingly, politics was personalised. Policies, debates and conflicts were described in terms of the wishes and actions of leading personalities. 'Personalisation is the secret of readability,' Hugh Cudlipp told one of his *Sunday Pictorial* columnists. 'So let's have more about Churchill and Attlee and less about Conservative and Labour.'[4]

The desire for spectacle was particularly evident during election campaigns. Before the emergence of modern opinion polling techniques charting the fluctuating fortunes of the parties, papers used prediction competitions, postal ballots and betting exchanges to generate interest in the weeks leading up to election day. In November 1923, for example, the *Mirror* offered the substantial sum of £1,000 to the reader who most accurately forecast the number of seats won by each party. Politics was recast as sporting competition. The leading papers transformed election night itself into a political festival. In 1906, the *Daily Mail* established a system of magic lanterns to project the election results for spectators on the Embankment and in Trafalgar Square, while firing off different coloured rockets to spread message to people further afield. In 1924 the *Daily Express* constructed two signs in moving lights, one at Trafalgar Square, the other at Shepherd's Bush: 'Thousands of people will be able to enjoy the thrilling experience of seeing the results in which they are personally interested on this ribbon of lighted letters,' the paper declared proudly. Such performances are a reminder that the political drama created by the popular press could leap from the printed page into urban space, not just with election-day light-shows but in the everyday use of placards and sandwich boards with the latest headlines, and street sellers encouraging prospective customers to 'read all about it'.[5]

Third, the tabloids sought to reduce the distance between politics and 'everyday life'. Inter-war popular newspaper editors were targeting audiences that had a high degree of scepticism about the importance and relevance of politics. Rather than present themselves as knowledgeable insiders, taking political debates on their own terms, popular journalists often distanced themselves from the world of Westminster, questioning the importance and relevance of certain types of political debate, and criticising politicians for being aloof and out-of-touch. 'Was a pregnant woman, whose husband could not possibly afford her fourth child, interested in a Parliamentary debate on foreign affairs which would obviously result in nothing at all?' asked Basil Nicholson, an influential features editor at the *Mirror* in the 1930s. Politics only received attention when the importance of the issues was transparent or when they obviously intersected with practical and concrete concerns, such as living standards, taxation, housing, education. By contrast, complex constitutional, religious or diplomatic issues often obtained little coverage. Popular newspapers reinforced the secularisation and domestication of British politics, and sought to wrest control of the political agenda from governments and parties when they diverged from issues deemed to be important to the public.[6]

A corollary of this scepticism was that the press often implied that genuine political wisdom rested with the people, rather than politicians; journalists were therefore attentive to popular opinion, and crafted their political rhetoric around representing 'the people'. Newspapers found numerous ways of monitoring the attitudes of their readers, from scrutinising their postbags to commissioning opinion polls. Perhaps the first formal attempt to measure the public's political views came in 1903 when Northcliffe's *Mail* surveyed attitudes on the topical issue of whether Britain should impose tariffs on foreign imports: this was, the paper boasted, 'practically a general election in advance'. A prize of £1000 was offered to the 'most industrious and successful collector of votes', and some 546,000 ballots were eventually counted – around half from people who could not vote in parliamentary elections – demonstrating a mood in favour of abandoning the liberal free trade policy. In 1929, the *Daily Mirror* established an elaborate nationwide canvass to discover the political attitudes of the newly enfranchised female voters, counting 376,000 ballots. Such polls may not have been representative, but they encouraged the discussion and expression of political views amongst many who were still new to democracy. From the late 1930s, the press devoted considerable amounts of money and space to the new 'scientific' means of surveying the public. The *News Chronicle* set up a formal relationship with the British Institute of Public Opinion ('British Gallup'), while other papers printed the results of Mass-Observation's pioneering surveys; the *Express*, meanwhile, established its own Institute to measure public feeling. After the Second World War, the results of the latest opinion poll became a staple of political journalism. More broadly, though, the tabloids repeatedly presented themselves as champions of the British people against a remote, elitist and out-of-touch political establishment. The greatest admiration was reserved for those leaders – above all Margaret Thatcher – who had a populist appeal.[7]

These strategies meant that popular political journalism was frequently crude and reductive, trying to persuade readers to support predefined positions rather than form their own judgement. It focused on personality and controversy rather offering the opportunity to analyse long-term developments and structural issues. By omitting the detail of day-to-day parliamentary business, it obscured the actual operation of the political system. These popularising impulses nevertheless emerged at a time when the boundaries between personal and political were still strictly enforced, and the personal attacks and scandal making of later periods remained largely unknown. Proprietors such as Beaverbrook were also prepared to invest heavily in teams of talented political correspondents and commentators who often demonstrated considerable skill in their task of simplification. The popular press was a vital source of political information, and, at its best, its populist energy and its restless insistence on action could place the spotlight on key issues, cut through parliamentary obfuscation, and challenge complacency.

Right-wing dominance 1900–1930s

The popular daily papers that emerged at the turn of century and quickly came to dominate the market – the *Mail*, the *Express* and the *Mirror* – were conservative, patriotic and imperialist, and established a right-wing dominance of Fleet Street that would never be entirely eroded. They reflected the views of their wealthy proprietors, but they were also shaped by the deeper structures of contemporary culture. It was far easier for 'patriotic' and politically orthodox publications to attract consumer advertising and mainstream acceptance than for radical socialist papers aimed at overturning the status quo. In the early decades of the twentieth century, moreover, the popular press's audience remained predominantly lower middle class – typified by the suburban clerk reading his copy of the *Mail* during his commute to work – and often receptive to conservative political ideas. There were some notable left-of-centre popular papers, such as the liberal *Daily News* and, from 1912, the *Daily Herald*, but the former was hindered by the divisions in the Liberal Party during and after the First World War, and the latter by the suspicions that surrounded a relative new party like Labour.

Early twentieth-century political life was dominated by debates about the role of the state: how it should intervene in the economy, and what responsibilities it had to its citizens. While the Liberal press supported the introduction of welfare measures, such as old age pensions and unemployment insurance, and the implementation of a more equitable tax regime, the *Mail* and the *Mirror* argued that the state's growth needed to be restrained for fear of extinguishing the individualism that was supposedly the source of national greatness during the Victorian period. They articulated the anxieties of the propertied classes about a growing tax burden and the increasing organisation of working-class trade unions, and suggested that only the Conservative Party could be trusted to run the run the economy. As the 1906 election campaign swung into action, the *Mail* proclaimed that the Liberal Party would 'attack capital' and 'assail private enterprise' if it obtained power. The opposition of the *Mail*, *Mirror* and *Express* could not prevent a crushing Liberal victory over a divided Conservative Party, however, and these papers were forced to wage an ongoing campaign against the reformist governments led by Campbell-Bannerman and Asquith. The *Mail* fiercely opposed Lloyd George's 'People's Budget' of 1909, which raised taxes to pay for welfare legislation. It was, the paper declared, a 'complete departure from the past traditions of British finance', and an 'audacious attempt to force socialism on the country without consulting the people'. The imposition of land duties, editorials dramatically insisted, would 'facilitate the confiscation of property' and encourage an 'exodus of British capital'. The *Mail* threw its weight behind the House of Lords' ultimately unsuccessful attempts to obstruct the budget.[8]

If the right-wing press perceived the reformist Liberals as being politically dangerous, the fledgling Labour Party, committed to a fundamental overhaul of capitalism, posed a far greater potential threat. Journalists repeatedly portrayed the party as the tool of jealous and mean-spirited trade unions pursuing their own goals at the expense of the rest of society. The only way to implement its policies would be to create an over-mighty state and crush dissent. The *Daily Mail*'s first detailed piece on the Labour Party in 1906 suggested that Labour's policies 'must of necessity conflict with the organisation of industrial enterprise', while the party's pursuit of 'new fields of taxation' would hit not only 'large capitalists' but also middle-class homeowners. By 1910 the paper was highlighting Labour's 'campaign of class hatred and plunder'. Before the First World War only the relative weakness of the Labour Party saved it from being attacked more consistently.[9]

Who deserved the franchise was another hotly contested political question before 1914. Many commentators in the right-wing press feared that extending the right to vote – especially to supposedly 'sentimental' and 'naïve' women who might be hoodwinked by the extravagant promises of the Liberal and Labour parties – would unsettle the political system. The campaign of Emmeline Pankhurst's Women's Social and Political Union (WSPU) was rarely treated with much sympathy. The *Mail* coined the term 'suffragette' to label the new breed of protestors, but Northcliffe encouraged his papers to minimise the publicity given to their campaign. The WSPU's violent direct action probably hardened opposition: by 1912 the *Mail* was denouncing the 'hysterical' window-smashers, arguing that 'every shattered paned has been responsible for the turning into enemies of thousands of potential friends.' The peaceful campaigning of the National Union of Women's Suffrage Societies (NUWSS) was often reported more favourably, and the *Daily Express* and the *Daily News* came out in support of the principle of female enfranchisement. It was left to the relatively marginal voice of the *Daily Herald* to provide a reliable platform for the more militant campaign. 'It is supremely pretentious and arrogant on the part of men to desire to keep the franchise to themselves,' the paper declared in

1913. Looking back in 1925, the *Herald*'s former editor George Lansbury was proud to recall that his staff had 'found time to support in every possible way the women's fight for freedom', even to the extent of harbouring activists on the run from the police.[10]

The First World War brought the suffrage campaign, and most other political controversies, temporarily to a halt. The intense pressures of fighting the first 'total war' eventually broke the mould of Edwardian politics, splitting the Liberal Party and increasing the strength of the trade union movement and, ultimately, the Labour Party. The war also brought into focus the rising power of the right-wing popular press. As discussed in Chapter 1, the *Daily Mail*'s persistent criticism of the Prime Minister, Henry Asquith, and the War Minister, Lord Kitchener, was widely believed to have destabilised the coalition and cleared Lloyd George's path to power. Lloyd George, who became Prime Minister in December 1916, seemed to personify a new breed of image-obsessed politician, and often appeared to be more concerned with securing his position in Fleet Street and public opinion than with this party. He appointed the leading 'press barons' to official positions, leading to accusations that he was buying the support of the popular newspapers. Lloyd George was not as beholden to Northcliffe, in particular, as critics made out, and broke with him after a devastatingly critical speech in the House of Commons in April 1919. Nevertheless, as Britain emerged uncertainly into the post-war world, the popular press had undoubtedly become a significant factor in political calculations – not least because new ways had to be found to reach out an electorate that had nearly tripled in size.

With hundreds of thousands of ordinary men and women working, fighting and dying for the national war effort, it became very difficult to justify restrictions on voting rights. By 1916 Northcliffe had been converted to the enfranchisement of women, even speaking to Lloyd George about it on behalf of the leader of the NUWSS, Millicent Fawcett. As the war entered its final stages in 1918, the press threw its weight behind the Representation of the People Act, which enfranchised all men over twenty-one (and those in military service over nineteen), and female householders, or wives of householders, over 30. Indeed, after the heated debates about female enfranchisement in the Edwardian period, it is striking how quickly and decisively the popular press rallied behind women as voters and candidates. During the election campaign of 1918, the press emphasised time and again the importance of women involving themselves in the political process, understanding the issues under discussion, and casting their vote. 'The need for the association of women in the deliberations and governance of national affairs was never greater than now', observed the *Mail* in November 1918: 'Now that we have admitted and realised the rights of women it seems almost incredible that we should have attempted to touch even the fringe of such problems [of social reform] while more than half of the population were excluded from any share in the management of the nation's affairs.' After 1918, the popular press would have to adapt itself to a new, more democratic environment, and it did much to integrate new voters into the national political culture.[11]

The war also transformed the status of the Labour Party, and, more broadly, socialism itself. With one of its leading MPs, Arthur Henderson, joining the wartime Coalition government, and the Liberal Party rancorously divided between the Asquith and Lloyd George factions, Labour gained credibility as the second party of state – a status that it would cement in the immediate post-war years. At the same time, the Bolshevik revolution of October 1917, with its associated violence, confiscation of property, and rhetoric about toppling regimes across the globe, significantly intensified fears of socialism in Britain. The reality was that the British Labour Party was a moderate, pragmatic and reformist movement determined to keep Communism at arm's length; papers like the *Daily Mail*, however, took every opportunity to associate it with foreign extremism, class hatred and social upheaval. The right-wing press invariably labelled the party and its members as 'Socialist' to reinforce the message that Labour was an ideological, sectional party, in contrast to the pragmatism and common sense of British Conservatism.

In the anxious climate of the 1920s, marked by political uncertainty and class tension, the right-wing popular press, led by the *Mail* and the *Mirror*, magnified the 'Red Peril' with vicious condemnations of Labour. Politics would not become so polarised again before the 1980s. The Labour Party, it was constantly suggested, could not be trusted because many of its members had Communist sympathies. A vote for Labour, insisted the *Mail*, was 'a vote for Bolshevism' which would 'threaten every man's house and furniture and every woman's clothes and jewellery'. Bolshevism meant the undermining of all standards of civilisation and decency, and the overturning of proper gender relations. Little more than two weeks before Labour's minority government under Ramsey MacDonald was to face public judgement in the 1924 general election, for example, the noted correspondent Sir Percival Phillips described the 'Cabinet's Moscow Friends' for the *Mail*. Phillips asserted that 'under the Moscow Dictatorship' women suffered 'cruelty, oppression and degradation': they were 'of less value than cattle', and were 'treated accordingly'. 'Women who cannot find employment,' he warned, 'are driven on the street in large numbers.' The *Mail* worked hard to associate the left with male violence and brutality, suggesting the Conservatism offered the safer home for the ordinary housewife.[12]

The high point of the 'Red Peril' scare came four days before polling day when the *Daily Mail* published the notorious 'Zinoviev letter' under the headline 'Civil War Plot by Socialists' Masters'. This forged letter, purporting to be from Comintern chief Grigory Zinoviev, offered financial backing for revolutionary activity to the Communist Party of Great Britain. The fact that MacDonald's Labour government had not taken any action to counter this unwelcome foreign intervention indicated, in the *Mail*'s eyes, that Labour were beholden to the Communists. The dramatic revelation of 'a great Bolshevik plot to paralyse the British Army and Navy and to plunge the country into civil war', the culmination of weeks of inflammatory rhetoric, seems to have successfully fanned public anxieties about the left. Fears of Communist infiltration alarmed more moderate papers like the *Express*, which did not usually denounce Labour with the violence of the *Mail* and *Mirror*. This time the paper warned voters 'that Socialism is Red on the extreme Left, and that the extreme Left always imposes its will upon the whole body'. 'If the moderate Socialists capture the voters,' the *Express* claimed, 'the Red Left will soon capture them.' The *Mirror* simply headlined its front page 'Vote British, Not "Bolshie"'. The heated political atmosphere led to the highest voter turnout of the inter-war period, and, although Labour's overall tally increased, the anti-socialist propaganda seems to have driven some former liberal voters into the arms of the

Conservative Party. The result was a crushing majority for Stanley Baldwin's Conservatives.[13]

Class tensions continued to run high for the rest of the 1920s, with industrial relations hitting a new low in May 1926 when the TUC called a General Strike in support of the miners' campaign to resist a worsening of their pay and conditions. Members of the printing union at the *Daily Mail* helped to spark the strike by refusing to typeset a leader condemning the industrial action, and the absence of the production workforce meant that most London dailies were reduced to printing single sheets rather than proper papers. The news vacuum was filled by publications printed by the government – the *British Gazette*, overseen in characteristically bullish fashion by Winston Churchill – and the unions. A worrying harbinger of the future for Fleet Street was the attention paid to the radio coverage broadcast by the fledgling BBC. The press was no longer the only national provider of news.

Whereas Stanley Baldwin, the Prime Minister, sought to heal the wounds of the General Strike with his relatively moderate brand of conservatism, the leading press barons called for more decisive action. Rothermere's *Daily Mail*, in particular, despaired of Baldwin's 'semi-socialist' administration and cast admiring eyes at the extreme right-wing movements transforming European politics. Rothermere penned articles lauding Mussolini as 'The Leader Who Saved Italy's Soul' and 'the greatest figure of our age', and declared his pride 'that the *Daily Mail* was the first newspaper in England, and in the world outside Italy, to give the public a right estimate of the soundness of his work'. As the economic situation worsened in the early 1930s, the *Mail* expressed its political frustration by publicising a variety of critiques of the British parliamentary system, from Labour MP J. M. Kenworthy's lament that 'for getting anything done that matters Parliament is hopeless' to the writer Sir Ernest Benn's suggestion that 'Our present troubles are the outcome of thirty years of stupid worship of the governmental idea'. Oswald Mosley informed readers that Italian Fascism had, by contrast, produced 'not only a new system of government but also a new type of man.' The search for foreign inspiration even led in October 1933 to an exclusive, and sympathetic, *Daily Mail* interview with Adolf Hitler, conducted by star reporter G. Ward Price.[14]

In 1934, Rothermere finally instructed the *Mail* to come out in support of Mosley's British Union of Fascists (BUF). In an infamous article headlined 'Hurrah for the Blackshirts', Rothermere described Italy and Germany as 'beyond all doubt the best-governed nations in Europe today' and insisted that thousands in Britain sought the 'spirit of patriotic pride and service' they saw in fascist Europe. While open propagandising for the BUF lasted only six months before differences of opinion forced a split, Rothermere and the *Mail* did little to conceal their continued approval of Hitler and Mussolini's domestic policies. The *Mail*'s idiosyncratic politics were becoming less appealing to the mainstream public, and its circulation stagnated while that of its more moderate Conservative competitor, the *Daily Express*, rocketed.[15]

Beaverbrook, for his part, was not dazzled by the continental dictators. His solution to Britain's political and economic ills was to strengthen the ties of empire, most notably by creating a tariff wall around the Empire to encourage greater trade within. In July 1929, the *Daily Express* announced on its front page the launch of 'a new and powerful minority movement', a 'party of Empire Crusaders', and by the end of the year an organisation, with officers and a register of supporters, had been created. In February 1930, Beaverbrook formed the United Empire Party to run candidates in elections. With the huge publicity operations of the *Express* and the *Mail* (Rothermere was an early supporter) behind it, and the financial backing of leading businessmen, the party posed a real threat to the Conservatives, who were still committed to maintaining Britain's free trade regime. This was the most direct challenge yet posed by the press barons and their popular papers to the political system, and when the United Empire Party won the Paddington South by-election in October 1930, it seemed that Baldwin was at risk of being toppled from the Conservative Party leadership. He survived by focusing disquiet on the undemocratic ambition of the press barons themselves, delivering in March 1931 the famous lines, penned by Kipling, that Beaverbrook and Rothermere were seeking 'power without responsibility – the prerogative of the harlot down the ages'. The speech was enough to derail the Empire Free Trade bandwagon, and marked the end of the most hubristic ambitions of the press barons. As was becoming clear, the right-wing popular press was not going to have things its own way for much longer.[16]

Reform and reconstruction: 1930s–1960s

From the early 1930s, the political balance of the popular press started to shift significantly. The key structural cause was the broadening of the newspaper market as the working classes were increasingly enticed into the habit of daily readership. The opportunities provided by this shift resulted in a transformation of fortunes for two already well-established papers, the *Daily Herald* and the *Daily Mirror*, and enabled them to provide a counterweight to the political and social conservatism of the *Mail* and the *Express*. At the same time, the political climate altered too. Having suffered so badly at the hands of the press in the 1920s, the Labour Party was determined to update its political communications strategy, most notably in backing the one paper – the *Herald* – that had the potential to be a faithful supporter. The defeat of the 'Empire Free Trade' campaign led to something of a backlash against the right-wing 'press barons', and, from the mid-1930s at least, the attempts to label the Labour Party as 'Bolshevist' appeared increasingly implausible now that a long-time Labour leader, Ramsay MacDonald, had served as Prime Minister of the Conservative-dominated National Government, and Labour had established its credentials as a respectable, moderate party of opposition. By 1945, Labour would fight the election on much more equal footing in Fleet Street, and it became clear that the scaremongering of the 1920s would no longer be effective.

Before the 1930s, the Labour Party's despair at the activities of the 'millionaires' press', 'doping' the unsuspecting public with right-wing propaganda, had been compounded by its frustration that the one loyal daily it could rely on, the *Herald*, found it so difficult to attract readers and achieve a profit. After the First World War, the *Herald* featured contributions from an impressive array of authors and intellectuals, such as H. G. Wells,

Rebecca West, E. M. Forster and Robert Graves, but its serious-minded editorial policy meant that it did not leaven its political material with much in the way of entertainment or human interest, and it rarely compromised its fierce commitment to socialism in order to appeal to moderate voters. Throughout the 1920s, and despite various editorial changes, its circulation fluctuated between 300,000 and 400,000 copies a day at a time when the *Mail* was selling over four times as many. Unable to sustain it independently any longer, and determined to see the paper reach a wider readership, the TUC sold half of its stake to the commercial publishers Odhams Press (owners of the *People*, a Conservative-supporting Sunday paper), with the hope that it could be given a populist makeover.[17]

In March 1930 the *Herald* was reborn as a brighter, bigger, and more commercially appealing paper. Although politically engaged trade unionists remained the core audience, the paper now had enough variety to attract a broader range of readers. Some old hands complained that the paper had compromised its political principles, lamenting that any socialism had to be included 'on the back of a bathing beauty', but it still contained more political reporting than its rivals. The difference now was the size of the audience. With a properly funded product and advertising, and with a big canvassing push, the *Herald*'s circulation quickly topped one million, and in 1933 it became the first daily to sell two million copies in a day. The 'millionaires' press' now had a challenge on its hands.[18]

By the mid-1930s the *Herald* found itself competing against an unexpected source of left-of-centre popular politics: the *Daily Mirror*. The *Mirror* had achieved great success as a picture paper under the proprietorship of Northcliffe and then his brother Rothermere, but as other dailies started integrating photographs into their pages from the late 1920s, much of *Mirror*'s original appeal was lost. Politically, it aped the *Mail* in almost every respect, including its (brief) support for Mosley's BUF in 1934. With Rothermere loosening the reins and with an influx of new editorial talent (see Introduction), the paper transformed itself into a brash working-class tabloid, and in the process repositioned itself politically.

In order to attract a working audience perceived to be largely uninterested in the intricacies of party politics, the *Mirror* developed a new model of political reporting. The coverage of routine parliamentary business was reduced even further than it had been in other popular papers – in 1937, only 8 per cent of the *Mirror*'s total news space was devoted to 'political, social and economic news', and even on the main news page, only 15 per cent of the *Mirror*'s stories were about public affairs. The coverage that remained, though, was more opinionated and provocative, with a greater use of feature articles, columnists, and readers' letters. The paper gradually developed a left-of-centre crusading rhetoric that expressed discontent with the political status quo and demanded a greater voice for its working-class constituency. It updated established populist traditions for a modern, mediated mass democracy.[19]

The most potent exponent of the new approach was the columnist William Connor, who wrote under the pen name 'Cassandra'. With his informal, plain-speaking style, and a seething impatience with pomposity, official inactivity and bureaucratic obfuscation, he communicated with his readers as if they were talking politics in a pub. In February 1937, for example, he complained that despite the advances of modernity, 'life is pretty grim to forty million out of the forty-five million people who live in these islands. They lack money, and because of it their bodies are diseased, their homes filthy, and their minds twisted and dull.' His anger really hit home when he observed sardonically that the baboons at London Zoo 'live cleaner, healthier and probably happier lives; special glass lets through ultra-violet rays and the food is expensive and well prepared in the modern cheerful monkey house.' Before the Second World War, Cassandra, like the *Mirror* more broadly, refused to support any political party, preferring to develop broad attacks on the political class for their inability to understand the needs of the people and bring about real change. In March 1939, for example, Cassandra criticised the past four Ministers of Labour, from both main parties, for sitting, 'like glorified clerks' watching the unemployment figures rise and fall: 'At no time have these ineffective public servants attempted to provide work on a measurable scale'. He criticised the lack of investment in programmes of public works, especially because 'idle capital is available in quantities that make Croesus look as if he was on poor relief'. Left-of-centre political positions were conveyed in a simple, but powerful, populist rhetoric that played on working-class frustrations with the rigidities of party politics and the harshness of social inequality.[20]

During the Second World War, the *Mirror* positioned itself as the 'Forces' paper', the authentic voice of the Tommy and his wife back home (see Chapter 1). While not yet fully embracing the Labour Party, the paper made clear its support for a far-reaching programme of social reconstruction, and it swung its full weight behind the Beveridge Report of 1942 which laid down the blueprint for the post-war welfare state. By the time of the 1945 general election, the *Mirror* was resolutely anti-Conservative, repeatedly reminding readers of the broken promises after 1918 and the misery of the mass unemployment: 'The land "fit for heroes" did not come into existence. The dole did. Short-lived prosperity gave way to long tragic years of poverty and unemployment. Make sure that history does not repeat itself.' The paper sought, in particular, to mobilise the wives, mothers and sisters of the men who had served in the war – many of whom remained overseas and unable to participate in the election – with its daily slogan 'Vote for Them': 'You know what the fighting man wants. You know which party is likely to give him what he wants. You know the only way to make his future safe'. By demanding a progressive 'people's peace', the country could 'March forward to new and happier times'. One Conservative cabinet minister's suggestion that the *Mirror*'s support was worth a hundred seats for Labour was a hopeless exaggeration, but it is nevertheless significant that in 1945, for the first time, the Labour Party went into a general election with the support of a truly popular paper that seemed to be connecting with parts of the electorate that were not firmly politically aligned. The *Mirror* helped Labour reach past its usual constituency of trade union-affiliated supporters.[21]

Another sign of the shift in the political climate was the limited impact of attempts to portray the Labour Party as extremists. The most controversial moment of the election campaign was a Churchill speech, broadcast on BBC radio, claiming that the introduction of socialism into Britain would require a 'Gestapo'. The *Daily Express* gave the provocative accusation front-page coverage ('They would dictate what to say and do, even where to queue' insisted one prominent headline) and raised the political temperature yet further the following day with another front-page story labelling Labour 'The National Socialists' – the name of the detested Hitler's party.[22] These scare tactics were reinforced by the paper's

repeated attempts to cast the party chairman Harold Laski as a dangerously radical power lurking behind the moderate face of Clement Attlee.
Given that several key Labour figures – such as Attlee, Bevan and Morrison
– had only weeks before been running the home front in the wartime
coalition government, this characterisation of the party was faintly ridicu-
lous. The *Express*'s assistant circulation manager told one of the company
directors that 'the paper is falling into disfavour among people who liked
it because it was an objective and fair newspaper, and who now regard
it as the most politically prejudiced paper in the country.' The *Express*'s
'adulation of Churchill and the Conservatives' was regarded by some 'as
being as absurd as the constant belittlement of Labour.' After their decisive defeat, some inside the Conservative Party accepted that the *Express*'s
attempts to 'bludgeon the electorate' had backfired. This was an important lesson that sensational political claims had to have some ground-
ing in public perceptions or anxieties if they were to gain traction with
the electorate.[23]

The decades after 1945 have often been seen as a period of relative
political consensus, with the Conservative Party reacting to the Labour
landslide by accepting the welfare state and the mixed economy, and the
Labour movement marginalising radical left or Communist voices. Popular
political journalists, preferring the drama and simplicity of stark contrasts,
kept up the rhetorical battle, especially in the late 1940s and early 1950s.
The *Express* and, to a lesser extent, the *Mail*, remained in favour of 'free
enterprise' and attacked the growth of state control. They provided a voice
for the increasingly powerful middle-class frustrations about the continuation, and indeed intensification, of rationing after the war, combined with
higher taxation and inflation (personified in the *Express* in Cummings's
sinister cartoon character 'Mr Rising Prices'). In contrast to the left's version of the 'hungry thirties', the *Express* looked back to the pre-war period
as one in which a middle-class family could enjoy a 'house with garden
front and back and a garage, all to be owned outright in a matter of years',
as well as a refrigerator, 'a not-too-expensive car', and 'money in the bank
to give the children a start'. In 1950, by contrast, 'the man who earns £1000
a year' had 'no such prospect': 'It is, by far, less worthwhile to earn £20
a week than it has ever been before.' The paper warned that the middle

classes 'have nothing to thank the Socialists for, and nothing but further punishment to expect from them.'[24]

There were also strong personal attacks on certain ministers. Aneurin Bevan, the Minister of Health and standard-bearer of the left, was a favourite target of the right, while in March 1950, Beaverbrook's *Evening Standard* stirred up intense controversy by (erroneously) linking John Strachey, the Minister of War, with the recently convicted Communist spy Klaus Fuchs (thereby prompting the resignation from Express Newspapers of James Cameron, one of its star correspondents). The *Herald* and the *Mirror* responded in kind, defending the government's record and warning that the Conservatives would shatter the dream of social reconstruction by pursuing a belligerent foreign policy. On polling day for the 1951 general election the *Mirror* ran a dramatic front page, headlined 'Whose Finger?', depicting a sketched hand holding a gun above photographs of Attlee and Churchill. The obvious implication was that Churchill was a warmonger who could not be trusted to maintain peace as Cold War tensions intensified. The message was reiterated inside, as the paper pointed out that 'there are forces at work in the world which he dangerously misunderstands', adding that Conservative leader was far too close to the US administration: 'Are we to wait for our foreign policy to come to us from across the Atlantic?' A furious Churchill sued the *Mirror* for libel, eventually accepting money and an apology for another, earlier, story.[25]

Yet if the rhetorical battles never ceased, the political temperature in Fleet Street did start to lower in the early 1950s as the punishing austerity of the post-war period eased and the differences between the parties narrowed. Churchill's election victory of 1951 ushered in thirteen years of Conservative government, and also a period of relative moderation in popular political journalism. During the 1950s the *Mirror* grew increasingly tired of Labour's ineffectiveness and infighting, and stepped back from some of the highly partisan approaches of previous years. After Labour's third successive election defeat in 1959, the *Mirror* dropped both its 'Forward with the People' slogan and Richard Crossman's political column. On the right, much of the *Express* and *Mail*'s election coverage was relatively even-handed, and there were few attempts to deny – as in previous decades – that Labour was a serious party of government. Beaverbrook's *Express* remained proudly right wing in tone, but it maintained an independent and somewhat idiosyncratic line, and often criticised Conservative leaders as much as Labour ones. It vigorously campaigned, for example, against Macmillan's attempt to join the European Common Market. The *Mail*, meanwhile, had become more centrist since the death of Lord Rothermere in 1940. Rothermere's son, Esmond, was a more liberal Conservative than his father, but he struggled to develop a distinctive political identity for the *Mail*, and his hiring and firing of numerous editors could not prevent the paper remaining in the shadow of the *Express*. The *Mail*'s approach at this time was typified during the 1964 election by its new star columnist, Bernard Levin, writing in support of Labour in direct opposition to the paper's editorial line: 'What after all has Sir Alec Douglas-Home to do with the twentieth century or the twentieth century to do with Sir Alec Douglas-Home?' Levin asked acidly. This less partisan style was influenced by the perception in Fleet Street that an increasingly affluent and educated public, exposed to the 'impartial' reporting of the BBC, wanted a more sophisticated and neutral tone in its newspapers.[26]

This modest reduction in partisanship had its limits, of course, and was soon forgotten when political opportunities presented themselves. The *Mirror*'s political fire was, for example, temporarily reignited by the appointment of the relatively youthful Harold Wilson as Labour Party leader in 1963 and the general election campaign against the faltering Conservative Party the following year. The paper pulled out all the stops in its coverage, and leading figures at the *Mirror*, notably Cecil King and Hugh Cudlipp, contributed to Labour's manifesto and advised on key speeches; Cudlipp later claimed to have coined Wilson's most famous phrase of the campaign, 'the white heat of the technological revolution.' The paper helped to portray Wilson as a modernising, classless figure standing against the aristocratic, elitist and out-of-touch Conservative leader, Sir Alec Douglas-Home. 'It is Eton, forever Eton, when the Tories are in power', the *Mirror* sneered: 'It is insane that the corridors of power in Westminster should be forever bolted and barred against scientists and engineers and intelligent grammar school boys'. But the paper was gravely disappointed by Wilson's performance in power, and particularly by his inability to improve economic productivity or prevent the devaluation of the pound in November 1967. In a startling reprise of the proprietorial interventions of the inter-war years, Cecil King penned in May 1968 a front-page editorial under the headline 'Enough is Enough', accusing the government of 'lacking in foresight, in administrative ability, in political sensitivity, and in integrity', and demanding Wilson's resignation. It was, in fact, King who was forced to resign: using the *Mirror* as a platform to make such a vitriolic and personal attack was deemed inappropriate in the media environment of the 1960s. The public political machinations of Northcliffe, Rothermere and Beaverbrook were regarded as belonging to an earlier age. The controversy suggested two things. First, it was evident that the political influence of proprietors and editors had not necessarily declined, but would in future have to be employed more discreetly. Second, it seemed that the *Mirror* had lost some of its political touch and was in danger of drifting away from its audience. The scene was set for Rupert Murdoch, a proprietor who both appreciated modern political realities and was prepared to take on the *Mirror* in the popular market.[27]

Right rises again: 1970s–1990s

During the 1970s the political style and balance of the popular press shifted significantly. These shifts were not apparent until the end of the decade, but the seeds were sown earlier in the changing fortunes of the two papers that most fully embraced the new style: the *Sun* and the *Daily Mail*. The *Sun's* relaunch in November 1969 under the ownership of Rupert Murdoch did not initially have a major impact on the paper's political approach. It supported Labour in the 1970 general election and remained relatively centrist for the next few years. Nor was it immediately apparent whether the *Mail's* fortunes would be revived by Vere Harmsworth's assumption of control from his father, Esmond, his appointment of David English as editor, and the subsequent relaunch in 1971 as a tabloid. Over time, however, it became clear that the *Sun* and the *Mail* had the energy and ability to capitalise on the more polarised political climate of the 1970s. Both recognised the potential for a more aggressive and opinion-driven popular political journalism. Increasing competition from television meant diverging from, rather than imitating, the impartiality of broadcast coverage. Murdoch and the *Sun*'s first editor, Larry Lamb, calculated that rather than trying to take popular journalism gradually upmarket, as the *Mirror* had tried to do in the 1960s, it made commercial sense to move downmarket. This did not just mean more sex and entertainment; it also meant an intensification of the tabloid political style, with even more of an emphasis on personalities, conflict and crusading; over time it would also include greater intrusiveness into private lives. The *Mail* developed a similar formula suited to the middle market. Both papers were gradually won over to the 'new right' policies developed under Margaret Thatcher as Conservative Party leader. By 1979, the balance of press opinion in Fleet Street had changed dramatically, and the right had an ascendancy and political confidence not seen in Fleet Street since the 1920s. The tabloids underpinned more than a decade of Conservative electoral success.

Edward Heath, a distant and technocratic Conservative leader who did little to foster warm relations with potential allies in Fleet Street, was unable to capitalise on the growing right-wing frustration with trade union militancy and rising inflation. The inconclusive February 1974 general election, called in response to the second major miners' strike in two years, and the subsequent election the following October, both saw the press return to the well-worn themes of the Labour Party being directed, behind-the-scenes, by undemocratic trade unions and sinister Marxist elements. 'A docile Prime Minster – that's what the Reds are seeking now' warned the *Daily Express*, while the *Mail* gave sensational coverage to claims that the Labour leaders were 'Puppets on a Union String'. The outspoken MP Tony Benn – or 'Benn the Bogeyman' in the *Sun*'s words – became the face of Labour extremism, as Anuerin Bevan and Harold Laski had been in the past. But the right-wing tabloids found it difficult to endorse Heath's corporatist approach, and were frequently critical of Conservative policies on prices and housing. In February 1974, the *Sun* eventually endorsed the Conservatives, but only after running a relatively neutral campaign which gave space to both sides, and describing itself as 'The Paper that isn't in any Party's Pocket'; the following October it despairingly advocated an all-party coalition. The *Mail* gave lukewarm backing to the Conservatives, while also offering praise for the Liberal Party. Labour only retained the support of the *Mirror*, but could console itself that its main rival remained unloved in Fleet Street.[28]

It fell to Margaret Thatcher, who replaced Heath as Conservative leader in 1975, to woo the tabloids and reignite their interest in the Conservative Party with her distinctive brand of 'new right' politics. The *Sun*, the *Mail* and the *Express* came to play a central role in Thatcher's rise to power by artfully constructing an image of a country on its knees due to political ineptitude and union recklessness. A key moment came in January 1979, when the James Callaghan, the Labour Prime Minister, returned from a summit meeting in balmy Guadeloupe to a freezing Britain suffering from a number of prominent strikes, most notably involving a range of public sector workers. His denial that he had complacently left a Britain in serious turmoil was transformed into the famous *Sun* headline, 'Crisis, What Crisis?' After that, the conservative tabloids developed a persuasive narrative of a government losing its grip: 'What the bloody hell's going on, Jim?' asked the *Express* in February. A series of different and essentially unconnected industrial disputes were transformed into a 'Winter of Discontent'. As Derek Jameson, the editor of the *Express* later admitted, 'we pulled every dirty trick in the book; we made it look like it was general, universal and eternal when in reality it was scattered, here and there, and no great problem.' Rarely has the press power to label and narrate been used to such significant effect: the imagery of the 'Winter of Discontent' was potent not just in the forthcoming general election, but throughout the following decade and into the 1992 election.[29]

As polling-day drew closer, the conservative tabloids rallied decisively behind Thatcher. 'She holds aloft the beacon of optimism', wrote the *Mail* admiringly: 'To read the Tory manifesto is to feel the spirits rise'. Under the rousing headline 'I Believe!', meanwhile, the *Sun* – which had been developing its own brand of blue-collar conservative populism under new political editor Walter Terry and leader writer Ronnie Spark – reported that Thatcher had 'declared her faith in a better, brighter, booming Britain', and had 'set the election alight' by promising to 'slash taxes, curb union power, combat crime and reform schools'. The positive coverage of Thatcher was complemented by unusually vehement and tendentious criticism of the Labour Party, the unions and the radical figures – notably Tony Benn – lurking behind the leadership. 'How Many Reds in Labour's Bed?' asked one *Sun* feature: 'Power of Wild Men will Grow if Uncle Jim is Elected Again'. One of the most sensational attacks was a front-page article in the *Mail* on 26 April 1979, under the headline 'Labour's Dirty Dozen', which supposedly exposed the '12 lies designed to frighten voters into staying with a bankrupt Labour Government'. Not only was this article a light reworking of a Conservative Central Office press release, many of these 'lies' – such as the claim that Thatcher would double VAT – were subsequently shown to be pretty close to the truth. On the eve of election day an unusually lengthy and florid editorial in the *Sun* called on its readers to 'Vote Tory This Time' as the only way to 'Stop the Rot'. It was addressed explicitly 'to traditional supporters of the Labour party', who, like Murdoch and Lamb, had become disillusioned with the left. Although it seems that more *Sun* readers voted Labour than Tory in 1979, the paper's endorsement was certainly significant, and may have helped to influence the young male skilled and unskilled working-class electors who swung behind the Conservatives in substantial numbers and helped to propel the party to victory.[30]

For more than a decade the conservative tabloids celebrated and sustained Britain's first female Prime Minister. 'Maggie', as she came to be known, was the first Conservative leader who was genuinely in tune with tabloid populism. With her relatively modest provincial background, her suspicion of traditional elites and institutions, her stark, confrontational and yet commonsensical political rhetoric, her unapologetic patriotism, and her resolute support for 'law and order' and family morality, she could have been invented by the right-wing popular press. Whereas most Tory patricians struggled to conceal their disdain for popular newspapers, Thatcher, encouraged by her public relations guru Gordon Reece, maintained warm relations with proprietors and editors, and rewarded them handsomely with honours and favours. Five months after the election, for example, the *Sun* asked the Prime Minister for a letter of congratulations to celebrate the paper's tenth birthday. Overriding the objection of her press secretary, Thatcher wrote 'The Sun is a friend! Will do'. More significantly, Rupert Murdoch's empire benefited from the Conservative government in some fairly conspicuous ways: the acquisition of *The Times* and *Sunday Times* was waved through in 1981–2, and the full support of the Metropolitan Police was offered when the News International operation was suddenly moved to Wapping in 1986, against trade union opposition.[31]

In office, Thatcher was not a great newspaper reader, but remained informed through the press briefings prepared by Bernard Ingham, her chief press secretary. Ingham usually started his summaries with the *Sun* and encouraged the view that the paper represented the views of the man in the street. Once she had ridden out the initial political and social turbulence provoked by her monetarist policies, and had triumphantly proved her mettle in the 1982 Falklands War (see Chapter 1), the conservative tabloids portrayed her as nothing less than the nation's saviour. At election time, they were unfailingly committed. In 1983, the *Mail*'s coverage was so partisan in its support for Thatcher that the journalists' union chapel requested that other parties be given fairer coverage, and the *Sun*'s backing was just as vigorous. With the *Sun* firmly installed as the nation's most popular paper, having overtaken the declining *Mirror* in 1978, and the new *Daily Star* shifting from its initial pro-Labour stance to support the Conservatives too, the political balance of the popular press was more unequal than at any time since the 1920s. In the 1920s, moreover, the leading papers had been sceptical of Baldwin and many of his colleagues; now the tabloids were enthusiastic cheerleaders for the Prime Minister. The *Daily Mirror* was the only counterweight to this right-wing populism.[32]

There were important shifts, too, in the nature of popular political journalism in the 1980s. These were most visible in the *Sun*, as Kelvin MacKenzie, installed as editor in 1981, responded to changes in the social and cultural environment and updated the tabloid template for a new era. The belief that circulation growth could be achieved by moving downmarket led to a further blurring of the boundaries between politics, entertainment and celebrity. Political reporting became more personalised, intrusive, outspoken and sensationalised. The culture of silence around politicians' private lives, which in the first half of the century had enabled the infidelities of prime ministers, party leaders and their wives to be discreetly kept out of the public eye, had started to break down at the time of the Profumo Affair in 1963, but it was not until the 1980s and 1990s that the tabloid-driven sex scandal became a regular feature of British political culture. A long line of senior politicians, including Cecil Parkinson, Jeffery Archer, Paddy Ashdown and David Mellor, were damaged by the exposure of private sexual liaisons, while in 1987, Peter Mandelson, Labour's Director of Communications, was unceremoniously outed by the *News of the World*. The renewed aggression of the tabloids was also evident in the co-ordinated campaign throughout the 1980s against the so-called 'loony left' – the umbrella term used to describe the union movement, militant local authorities and minority rights campaigners. The right-wing tabloids played a crucial role in maintaining public support for the government during its campaign against Arthur Scargill and the miners' unions during the bitter strike of 1984–5, and magnified the divisions on the left by featuring, and demonising, 'extremist' figures such as Tony Benn and the Ken Livingstone, leader of the Greater London Council (1981–1986) and subsequently Labour MP.

But essential to the *Sun*'s commercial success was the way that it skilfully balanced its political aggression with a cheeky humour that resonated with an audience that felt a limited engagement with the world of politics. In 1987, for example, the paper ran the headline 'Why I'm Backing Kinnock, By Stalin', based on the speculations of a psychic employed to discover voting intentions from 'beyond the grave'. During the following election campaign, the *Sun* argued that Elvis Presley and Queen Victoria would have supported the Conservatives – the latter would 'not have been amused' by Kinnock the 'ginger jester'. Packaging politics as a form of entertainment enabled the *Sun* to engage its many readers who felt no strong party political affiliation, but who exhibited, as one study suggested, a 'strong conservative apolitical self-identity'.[33]

The market dominance of an energised and committedly right-wing tabloid press undoubtedly played a major part in underpinning Margaret Thatcher's success in the 1980s. Yet the relationship went deeper. The tabloid press was woven intimately into the fabric of Thatcherite political culture. The *Sun* and the *Mail*, in particular, with their combination of brash conservative populism, capitalist cheerleading, glitzy consumerism and self-confident moralising, represented the Thatcherite message more faithfully and completely than any other media channel. Such a passionate relationship inevitably could not last. John Major was initially given support as Thatcher's anointed successor, and was backed in the 1992 general election campaign with all the weapons of tabloid political journalism. The Labour leader, Neil Kinnock, was subjected to merciless criticism, and his party's tax plans were cynically distorted ('£1000 A Year Cost of Labour'). The *Sun*'s polling day front page pictured the Welshman's head in a lightbulb alongside the headline 'If Kinnock wins today will the last person to leave Britain please turn out the lights'. When a Conservative victory was declared in what had been seen as a close race, Murdoch's daily famously boasted 'It's The Sun Wot Won It'. Yet Major could never live up to the expectations created by Thatcher, and when, in October 1992, he was dramatically forced by the currency speculation of 'Black Wednesday' to drop his flagship economic policy of involvement in the European Exchange Rate Mechanism, the press turned against him. The redrawing of the boundaries between public and private that had become apparent during the 1980s now worked against him as his party was engulfed with a wave of scandals and accusations of sleaze. The traditionally tense relationship between the right-wing press and Conservative leaders finally reasserted itself – indeed when Major stood for re-election as party leader in 1995, there were widespread calls for his defeat. When he emerged victorious, the *Sun* predicted that future electoral defeat was inevitable: 'Chickens Hand It To Blair'.[34]

Shift to the centre? 1990s–present

Defeat in the 1992 general election was a traumatic experience for the Labour Party. Its fourth electoral reverse in a row left many wondering whether the party would ever be able to win over the British public – especially as it had failed to convince them when running a relatively disciplined campaign against an inexperienced leader overseeing an underperforming economy. The modernisers who rose to the top of the party after the untimely death of John Smith in 1994 – Tony Blair, Gordon Brown, Peter Mandelson and Alastair Campbell – were convinced that Labour needed significantly to alter its public image, and hence its relationship with the media: this was the only way it could compete for the electoral middle ground. Tony Blair was a young, articulate and telegenic leader who had already impressed the conservative press with his firmness on law-and-order while serving as shadow Home Secretary. His 1993 pledge to be 'tough on crime and tough on the causes of crime' demonstrated his awareness of the need for soundbites that would play well across the political spectrum. Blair and the modernisers worked hard to neutralise the issues that the right-wing tabloids had ruthlessly exploited in the past, notably rewriting Labour's 'Clause 4' commitment to public ownership to demonstrate its adherence to the market economy, and pledging not to raise income tax to counter suggestions that the party would resort to its traditional 'tax-and-spend' stance. Mandelson and Campbell, in particular, professionalised Labour's media operation, crafting memorable campaign pledges and establishing a rapid rebuttal unit. New lines of communication were opened up to proprietors and editors, most notably in July 1995 when Tony Blair travelled to Hayman Island in Australia to meet Rupert Murdoch and address a New Corporation conference. Gordon Brown's work ethic, fiscal caution and social conservatism, meanwhile, gradually won the respect of *Mail* editor Paul Dacre. With so many right-wing journalists thoroughly disillusioned with Major's weak and divided administration, key Labour figures had a rare opportunity to gain an extended hearing in the pages of usually hostile titles.

The result was that Labour, for the first time ever, went into the 1997 general election with the support of the majority of the press. The decisive moment was the front-page announcement, the day after Major set the polling date, that 'The *Sun* Backs Blair'. Despite the reservations of Trevor Kavanagh, the *Sun*'s political editor, and continuing concerns about Labour's links with the unions and its policies on Europe, the paper threw its weight behind the party and generously opened up its columns for Blair to communicate directly with its readers. Blair used this opportunity to try to neutralise suspicions of his Europeanism, declaring his 'love' for the pound, and pledging to 'see off Euro dragons'; the paper also helped contain fears of radicalism with front-page headlines such as 'Blair Kicks Out Lefties'. The *Sun* also continued the assault on Tory 'sleaze' by dramatically revealing how the Conservative MP Piers Merchant had been 'having a sordid affair with a 17-year-old blonde Soho nightclub hostess'. Merchant worsened the situation for his party by resisting strong pressure from the party leadership to step down, enabling the *Sun* to portray Major, once again, as a 'weak' figure who 'cannot run his party' and was therefore 'in no position to run the country'. When the *Sun*'s support was combined with the enthusiastic backing of the *Mirror* and the *Star*, Labour had a clear lead in the tabloid market; the *Mail* and *Express*, moreover, while opposing Labour, were often fiercely critical of the Conservatives, and especially their divisions over Europe. The *Mail* admitted that Major was 'an ineffectual leader' whose 'incompetence' had undermined his administration. The extent of the political realignment was vividly symbolised by *Mail* owner Vere Harmsworth, the third Lord Rothermere, moving across to the Labour benches in the House of Lords. His fiercely anti-socialist grandfather, who had been attracted by fascism rather than submit to Conservative dithering, would have been astonished.[35]

Nor was this realignment temporary. As Blair and Brown demonstrated their political and economic caution, and the Conservatives struggled to develop a convincing strategy to regain power, the arguments for supporting Labour remained persuasive. Labour went into the 2001 general election with an even greater level of press backing, having supplemented the support of the *Sun* and *Star* with the endorsement of the *Express* papers, as well as *The Times*. The *Express*'s shift was as historic as Rothermere's crossing of the benches, as the paper noted: 'after 100 years of support for the Conservatives in every general election since 1900 we urge you to vote Labour today'. The feebleness of the Major government had become an image almost as damaging to the Conservatives as the 'Winter of Discontent' had been for Labour. 'We need only to recall the dying days of the last Tory government to recognise that this is a party which has run out of steam,' observed the *Express* when justifying its switch: 'John Major and his cabinet simply had nothing left to offer but more sleaze and incompetence.' With the Conservatives suffering an electoral drubbing nearly as severe as in 1997, it seemed as if Britain's political centre of gravity had decisively moved.[36]

In many respects, however, these realignments were not as deep-rooted as they appeared. The Labour modernisers had compromised so much in their bid for the political centre ground that many no longer saw them as a left-wing party; they certainly did not threaten the fundamentals of the Thatcher settlement. Having been so badly scarred by the defeat of 1992, the New Labour generals were inclined to exaggerate the power of the tabloid press, and frequently deferred to it rather than challenge it. Gordon Brown's mildly redistributive tax measures were rarely trumpeted as proudly as tough law-and-order measures such as the introduction of the Anti-Social Behaviour Order (ASBO), and the party refused to take on deeply entrenched tabloid euro-scepticism. Murdoch's *Sun*, for its part, was always keen to back a winner, and had little desire to set itself outside the mainstream of British public opinion by adhering to a Conservative Party lacking credibility and decisive leadership. Both sides had much to gain from a marriage of convenience, but there was always a risk that the passion would gradually fizzle out. Furthermore, the focus on presentation and media image that was an essential part of Labour's rehabilitation was, as Campbell and Mandelson later admitted, taken too far into government. The perception that New Labour was a triumph of style over substance, and that many of its achievements had been spun by a cynical but talented public relations team, became a powerful and tenacious narrative that the *Mail*, in particular, used against it.

Damaged by the fall-out from the Iraq war, and weighed down by the increasingly conspicuous internal rivalry between Blair and Brown, press support gradually leaked away, with the *Express* and *Star* defecting in 2005, and the *Sun* following suit in 2009. David Cameron, who assumed leadership of the Conservatives in 2005, imitated many of the strategies that had been successful for New Labour, sharpening up the party's media operation, wooing key figures in the press, notably News International's Rebekah Brooks, and directing his appeal to the political middle ground. The *Sun*'s enthusiastic promotion of 'Cam the Man' helped to soften the Conservative leader's elite image, just as the relentless attacks on 'Prime Sinister' Gordon Brown reinforced the negative impressions conveyed by the latter's stumbling media performances.

Despite the media interest in the *Sun*'s declaration of support for the Conservatives – announced to upstage the Labour Party conference in September 2009 – this shift in allegiance was not as significant as the paper's backing of Blair had been in 1997. The political power of the tabloids, demonstrated so often across the century, and a major factor in the shifts of the 1980s and 1990s, was waning. The rise of the internet and social media hastened the long-term decline in newspaper circulations, while the decision to run a series of televised leaders' debates consolidated television's status as the centrepiece of the electoral campaign.[37]

With evidence accumulating that younger readers, in particular, were disengaged from party politics, the tabloids reduced further their coverage of public affairs in favour of giving greater priority to celebrity culture. The *Daily Star* was the paper that made the fewest attempts to conceal its disdain for Westminster. On polling day in June 2001, for example, the paper boasted that it had an 'election-free front page', concentrating instead on pictures of a topless celebrity and the arrest of the popular entertainer Michael Barrymore. An editorial inside, entitled 'Goodbye to boredom', described the paper's relief that 'for the first time in weeks, you can turn on the telly and NOT see a bunch of politicians wheedling for your vote.' In May 2005, the paper similarly reported that 'Britain is finally ready to party today after the most boring general election in history fizzled to an end. The fed-up nation breathed a sigh of relief as the ballots closed – and urged dreary Tony Blair, Michael Howard and Charles Kennedy to put a cork in it.' The expenses scandal of 2009 – a huge scoop that slipped through the fingers of the *Sun*, and was broken instead by the *Daily Telegraph* – consolidated and further encouraged the press's cynical view of politicians, although, for the *Star*, it at least gave readers a motivation for voting. 'Time to give 'em a kick in the ballots!' ran one front-page article, urging readers to 'remember all the broken promises, the fiddled expenses and the negative campaigning' and exercise their power 'over the least-liked bunch of MPs for a generation'. While the *Star* took the anti-politics approach further than any of its rivals, few tabloid editors believed that political coverage was a priority in an era of inexorably declining circulations, and the coverage that remained was increasingly dutiful in tone.[38]

In many respects, the political disengagement and apathy of recent years is nothing new. Newsrooms have long been keenly aware of what *Express* editor Arthur Christiansen called the 'immense reader-resistance' to 'heavy' political content. Tabloid journalists have always tried to make politics accessible, dramatic, and relevant, and have been sceptical of the more remote and introverted aspects of Westminster life. Yet the wider media environment in which the tabloids operated has shifted considerably over the decades, and is now serving both to weaken the political commitment of many papers, and to foster cynicism and distrust. Until the Second World War, the popular press was the chief source of political information for most ordinary people, and it was not until the 1960s that television broadcasting overcame its initial caution in covering politics. It was not surprising that editors and proprietors made bold claims about the influence of their papers, and that such claims were accepted. Even as politics became more television-centric, broadcasting was constrained by its duty of impartiality, allowing the partisan press to play a major role in setting the political agenda with its campaigns, critiques and scandal-mongering. The compromises associated with the rebranded New Labour in the 1990s showed how anxious politicians still were about the political power of tabloids. Since the turn of the twenty-first century, however, the gradual circulation decline of the tabloids has become decidedly more precipitous, 24-hour news channels provide almost obsessive coverage of breaking political stories, and the internet provides the platform for an ever-bubbling cauldron of opinionated blogs and social media sites. While an element of political content remains essential in retaining a tabloid identity, it has become harder for popular newspapers to provide distinctive coverage, and correspondingly more and more tempting to focus on celebrity, sport and entertainment.

As the tabloids have declined, moreover, they have become easier to attack. The close personal and professional relations between journalists and politicians revealed by the Leveson inquiry and the trials of former *Sun* editors Rebekah Brooks and Andy Coulson were embarrassing for both sides. As the revelations of journalistic misconduct mounted, politicians felt the need to distance themselves from the tabloids. David Cameron's reputation was seriously tarnished by Coulson's enforced resignation as his Director of Communications in January 2011, and by his subsequent criminal conviction in July 2014. Rupert Murdoch's aura of power and mystery was also considerably weakened by his faltering appearance before the Culture, Media and Sport Select Committee, and politicians across the political spectrum queued up to denounce his hold over British life. The tabloids' sense of authority and self-importance was very difficult to preserve in these circumstances and while their skill and inventiveness ensures that their political impact should never be entirely discounted, little more than twenty years after Murdoch's red-top cheekily declared 'It's The Sun Wot Won It', such claims seem to belong to another era.

CHAPTER 3

Monarchy and Celebrity

Tabloids are built on 'human interest', the basic curiosity we have about other people. Always tell the news through people, Lord Northcliffe told his staff, 'because people are so much more interesting than things'. He insisted that his papers provide 'Interviews, Descriptions of People and articles of the personal type'. The gradual integration of photography into newspapers reinforced this focus on the individual, because it was much easier to create an emotional connection with a familiar face than a mere name on a page. In their drive for these intimate, human stories, popular newspapers subverted the elite press's traditional hierarchy of news values based on ideas of public importance and historical significance. An item about a notable individual – a marriage or divorce, a triumph or disaster – could therefore be deemed worthy of more space than a political or diplomatic development, because human drama could generate more reader interest and enthusiasm than the apparently remote happenings of the public sphere. By having a regular cast of characters – royalty, aristocrats, socialites, politicians, actors and entertainers, sportsmen and women – whose trials and tribulations could be chronicled, newspapers both guaranteed themselves a steady supply of stories and provided their audience with many of the satisfactions of reading fiction or gossiping with friends. For urban, mobile individuals often without deep roots in a local community and consumed with the daily grind, celebrity culture enabled vicarious participation in a glamorous world and enjoyable, consequence-free, opportunities to sympathise or condemn.[1]

Across the twentieth century the members of the royal family dwarfed all others in their pulling power and news value. Symbols of the nation and at the heart of public ceremonial, they had a reach unmatched by celebrities reliant on skill or beauty. With the monarchy seeking to justify its role and retain public support in the new mass democracy, there was an acceptance that it needed to work with media: publicity was an essential element of its symbolic role. At the same time, retaining the necessary mystique and authority required a certain distance, and there was a strong desire within the royal family not to be brought down to the same level as other celebrities. In the first half of the century, the monarchy could rely on a significant degree of deference in the press, most dramatically demonstrated by the long press silence about one of the biggest stories of the century, Edward VIII's relationship with a divorcée, Wallis Simpson. After the Second World War, the popular press, led by the *Daily Mirror* and the *Sunday Pictorial*, reacted against the inter-war caution and gradually became more questioning and intrusive. Princess Margaret's romance with Group Captain Peter Townsend was pursued with an insatiable appetite, and there was also a gentle mockery of some of the monarchy's stuffier practices and traditions. During the 1980s the boundaries between monarchy and celebrity collapsed entirely as the tabloids became fixated with the glamorous and media-savvy Princess Diana. As Diana's marriage to Prince Charles unravelled, the press took ever-greater risks to pursue the story, as well as becoming increasingly critical of the financial burden of the extended royal establishment. Diana's death in 1997 after being pursued by paparazzi photographers through the streets of Paris brought home with shocking immediacy the costs of intrusive celebrity journalism. In subsequent years, the monarchy learned how to manage its media image more effectively, and insisted on restrictions on the coverage of the younger royals, but the apologies and promises made by Fleet Street after Diana's fatal accident were soon forgotten.

If the members of the royal family had a guaranteed news value, they were, with few exceptions, reserved, dutiful and conservative individuals, and the press, even at the end of the period, inevitably operated under some constraints when covering them. Other celebrities provided greater opportunities for the press to indulge fantasies of sex, glamour, skill, consumption and transgression. The Society figures who dominated the gossip columns of the first decade of the twentieth century were soon replaced by the stars of cinema and, later, the music and television industries, whose attractiveness, extroversion, wealth and global mobility generated endless opportunities for fresh stories and 'intimate' interviews. For the first two-thirds of the century, most 'revelations' and 'confessions' were carefully staged, but as celebrity culture intensified and the press felt the heat of competition from television, editors, journalists and photographers became more daring in their search of scoops. In the 1980s, Kelvin MacKenzie developed the 'kiss-and-tell' into a central element of the tabloid model, while technological developments such as the mobile phone and online database increasingly gave unscrupulous reporters and private detectives new opportunities to dredge up stories. Yet this greater intrusiveness carried serious reputational dangers for the press. Although circulation figures demonstrated the public's appetite for celebrity gossip, many readers regarded their consumption of this material as a guilty pleasure, and they often had little respect for those who produced it. The popular press's ever more vigorous pursuit of the celebrity agenda was often at the expense of the trust that had allowed journalists to educate and inform, rather than merely entertain, their readers. The findings of the Leveson inquiry, published in November 2012, generated widespread outrage and damaged the tabloid brand more seriously even than Diana's death.

The tabloid press played a central role in entrenching both monarchy and celebrity at the heart of British popular culture, much to the despair of numerous political and social commentators. In doing so it helped to normalise inequalities of status and wealth. If particular individuals were often criticised for their extravagance, remoteness or hubris, newspapers sustained the mythology surrounding the royal family and the fantasies underpinning the glamorous whirl of celebrity. Overt republicanism was generally treated as an oddity, and wide-ranging critiques of celebrity culture were marginalised. Nevertheless, the assumptions surrounding celebrity journalism changed significantly across the century, and, for all the surface trivia, this was a genre in which cultural meanings and identities were negotiated and morals and standards defined. Examining the representation and discussion of public figures enables us to chart the changing boundaries of public and private, and the shifting understanding of respect, deference and social distance.

Duty and distance: The monarchy before the Second World War

The popular press that emerged at the end of the nineteenth century played a vital role in a patriotic and populist rebranding of the monarchy after decades of controversy and declining public esteem. In the 1820s and 1830s, George IV and William IV had been savagely lampooned and satirised by journalists and cartoonists. Queen Victoria's retirement from public life after the death of Prince Albert in 1861 provoked much adverse comment, and the rakish activities of her son, the Prince of Wales, drew the scorn of public moralists. In the final quarter of the century, however, sympathetic politicians, courtiers and commentators presented the monarchy as the focal point of Britain's expanding empire, a source of unity in an increasingly contentious and class-based political system, and a symbol of tradition and stability in a rapidly modernising and urbanising society. Victoria's golden and diamond jubilees, and the coronations of Edward VII and George V, were celebrated with lavish rituals that emphasised the power and prestige of Britain's global empire. The national and international impact of these public ceremonials relied substantially on the willingness of the press to bring the magic of monarchy to a wider audience.[2]

In June 1897, little over a year after its birth, for example, the *Daily Mail* filled its pages with extravagant celebrations of Queen Victoria's Diamond Jubilee. For weeks in advance of the main events, special 'Diamond Jubilette' columns provided snippets of information about members of the royal family, and when the day arrived the paper offered 'the Complete Procession Guide', including a timetable of the Queen's estimated progress. Northcliffe recorded in his diary that the cavalcade through the heart of London, which featured over 50,000 troops from across the empire, was 'the most magnificent spectacle I ever beheld, or can ever behold', and he ordered the production of 100,000 copies of an eight-page souvenir edition, printed in gold ink. The paper spelled out the implicit messages of the ritual – the 'Greatness of the British Race' and the glory of Empire – and insisted that 'we ought to be a proud nation today'.

'It makes life newly worth living', the article concluded, 'to feel that one is part of this enormous, this wondrous machine, the greatest organisation the world ever saw.' Accompanying the text was a full-page line drawing of the view from St Paul's Cathedral, described as 'the largest news illustration ever printed by any daily paper in this country'. The *Mail* ensured that readers around Britain could visualise, and participate in, this festival of national communion.[3]

This combination of fantasy, patriotism, pride and deference marked the popular press's coverage of the monarchy for decades to come. Court circulars and gossip columns recorded the trivial details of the royal family's routine, while important ceremonial occasions or glamorous international tours received pages of eager reporting. Deaths were met with black columns and conspicuous solemnity. Although always on the look-out for intimate details to humanise these rather distant figures, Fleet Street reporters were cautious about revealing anything that went beyond the anodyne. Edward's VII's colourful past was discreetly overlooked, for example, and he was presented as a dignified and statesmanlike figure, 'the Peacemaker'. In 1910, the *Daily Mirror* caused some controversy by recording Edward's death with a full front-page of the late king lying on his deathbed. Despite the accusations of insensitivity, though, this was an official picture and its use had been authorised by Queen Alexandra, the king's widow. The accompanying report was reverential, observing the 'manliness and lofty dignity of King Edward's features'.[4]

George V, Edward's eminently respectable successor, had little appetite for the modern mass media. He was suspicious of the press and resisted for some years the opportunity to broadcast a radio message at Christmas. As the head of the nation during the Great War, and the leader of public commemorations after 1918, however, he was treated with considerable respect and deference, and his staff worked diligently to maintain favourable publicity. During the 1920s, though, the press found the king's sons more interesting and approachable. Prince Albert's marriage to Lady Elizabeth Bowes-Lyon was enthusiastically celebrated – 'because all know that he is marrying for love, and because he has chosen a British bride', gushed the *Mail* – as were the births of daughters Elizabeth and Margaret. They were

presented as exemplifying a typically British domestic happiness and stability. But it was the handsome and charismatic Edward, Prince of Wales,
who attracted the bulk of the headlines. His royal tours to India and the
dominions were orchestrated as media events that projected him as the
focal point of empire. But he was also a modern figure who seemed to pos-
sess all the glamour of Hollywood stars, and became similarly influential
in setting fashions. His photograph became so familiar that Beaverbrook
felt obliged to remind the *Daily Express*'s editor that 'the Prince of Wales
should not appear on the front page unless there is definite news of importance concerning him'. British newspapers were happy to retail gossipy
snippets – 'The Rambler' told the *Mirror*'s readers, for example, that the
Prince teased his sister-in-law 'in a happy, brotherly fashion about her
height' – but they were unfailingly respectful in the language they used to
discuss his private life, and usually refused to speculate about his personal
relationships. Most significantly, a discreet veil was placed over his affairs
with married women, such as Mrs Freya Dudley Ward, and from 1934,
Mrs Wallis Simpson.[5]

The mesmeric hold the monarchy had over the British press was demonstrated by Fleet Street's remarkable willingness to maintain its silence
about Edward's relationship with Wallis Simpson after his accession to the
throne in January 1936, despite the considerable attention it was receiving
in newspapers abroad, and especially in the United States. Edward's infatua-
tion with a divorcée was, without question, one of the tabloid stories of the
century, but the deferential British press believed it had a duty to protect
the dignity of the monarchy by not circulating damaging rumours; perhaps
more importantly, editors feared a fearsome backlash from readers if they
broke the scandal, especially given Edward's popularity. Globalisation,
technological innovation and more intense commercial competition would
soon make it impossible to close down such a monumental story; even
in the mid-1930s, it was barely possible to contain the rumours. By the
summer of 1936, numerous clippings from foreign papers were circulating
privately in Britain, and many letters were written to London newspapers
enquiring about the gossip, to no response.[6]

The international frenzy intensified in August after photographs
appeared of Mrs Simpson accompanying Edward on a Mediterranean

cruise aboard the steam yacht *Nahlin*. One set of pictures appeared in the British press, but with no explanation of Simpson's significance. In October, the king asked Lord Beaverbrook to use his influence to keep publicity of Mrs Simpson's divorce hearing to a minimum, with the result that only very small circulation publications such as *Cavalcade* and *News Review* offered any hints about the developing scandal. The leading figures in Fleet Street were generally united on the need for reticence. Howell Gwynne, the widely respected editor of the *Morning Post*, told his colleagues that 'in such a delicate matter as this, the Press should follow the Government and not dictate to it'. He also believed that silence was necessary because the 'sensational press' would be unable to handle the story 'with dignity and caution'.[7]

Fleet Street's discipline was maintained until 2 December 1936, when the Bishop of Bradford referred to the crisis in a speech: this was read by editors as the moment finally to bring the story into public arena. The press made up for lost time, filling countless pages with details about Wallis Simpson's life story, speculations about Edward's intentions, and views on the constitutional situation. This was a fantastic human drama, involving a stark conflict between duty and love. The king, no stranger to intense press scrutiny, was taken aback by the scale and tone of the coverage: 'what stared at me from the newspapers that were brought to my room on Thursday morning really shocked me,' he later recalled. 'Could this be the King, or was I some common felon? The Press creates: the Press destroys.' Many of the leading popular papers were actually sympathetic to the king's plight, at least initially. The *Mail* and *Express*'s support was largely due to proprietorial direction. Rothermere and especially Beaverbrook had personal connections to the king and his circle, and shared an intense dislike of Baldwin. For the *Mirror*, on the other hand, the crisis was an opportunity to sharpen the populist credentials it was trying to develop as part of its editorial reinvention. The paper suggested that the political class was conspiring against the wishes of the public to remove a popular king, and used its front page to demand that the people be allowed to participate in the decision-making process: 'Tell Us The Facts, Mr Baldwin! ... The Country Will Give You the Verdict'. The paper made a point of emphasising its attentiveness to the opinions expressed by its own readers: 'Sympathy for the King facing the greatest crisis of his life is voiced in the hundreds of letters that have poured into the *Daily Mirror* office from all parts of the country ... Not one per cent of the letters received criticise the King in his choice of Mrs Simpson'. Research by the historian Susan Williams suggests that the *Mirror* may well have been in tune with the majority of the public on this issue.[8]

By contrast, the rest of the national press, and the majority of the provincial papers, shared Baldwin's view that Simpson's past meant that she would not make a suitable queen, and agreed that a morganatic marriage was not an appropriate solution to the crisis. Once Edward had made his decision to abdicate, the divisions in Fleet Street quickly closed and the whole spectrum of the press patriotically rallied in support of King George VI. The *Express* admitted on 12 December that it 'would have preferred an alternative to abdication' but turned its attention to the new king: 'Nobody doubts that he will show the same high character and worth as his father. He is happy in the love of a wife and family. The British people will try to make him happy in the regard of a nation'.[9] The overwhelming desire to preserve the revered national institution ensured that there was no desire to dwell on the crisis.

After the dangerous unpredictability of Edward, Palace officials encouraged the media to focus on the contented domestic stability projected by King George VI, Queen Elizabeth and their young daughters. In the short-term, this strategy was successful, but the popular press would never again treat the monarchy with quite such cautious deference. Tom Harrisson, founder of the survey organisation Mass-Observation, noted that the press suffered a 'big knock' to its prestige 'when the Simpson crisis blew up and the public found major news had been withheld from them for months'[10] After the Second World War, a generation of younger journalists, led by Hugh Cudlipp at the *Mirror*, would start testing the boundaries of acceptable reporting and scrutinise the monarchy with a keener eye.

Society, gossip and the emergence of modern celebrity

If the monarchy, at the apex of the social hierarchy, inevitably attracted considerable attention, the aristocratic and upper gentry families that stood immediately beneath them also remained an object of press fascination well into the twentieth century, despite the gradual weakening of their political and social power. Proprietors such as Northcliffe, Rothermere and Beaverbrook had socially conservative instincts, sought acceptance by respectable society, and gratefully received honours and baubles; they also recognised the vicarious enjoyment that could be obtained by reading about wealthy lifestyles and luxurious goods. Women were thought to be particularly interested in gossip and celebrity news, and Northcliffe was convinced that most were fundamentally aspirational: 'Nine women out of ten would rather read about an evening dress costing a great deal of money – the sort of dress they will never in their lives have a chance of wearing – than about a simple frock such as they could afford'. Most popular papers thus filled their gossip columns with snippets about the privileged and wealthy, in the process helping to sustain and even glamorise the inequalities that disadvantaged their own readers. Many commentators were struck by the remarkable persistence of this curiosity about the social elites. For Paul Cohen-Portheim, a German writer describing his experiences of England in 1930, 'The interest which the whole nation takes in Society is astonishing ... Every newspaper tells you about their private lives, every illustrated paper is perpetually publishing photographs of them ... Their parties and their dresses, their weddings, christenings and funerals, their house and their travels are all described and depicted.' Aldous Huxley, the noted author, was likewise astonished that the middle-classes were 'prepared to listen to the privileged class congratulating itself'.[11]

Some left-wing papers, notably the *Daily Herald* and *Reynolds's News*, did try to puncture the glamour of Society by juxtaposing images of its ostentatious luxury with evidence of poverty and distress. Photographs from Ascot, printed in the *Herald* in 1925, emphasised that Society was 'flaunting its wealth, mostly unearned', while 'official figures were revealing the increasing suffering of the working class'. Many of the 'highest in the land' were 'self-centred and self-indulgent', the paper claimed: 'No day passes without proof being given of the extent to which the canker of luxurious life, requiring vast sums of money to satisfy it, has eaten into that class'. The bulk of the popular press, however, reported on Society with respect and admiration. Social diaries and gossip columns flattered readers that they were part of a privileged circle privy to the latest developments in the world of the upper classes. Indeed, in order to obtain the most accurate and colourful snippets, popular newspapers signed up columnists who were at ease moving in the circles they described. In 1926 the *Sunday Express* hired, at great expense, the young Irish aristocrat Lord Castlerosse to write the paper's 'Londoner's Log'. Castlerosse quickly became one of the paper's most popular writers, and other aristocratic columnists – notably Lady Eleanor Smith and Lord Donegall – soon followed. Society was publicising itself from within.[12]

Yet for all the promises of 'intimate' revelations from insiders, columnists remained very discreet about marital infidelities and sexual misdemeanours, particularly in comparison with brash American columnists such as Walter Winchell. Beaverbrook insisted that the *Express*'s gossip column, 'Talk of London', should provide 'good clean wholesome news about People who matter': there was no question that it should include intrusive stories about sexual relationships, unless these details had entered the public arena in other ways, such as through divorce proceedings. It was relatively easy for well-connected individuals to prevent the publication of embarrassing stories. Patrick Balfour, a gossip writer, did not disguise the fact that 'if you ask a social columnist, politely, to keep his mouth shut it is quite on the cards that he will do so'. He advised readers that the 'safest way to prevent a story appearing in a newspaper' was simply to 'ring up the editor, tell him the story, and ask him not to print it'. Important public figures – Lloyd George is a good example – could keep mistresses confident that they would not be exposed even by their enemies in the press. Fleet Street memoirs abound with anecdotes of favours being called in and stories being suppressed: of Riddell, the proprietor of the *News of the World*, protecting the 'important men' whose names were found in the records of a Westminster brothel, or Beaverbrook covering up for F. E. Smith (later

Lord Birkenhead) when he was caught with a prostitute and gave a false name to the police.[13]

The weakening of the appeal of news about the social elites, evident by the 1930s, was less the result of a growing popular impatience with tittle-tattle about toffs, and more the result of the emergence of a more glamorous, democratic and consumerist class of celebrity: the film star. In the years after the First World War, with cinemas rapidly opening up around the country and attendance figures booming, films moved to the heart of British popular culture. In July 1919, Northcliffe was suddenly struck by the extent of the cinema-going craze, and urged the *Mail* to capitalise on it: 'I wish we had more film matter with pictures. I had no notion the topic of public conversation among all classes films have become.' He soon asked for 'film notes' to appear daily.[14] The *Mail*, and the rest of the popular press, took up the invitation with gusto. Even more than the films themselves, though, newspapers were interested in the personalities. The movie industry was firmly based on the star system, and Hollywood studios spent considerable amounts of money publicising their leading men and women. In a world of static imagery, viewers often experienced an intense and intimate sense of connection with the stylish and self-confident figures dazzlingly displayed before them on the silver screen, and they had a considerable appetite to read more about them.

Leading men were presented as being so extraordinarily charismatic and magnetic that they were able to entrance legions of female fans. Rudolph Valentino, who rose to fame as the star of the desert romance *The Sheik* (1921), was the 'hero of the female population of five continents'; French actor Maurice Chevalier had 'stormed ten million feminine hearts', while John Gilbert, 'the screen's greatest lover', was the 'idol of twenty million women'. Newspapers played along with the attempts of studios to generate hype. When Tyrone Power came to London in 1939, the *Express* revealed how he had to notify Scotland Yard of his route 'all because he has a beautiful face that everyone recognises'; he kept on being made 'prisoner' by his 'girl fans'. The press neither exposed the careful marketing machinery employed by the studios, nor did they question the public images created for the stars – there was no hint of Tyrone Power's homosexuality, for example. Newspapers and their advertisers had little inclination to risk the financial benefits they enjoyed from the interest in cinema.[15]

Female stars were discussed even more intently in terms of their visual appearance and sexual allure. The fashions, hairstyles and mannerisms of actresses such as Clara Bow, Jean Harlow and Greta Garbo were photographed, scrutinised and debated. As a *Mail* feature argued in 1935, after the war 'cinema took over the role of instructor' in matters of beauty because 'every woman sees a wish picture of herself in the glamorous heroine of the film she is watching'. These leading ladies were integrated into an expanding commercial nexus supporting the interrelated interests of the cinema, press, fashion and cosmetics industries. Newspapers encouraged glamorous actresses to reveal their style 'secrets' – although the difficulties of achieving the 'screen look' without the Hollywood budget (and photographic trickery) were glossed over. The *Mirror*, for example, invited Rudolph Valentino's lover and Hollywood *femme fatale* Pola Negri to advise the 'Girl Worker' on the 'Best Way Of Planning An Attractive Wardrobe' and how to 'Look Your Best During Business Hours': 'it cannot be denied,' she declared, 'that a neat, smart, well-turned-out appearance does help us to rise in the world.' In 1935, meanwhile, the *Daily Express* produced a 'Film Book', which provided 'film fashions', 'secrets of make-up' and 'some of the methods of slimming used by well-known players to meet the exacting demands of the camera'. Maintaining 'sex appeal' – a term coined in this period that quickly became ubiquitous – meant keeping up increasingly exacting standards, and was underpinned by educated consumption, buying the cosmetics and beauty treatments endorsed by actresses: '"After my nightly cleansing with Pond's Cold Cream," says Miss Betty Balfour, the famous Cinema star, whose complexion is as fresh as the petals of a rose, "the skin of my face, neck and hands seems so deliciously soft and refreshed"'.[16]

The unattainable glamour of Hollywood was sometimes critiqued by left-wing papers. One commentator for the *Daily Herald* observed in 1923 that 'whatever the plot', American films offered 'to the tired eyes of work-saturated wage slaves pictures of material riches, luxury and senseless splendour'. He argued that by unapologetically displaying what was out of reach of the ordinary worker, 'The pictures should make revolutionists'. For all those alienated by the flaunting of wealth, however, many more seem to have enjoyed the escape into a fantasy world of romance and sensual pleasure. The mainstream press powerfully reinforced the aspirational and escapist culture that Northcliffe had recognised in his audience.[17]

Cinema stars' value to gossip columnists was magnified by their propensity to have complicated and turbulent private lives, providing plenty of opportunities for revelations and speculations. 'Greta Garbo's Vow Never To Marry – Romance Revealed In Tomorrow's "Sunday Express" – Intimate Truths' blazed an advertisement in October 1931. In 1935 English actress Elizabeth Allan's protestation that she was 'happily married' –'Clark Gable Means Nothing To Me' – was front-page news in the *Express*. The preoccupation with film stars was the clearest symbol of how the tabloids had uprooted traditional news values. The journalist and historian Robert Ensor, reflecting in 1947 on the tendencies of inter-war journalism, observed that 'film-stars came to be for the popular Press nearly the most important persons living; and a "romance" between two of these idolised beings was an event which few could outclass in attraction'. The Royal Commission on the Press two years later similarly expressed its distaste that such papers presented 'the matrimonial adventures of a film star as though they possessed the same intrinsic importance as events affecting the peace of a continent'.[18]

The elevation of film stars to such an elevated status inevitably encouraged dreams of celebrity among newspaper readers. Dick Richards, the *Sunday Pictorial*'s film critic, revealed that he was bombarded by letters from 'screen-struck girls' seeking to imitate their idols:

> They project themselves into a romantic clinch with Stewart Granger or John Mills. They imagine themselves floating around in elegant cars and lush furs, the adored of autograph-haunting fans ... the letter invariably begins: 'Dear Mr Richards, – It has always been my ambition to be a film-star ...' Not, you will note, to be an actress. But to be a film star, which sounds so much easier.

Richards declared himself 'so tired of trying to reason with people who, either through conceit, or because they need money, or because they're the victims of flattering friends, or because, owing to the drabness of their lives, they're trying to clutch at a mythical, glamorous bubble, want to find a primrose path to screen stardom. I cannot help them.' The lust for stardom that Richards identified was a necessary part of the celebrity culture that the tabloids had done so much to create – and it would only intensify in the future.[19]

Growing intrusiveness: Monarchy in mid-century

In the years after the Second World War, the deference and restraint that characterised the popular press's coverage of monarchy and celebrity were gradually eroded. This was partly a reflection of changing social relations, as the electoral success of the Labour Party, the growing strength of the trade unions, the construction of a welfare state, and the achievement of close to full employment, gave greater political and cultural strength to the working classes. Papers such as the *Mirror* and *Pictorial*, seeking to represent and project this working-class voice on behalf of their readers, were critical of the old-fashioned attitudes and hierarchies they believed were hindering social improvement, and began to take a less respectful approach to the monarchy. 'It was more than light-hearted impudence,' Cudlipp later recalled, 'it was a reflection of the new healthy mood of questioning authority, especially the Establishment. The mood was no longer docile acceptance and silent reverence.' Changes in the media environment also encouraged a greater intrusiveness. The rise of television, which could hardly be ignored after 20 million people watched the BBC's broadcast of Queen Elizabeth's coronation in June 1953, meant that popular newspapers could not so easily entice readers with the lavish but rather passive coverage they had provided in the past. To offer something distinctive, they delved into the tabloid toolkit of speculation, gossip and scandal in an attempt to find the 'stories behind the story'. This certainly did not mean that all caution was thrown to the winds, and there continued to be far more editorial restraint than there would be in the final decades of the century; there was, though, a notable change in the tone of the reporting.[20]

This 'new healthy mood of questioning authority' was evident when rumours about Princess Elizabeth's romance with Prince Philip of Greece circulated in the winter of 1946–47. Brushing aside denials from the Palace that an engagement was not imminent, the *Sunday Pictorial* surveyed readers on the question 'Should Our Future Queen Wed Philip?', arguing that the British people should have the opportunity to express their views, 'not after the event as was the case with another Royal crisis in 1936 but before it'. This was an important turning point in the relationship between press, public and monarchy. By conducting the first formal poll on the internal affairs of the royal family, the *Pictorial* was seeking to establish the principle that the people had a right to be informed and consulted on royal matches. The paper employed a powerful democratic rhetoric in opposition to the culture of secrecy that surrounded the Palace and Cabinet on royal affairs, declaring that everyone who had voted in its poll had 'rendered a valuable service to our democratic system', by providing 'the authorities with a gauge of popular feeling'. In the end, sixty-four per cent of readers were in favour of the marriage if the couple were in love, but in many respects the result was less important than the fact that (a section of) the public had been given a chance to speak. The poll generated coverage across the world, notably in the United States and Greece, and was condemned by many as an impertinent contravention of the unspoken rules governing relations with the monarchy. 'Many people are saying that the *Sunday Pictorial's* intrusion into the Royal Family's affairs is a breach of good taste', wrote Arthur Christiansen, the *Daily Express* editor, to Beaverbrook, 'but people often read things that are in bad taste.' The experienced Christiansen recognised that outraged protests only tended to stimulate public curiosity about major human-interest stories, and over the coming decades editors would increasingly seek to manufacture such outrage to generate publicity.[21]

Unwilling to wait for official announcements from the Palace, the press also began to compete more aggressively for royal exclusives. On 9 July 1947 the *Daily Mail*, relying on sources in Greece, announced the engagement of Princess Elizabeth and Philip Mountbatten. The story was initially denied by the Palace press office, before its accuracy was officially confirmed the following day. The following March, the *People* reported on its front page that Elizabeth was expecting her first child in October, news that was officially verified only in June. Another breach of traditional protocols came in 1950 when Marion Crawford, a former governess at the Palace, serialised her recollections as *The Little Princesses*; *Woman's Own* won the rights to the British serialisation, but the popular press followed up the stories she provided with enthusiasm. When George VI died in February 1952, there was a further wave of controversy after several popular papers printed candid photographs of grieving members of the royal family. The *Mirror* photographer caused particular fury by leaving his allocated position and snapping a shot of Prince Philip kissing the Queen Mother. John Gordon, the editor of the *Sunday Express*, confided privately to Beaverbrook that the press had crossed previously established Fleet Street boundaries by printing '"blown-up" close-ups of the women in the royal family in deep black and obviously deeply moved'. 'I am inclined to think', he added, 'that newspapers which are rather sadistic in their drive to extract the last ounce of emotion out of personal grief, over-reached themselves'. The tense relations between the press and Palace were not helped by the obstinate position adopted by Commander Richard Colville, the Palace press officer from 1947 to 1968, and known in Fleet Street as the 'Abominable No-Man'. Colville was disdainfully dismissive of journalists: as the historian Ben Pimlott has observed, he refused 'to treat even the most modest press request for personal information as legitimate'. Unable to appreciate the benefits of feeding the media's appetite for news with authorised stories, however, he only intensified his efforts to prevent information leaking out.[22]

The individual who would bear the brunt of the press's new aggressiveness was not the new Queen, though, but her sister, Princess Margaret. Her mercurial character and turbulent personal life provided plenty of licence for speculation, and the press saw her as a safer target because she was not directly in line to the throne. Princess Margaret's romance with Group Captain Peter Townsend, an equerry to the Queen, not only became one of the biggest tabloid stories of the decade, it was successfully mobilised by elements of the press to fuel a populist critique of a hidebound and out-of-touch establishment. The relationship was first revealed to British readers by the *People* in June 1953, less than two weeks after the coronation. With echoes of 1936, the paper referred to 'scandalous rumours' being circulated abroad that 'the princess is in love with a divorced man and that she wishes to marry him'. The *People* feigned to believe that the rumours were 'utterly untrue' and demanded an official denial. This time, however, the British press drove the story forward itself rather than simply waiting for events to unfold. In royal circles, many considered the older and previously married Townsend an unsuitable match, but in Fleet Street there was considerable sympathy for the dashing RAF officer who had served valiantly during the war, and was the innocent party in a divorce; several journalists presented him as a symbol of the talented individuals whose hopes were all too often crushed by the snobbery and moral conservatism of the traditional elites. The *Mirror* and the *People* portrayed Townsend's sudden appointment as Air Attaché to the British embassy in Brussels as a clumsy attempt by the Palace to exile him, and whipped up sympathy for the 'ace pilot'. There were reports that the government had decided to block the prospective marriage, prompting exasperated cabinet members to consider issuing a statement calling an end to the 'deplorable speculation and gossip'. Most significantly, the *Mirror* mobilised public opinion. Following the precedent set by its sister paper in 1947, the *Mirror* decided to conduct a poll of readers so that 'the voice of the British people' could be heard. Within four days over 70,000 responses had been received, with more than 96 per cent in favour of the marriage.[23]

The *Mirror*'s poll provoked a storm of criticism, just as the *Pictorial*'s had in 1947. The *Mirror* was equally unrepentant, dismissing the 'pompous, self-appointed arbiters of "good taste"' who had accused the paper of the 'frightful crime of telling the public the things the public is entitled to know!' Fleet Street, united in silence in 1936, was now seriously divided. The General Council of the Press, the new self-regulatory body set up as a result of the recommendations of the Royal Commission of 1949, was just about to have its first meeting, and it wasted no time in condemning the poll as 'contrary to the best traditions of British journalism'. *The Times* similarly made clear its disgust for scandalmongers involved in 'the cruel business of prying into private lives'.[24]

Condemnation from elite sources tends only to spur on tabloids, especially when they are confident they have public opinion on their side. Such was the case with the *Mirror*, which, on the eve of the Princess's twenty-fifth birthday – the age when she no longer needed the Queen's consent to marry – ran its infamous front-page headline, 'Come On Margaret! Please Make Up Your Mind!' The Press Council intervened once again, resolving that 'Such coarse impertinence was an insult to the Princess and an offence against the decencies of British public life'. But the *Mirror* protested that these 'decencies' and 'good manners' were elitist, class-bound concepts designed to silence the popular press: the 'vulgar frankness' of the *Mirror* was the natural idiom of the readers it was addressing. Furthermore, it was exactly this snobbery that was responsible for the Palace's disapproval of Townsend: 'The young man concerned has committed two offences: he was born a member of the middle class and he divorced a wife who deserted him'. Rejecting him as an appropriate partner on those grounds 'strikes the overwhelming majority of the public as being a piece of archaic humbug'. Pursuing this story, and championing the cause of a man 'outside the established slate of royal bridegrooms', was part of the *Mirror*'s ongoing crusade against the rigidities of British society. It also reflected the paper's underlying sentimentality. The public seemed to desire a happy ending to the royal romance, and the *Mirror* was impatient with those placing obstacles in the path of true love.[25]

If the *Mirror* provoked the greatest consternation in royal and political circles with its populist agenda and demotic presentation, its rivals pursued the story with a similar eagerness. When Peter Townsend returned to Britain on 12 October 1955, the press went into a frenzy. Pleas from the Palace to respect Princess Margaret's privacy were brazenly ignored. When Margaret and Townsend spent a weekend at Allanbay Park in Berkshire, they were surrounded by photographers and reporters. Some papers chartered aircraft to monitor the house from above, and £1,000 was offered in an attempt to bribe a butler. One loyal *Daily Herald* reader, who had bought the paper since 1928, gave it up in disgust on 15 October when it devoted three of its eight pages, including the front page, to the romance, while covering the final day of the Labour Party annual conference in a seven-inch, one column report on page six. The pursuit of Margaret increasingly overrode deference to the institutions of state. When the Palace refused to follow the press agenda by releasing a statement, it was fiercely lambasted: 'Never has the Royal Family been led into such stupidity', declared the *Mirror*. In the aftermath of Margaret's eventual decision not to marry Townsend, the popular press channelled much of its consternation at the Church of England and its teachings on divorce. The *Express*, the *News Chronicle*, and the *Mirror* all produced editorials critical of Church policy. 'The serious upshot of the whole affair in Parliament and the country is a demand for disestablishment' argued Kingsley Martin in the *New Statesman*. The *Mirror* printed several angry letters in its correspondence columns. 'I am ashamed to be British. I vow I shall never set foot in a church again', wrote one reader. 'Throw out this Church which sanctifies arranged marriages but will not allow couples in love to marry', insisted another.[26]

As several contemporary commentators observed, the coverage of Princess Margaret's relationship with Peter Townsend marked a decisive shift towards the monarchy as 'soap opera'. The tabloid approach to covering the royal family had developed in two significant ways. First, editors were increasingly prepared to ignore established protocols and take risks. In October 1956, for example, the *Daily Sketch* printed a report about a private party for the Duke of Kent's twenty-first birthday which had been obtained by a female journalist smuggling herself in by hiding in the boot of a car. In February 1957, the *Mirror* was even bold enough to print rumours emanating from the United States about the Queen's own marriage. While describing the rumours as 'malicious', the paper's front page headline – 'Fly Home Philip!' – called for the Prince to return home to scotch the story. Princess Margaret was, unusually, able to keep her engagement to Anthony Armstrong-Jones a secret before the official announcement in February 1960, but her marriage was not a happy one and would be subject to increasing scrutiny.[27]

Second, the populist critique of the outdated and undemocratic culture of secrecy surrounding the Palace had become well established, particularly in the *Mirror* and the *Express*. In 1956, the novelist and *Mirror* columnist Keith Waterhouse produced a series of articles entitled 'The Royal Circle' arguing that the clique of people 'surrounding the throne is as aristocratic, as insular and – there is no more suitable word – as toffee-nosed as it has ever been'. The following year, the *Mirror* gently mocked another royal tradition by creating its own 'Debs' Ball' for working-class girls; within months the Palace had declared an end to royal presentation parties for debutantes. Criticisms of Britain's fawning relationship with the monarchy, made by prominent figures such as Lord Altrincham and Malcolm Muggeridge, were given front-page coverage (in contrast, it is worth noting, to the silence of the BBC). The *Express*, meanwhile, campaigned persistently against the

restrictions placed on divorcees at royal functions, and criticised the waste
and expense that characterised royal travel arrangements. In March 1962,
Sir Martin Lindsay, a Conservative backbench MP, even tabled a motion
in the House of Commons accusing Lord Beaverbrook of conducting
a 'sustained vendetta' against the royal family, highlighting 'more than
seventy adverse comments on members of the Royal Family who have no
means of replying'. Prince Philip did actually reply, being caught off record
denouncing the *Express* as a 'bloody awful paper'. The press's affection for
the royal family had by no means evaporated, and the bulk of its coverage
remained respectful, but the distance between royalty and celebrity was
narrowing and the reporting shifted accordingly.[28]

Mid-century celebrity culture

If the rise of cinema enabled the development of modern celebrity culture,
the mid-century popularisation of television saw this culture intensified
and extended. A new set of individuals rose to fame and fortune by being
beamed directly into the nation's homes, and cinema stars now had to
worker harder to maintain the public's attention. At the same time, the
boundaries between public and private were shifting in both the United
States and Britain, as the discussion of sex became more explicit. A market
started to emerge for intimate revelations and confessions, and gossip magazines such as *Confidential* in the United States demonstrated the success
that could be achieved by a more aggressive and unashamed pursuit of
private information. As the newsprint restrictions imposed by rationing
finally started to ease, extra space was devoted to celebrity news and features.
Gossip columns, such as those by the *Express*'s William Hickey and the
Mail's Paul Tanfield, fought for the latest celebrity stories, while the Sundays
increasingly competed to secure high-profile celebrity serialisations.[29]

The shifting tone and nature of the daily gossip in the 1950s and 1960s
is brought into focus by the anguished debates contained in the editorial

archives of the *Express* and *Evening Standard*. Beaverbrook, entering old age but still interested in the detail of his papers' content, repeatedly complained about the people the *Express* and the *Standard* were publicising, and he was supported by some of his fellow directors. In July 1956, for example, Beaverbrook lamented an 'Over emphasis on insignificant television personalities', while Arthur Christiansen denounced the *Express*'s front page story about Diana Dors and the TV hairdresser Raymond as 'Fleet Street journalism at its worst'. 'Raymond is London's biggest publicity seeker,' Christiansen concluded, 'The story is a publicity stunt and nothing else. These views have been conveyed to the night staff.' A few months later, Beaverbrook wrote again insisting that Diana Dors was not worthy of front-page or diary coverage. 'I agree that Diana Dors is a singularly vulgar creature,' protested Percy Elland, the *Standard*'s editor, 'but there is certainly an immense interest in her affairs'. Two years later, Harold Keeble, another *Express* director, wrote a long memorandum suggesting that the paper should 'shift the emphasis of the William Hickey column away from its present obsession with largely worthless social figures and try to build up more exclusive news about more important and fundamentally more interesting people':

> Since we took the decision to 'splash' Hickey all across Page Three, we have got ourselves locked in a stupid war with Tanfield of the *Daily Mail*. Both papers are now writing about identical people. One day we get a 'scoop': the next day the *Mail*. But the merry-go-round remains the same. And my suspicion is that the public is growing weary of Tessa Kennedy, Mark Sykes, Dominic Elwes, the Duke of Kent, Eva Bartok, Suna Portman – the whole gang who now make up the 'licensed target-list' for gossip columns. Why should anybody be interested in Mark Sykes and Suna Portman? Yet our cuttings on them nearly fill an envelope because neither the *Express* nor the *Mail* will let go. And thus bigger and bigger headlines are devoted to sillier and sillier people.

This was an acute analysis of how celebrity culture encouraged a self-reinforcing competitive cycle from which it was very difficult to step away. With more space to fill, rival papers simply worked harder and harder to secure the scoops they convinced themselves that the audience demanded. With editors unwilling to cede any potential advantage to their competitors, though, high-minded memos had little impact. Two years later, Max Aitken, Beaverbrook's son, was writing about Hickey 'drifting back into models and un-known actresses.' As Aitken noted, this was 'always a temptation, especially when there is not news'. It was not a temptation the tabloids would learn to master.[30]

Sunday newspapers competed on major features and in-depth serialisations rather than on the latest news. Still too cautious to run detailed unauthorised stories about private lives, the weeklies increasingly worked with celebrities or their agents to produce racy confessionals and reminiscences. A new era of competition was heralded by the *People*'s payment of £40,000 for Errol Flynn's memoirs in October 1959. Serialised immediately after his death under the title 'My Wicked, Wicked, Life', the paper boasted that Flynn's story was the 'frankest confession ever made by a famous star'. Running for over two months, articles described Flynn's sexual escapades, drinking, and drug-taking under headlines such as 'Twin Lovelies Ambushed Me At Night ... I Gave In' and 'Three Weeks Of Orgy – With Barrymore The Sex-Mad Drunk'. 'My favourite occupation is still love, prolonged bouts of love', wrote Flynn, adding that it was 'impossible to count the women I have known, loved, been loved by, or just taken by'. The memoir was hugely popular, increasing the *People*'s circulation by almost 200,000 copies and enabling it to overtake the *Pictorial* to become the second most popular Sunday.[31]

Stafford Somerfield, the newly appointed editor of the most popular Sunday, the *News of the World*, demanded a series of articles that would create a similar impact and make readers' 'hair curl'. The result was the purchase of the rights to Diana Dors's autobiography, *Swinging Dors* for £36,000. Running for two months from January 1960, Dors's 'frank and full account of the men she loved and the wild life she has lived' was every bit as titillating as Flynn's memoirs. She admitted that she when she was younger she had been 'a naughty girl', and that at her parties 'off came the sweaters, bras and panties. In fact it was a case of off with everything – except the lights'. She revealed that – unknown to her – her home with her former husband Dennis Hamilton had hosted parties in which Hamilton and his friends had sex with young women while guests looked on through a two-way mirror; it had also been a venue for 'blue movies' starring 'couples I had called friends and who are still well known in the West End'. There was a thin veneer of morality coating the articles. Dors claimed that her 'wild life' was 'all behind' her – 'today I'm a happy wife. Soon I hope to become a devoted mother' – and she held Hamilton responsible for the most raucous activities. At the same time, she made no apologies for her own actions and taunted her critics for the lack of fun in their lives. Dors's memoirs – liberally illustrated with titillating photos of her – offered a provocative celebration of female sexual pleasure in a paper more accustomed to focus on the punishment of sexual transgression. The series was an immediate hit with readers, adding over 100,000 copies to a previously falling circulation. In a desperate bid to prevent readers defecting for the Dors story, the *Sunday Pictorial* ran concurrently a series on the life of Dennis Hamilton, recounting in detail his voyeuristic use of mirrors and peep-holes. In the spring of 1960 few working-class newspaper readers can have avoided discovering something about the sex lives of Dors and Hamilton.[32]

This new tendency for celebrity confessions dismayed the Press Council, which in its meeting of March 1960 denounced the 'debased standard of articles' represented by the Flynn, Hamilton, and Dors memoirs. The Council declared that these features 'sank below the accepted standards of decency' and criticised the Dors and Hamilton articles, in particular, for containing 'material that was grossly lewd and salacious'. Once again, however, the papers involved were unrepentant, and these sexualised serialisations proliferated. Within months the *News of the World* had bought Brigitte Bardot's life story and paid £15,000 for the rights to Jayne Mansfield's memoirs. The gradual normalisation of these accounts of exotic and tempestuous sexual activities – previously only to be found in court reporting – paved the way for Fleet Street's intense interest in the Profumo scandal of 1963. As Lord Denning remarked in his report into the circumstances leading to Profumo's resignation, public figures were increasingly vulnerable because 'scandalous information about well-known people has become a marketable commodity'. The *News of the World* scooped its rivals by paying Christine Keeler for her story, the five-part 'Confessions of Christine'. Across Fleet Street, reporters were dispatched to investigate the activities of Keeler, Stephen Ward, and their associates, in a bid to uncover further scandal. Readers were presented with a flurry of vague stories and unsubstantiated rumours about incriminating photographs taken at high-society orgies. Ultimately, though, the press did not go so far as to satisfy public curiosity by naming the high-profile individuals linked to the most sensational stories. Tabloids still remained far happier using their chequebooks to secure approved accounts than risking libel damages with unsubstantiated accusations – indeed, Fleet Street was reminded of the dangers when the *Sunday Mirror* was forced to pay £40,000 to Lord Boothby in 1964 after stories linking him to Ronnie Kray. Celebrity sex lives had now entered the public domain, but usually only with a significant degree of consent and connivance.[33]

The convergence of royalty and celebrity:
The pursuit of Diana

From the late 1970s there was a convergence between royal and celebrity journalism, and many of the restraints holding back tabloid editors finally snapped. Rupert Murdoch's relaunch of the *Sun* in November 1969 shook up the market by introducing a competitor willing to exploit celebrity, sex and scandal with unprecedented aggression. As a republican and self-perceived outsider to the British establishment, Murdoch had few qualms about exposing members of the royal family to the same level of scrutiny as other stars. The steady conversion of popular newspapers to the tabloid format, and the introduction in November 1978 of the *Daily Star*, another self-consciously populist title, intensified the competition still further. A new generation of tabloid editors, typified by the *Sun*'s Kelvin MacKenzie, thrived on the establishment outrage they provoked, and saw legal damages as a necessary price of keeping ahead of the competition. Under Thatcher and Reagan, moreover, the flaunting of wealth became more socially acceptable, and global celebrity culture shifted onto a new level with the arrival of MTV and glossy celebrity magazines such as *Hello!*. New technologies – long lens cameras with greater range, computer databases, mobile phones – all provided fresh opportunities to trace, monitor and scrutinise the private activities of celebrities, and tabloid journalists and their associates had few misgivings about exploiting their potential, as later court cases and investigations would make clear.

It was no surprise that the relaunched *Sun*'s first front-page featured, alongside its revelations about a 'Horse Dope Sensation', a speculative royal report: this was one of the surest ways of seeking to build its audience. 'Where are Charles and Lady Leonora?' asked the headline, suggesting that 'The mystery of Prince Charles and Lady Leonora Grovesnor deepened last night', despite the latter's insistence that it was 'silly' to suggest they were about to be engaged. There was a new competitor for the big royal stories, and, even if it was less well connected than some of its rivals, it would gradually show itself to be ruthless in search of exclusives. The *Sun*'s first significant royal scoops related to Princess Anne's relationship with the horseman Mark Phillips in January 1973. The paper demonstrated how it was gradually blurring the boundaries between royalty and pop stars when it offered readers the opportunity to 'Take the royal boyfriend home with you!' by buying a 30 by 20 inch souvenir poster of 'Princess Anne's handsome young escort' for 20 pence. For the *Sun*, Phillips was an object of fantasy to be commodified and displayed on bedroom walls alongside musicians and actors.[34]

The *Sun*'s stablemate, the *News of the World*, meanwhile, led the pack with its coverage of Princess Margaret's disintegrating marriage. In February 1976 the paper's front page was dominated by photographs of a swim-suited Margaret enjoying the Caribbean island of Mustique with the young socialite Roddy Llewellyn, 17 years her junior. 'It is the third holiday that this Old Etonian ... has shared there with the 45-year-old Princess', noted the paper knowingly: 'Each day, Margaret and Roddy walk arm in arm on the beach, where they spend many hours', and Roddy was intimate enough to rub 'suntan oil on her bronzed shoulders.' The photographs produced a storm of comment and conjecture in Fleet Street, led by the *Express*'s star columnist Jean Rook, whose blunt article suggesting that Margaret was making a 'fool of herself' and her husband gave editor Roy Wright considerable concern before he eventually decided to run it. Two weeks later, the *Express* broke the news that Princess Margaret and Lord Snowdon were splitting up.[35]

This separation was merely the prelude to a rerun of Margaret's 1950s romance, as the tabloids pursued any hints that she would formalise her relationship with Llewellyn. 'Will the Princess marry Roddy? It's Make Your Mind Up Time For Margaret!' declared the *Sun* in March 1978, in a self-conscious echo of the *Mirror's* 1955 headline, while the following month it announced: 'The Queen Tells Margaret: Give Up Roddy Or Quit'. As in 1955, Margaret chose duty over love. This romantic sequel was messier, sleazier and more far more damaging to the royal family than the glamorous fantasy surrounding the young Margaret's liaison with Peter Townsend. 'Nobody objects to the Queen's little sister enjoying herself,' mused the *Sun's* Jon Akass in April 1978, 'It is just that there does not seem to be any good reason why we should foot the bill'. Amidst the economic dislocation and strikes of the 1970s, the costs of the monarchy were criticised by papers on the left and right. 'Admiration is no longer automatic and there is no reason why it should be', added Akass. 'The syrupy adoration which oozed over the royal family in the immediate post-war years was an aberration, an historical oddity.' When the *Daily Star* launched in November 1978, it too sought readers through the trusted means of the big royal exclusive, providing a lavish serialisation of 'Roddy Llewellyn's Own Story'. He wrote of the 'nightmare' of being in the tabloid spotlight and knowing 'that in my childhood haunts, in the places where I went to school, and where I did my growing up, highly paid journalists from all over the world have been raking over my past – and generally managing to get it wrong.'[36]

Intense as was the spotlight placed on Margaret and Llewellyn, it could not match the dazzling wattage that shone on Prince Charles and Princess Diana in the following decades. Guessing the identity of the heir to the throne's romantic partners became one of the chief tabloid sports of the 1970s, with countless contenders profiled and investigated. On several occasions, papers jumped the gun, most spectacularly in June 1978 when the *Express* confidently declared on its front page 'Charles to Marry Astrid – Official'. The formal engagement to Princess Marie Astrid of Luxemburg 'will be announced from Buckingham Palace next Monday', the report announced, adding that the Queen and Prince Philip had consented to a 'novel constitutional arrangement' whereby any sons would be brought up Protestant, while daughters would be Catholic. The Palace's annoyance was communicated to the *Express* at board level, but the paper's editor, Roy Wright, unwisely assured the public that the story would be vindicated. The *Sun* eventually won the search for the bride, revealing on 8 September 1980 that 'He's In Love Again: Lady Di is the new girl for Charles'. There were clear signs of the tabloid scrutiny and duplicity to come only ten days later when Diana was photographed posing in the sunlight showing, in the *Sun*'s unusually coy formulation, 'she was not wearing a slip under her cotton skirt.' One photographer tried to enter the kindergarten where she worked by climbing through the lavatory window. Two months later the *Sunday Mirror* provoked huge controversy with its front-page splash, 'Royal Love Train', claiming that Prince Charles had spent the night with Diana on a train parked in sidings outside Chippenham. The Palace officially denied the story and forty-five MPs signed a motion criticising the speculation, although later suggestions that the mystery woman aboard the train was Camilla Parker Bowles rather than Diana explained why the *Sunday Mirror* was so confident in its scoop.[37]

Charles and Diana's marriage ceremony in July 1981 was explicitly presented as a 'fairy-tale wedding' to cheer up a public suffering amidst severe economic problems and urban disturbances. 'For the next couple of days we can, and should, set aside in our minds those all-consuming national concerns of recession and riot,' insisted the *Express*. It suggested that the national rejoicing accompanying the wedding was a 'tonic which, like the sun breaking momentarily through some gloomy clouds, will raise our spirits for the difficult days to come'. Rarely was the monarchy's role as a focus for national unity more evident. Diana's youth, beauty and warmth made her the perfect fairy-tale princess, and editors found her pictures irresistible. Her spontaneity and informality provided a welcome contrast with the stuffier aspects of royal protocol, and she appeared to be a modern, up-to-date figure – a 'princess of the people and a princess of our times' declared the *Mirror* admiringly in 1982.

Such attributes meant that she would never be able to escape the press glare. Despite Palace requests for sensitive treatment after the announcement of her pregnancy, for example, the *Sun* and the *Star*, then at the high point of their commercial competition, continued the pursuit. In February 1982, both published long-lens shots of the visibly pregnant Diana relaxing in a bikini on a private holiday on a remote Caribbean island; the *Sun*'s description of her as 'stunning' in her 'revealing outfit' came close to eroding the boundaries between princess and 'pin-up'. The Queen was immediately critical of the press's 'tasteless behaviour'. The *Sun* offered a lukewarm apology for causing offence, but reprinted the photographs and declared its 'legitimate interest in the Royal family not merely as symbols, but as living, breathing people.' The *Sun* effectively made clear that royal status no longer provided any special protection from the pressures of celebrity. Indeed, the marriage of Sarah Ferguson to Prince Andrew in July 1986 allowed the fairy-tale wedding and modern princess narratives to be given another spin. 'He was born a Royal but, on the day, she was the star', fawned the *Mirror*: 'Sarah was beautiful. Her dress was stunning, her smile radiated happiness.' While the Duchess of York – more commonly known as 'Fergie'– was not pursued quite as intently as Diana, it was not long before she was exposed to snide and critical comments about her appearance and personality, and she would eventually be the subject of several tabloid stings.[38]

If the tabloids enjoyed writing the fairy tales, they found unravelling them even more compelling. The frenzied accounts of the breakdown of Prince Charles's, and then Prince Andrew's, marriages demonstrated how completely the press's inhibitions had been jettisoned since the 1930s. Rumours about Charles and Diana's increasingly frosty relationship had circulated since 1987, and by 1990 tabloids devoted considerable space to reports that the couple were leading 'separate lives'. The *Sunday Times*'s serialisation of Andrew Morton's biography of Diana – later revealed to have been compiled with her assistance – opened up the floodgates. The tabloids greedily circulated stories of affairs, heated arguments and suicide attempts, and tried to outdo each other with the latest revelations. In August 1992, the *Daily Mirror* published intimate photos of a topless Duchess of York having her toes sucked by her financial advisor John Bryan. Sales rose by around half a million copies. The *Sun* responded by printing details of a bugged telephone conversation – 'the Squidgy tapes' – between the Princess of Wales and friend James Gilby, which it had had in its possession for two years. A hotline was established so that readers could listen to the recording themselves. The following January, the *Sun* and the *Mirror* caused further embarrassment by publishing extracts of a bugged conversation between Charles and Camilla Parker Bowles. The refusal to adhere to traditional protocols was perhaps most starkly illustrated when the *Sun* published in advance – for the first time ever – the Queen's Christmas address, making her 'annus horribilis' even worse. The newly established Press Complaints Commission, lacking any punitive sanctions, could do nothing to stop the stories when every revelation was eagerly snapped up by a public fed for so long on the fantasy of monarchy.[39]

It was only with Diana's death in a car accident in August 1997 that the tabloids were forced to reflect on the ethics of their pursuit of the Princess. The anguished reaction of Earl Spencer, Diana's brother, that he 'always knew the press would kill her in the end' immediately put the press on the defensive. The *Sun* pointed out the that tragedy had happened in the country with the 'toughest privacy laws imaginable' and protested that in a global market tougher British privacy legislation would achieve little: 'No British law could prevent editors in America, Asia or Africa from reaching for their chequebooks'. Nevertheless, with Spencer renewing his denunciation of paparazzi in his funeral eulogy, lamenting that Diana had become the 'most hunted person of the modern age', the *Daily Mail*, amongst others, pledged to renounce the use of paparazzi shots, while the *Sun* declared that it had 'no intention of carrying photographs which invade the privacy of Princes William and Harry'. Diversion proved to be a more effective tactic, however. The press prevented a more searching examination of its own role in Diana's unhappiness by voicing the public's frustration at the Palace's formal and stilted response to her death. 'Where Is Our Queen? Where Is Her Flag?' demanded the *Sun* as the Queen remained in Balmoral and Buckingham Palace officials did not initially accede to widespread calls to fly a flag at half-mast. The *Sun* warned that the monarchy, seemingly out of touch with the more emotionally expressive culture of the time, was at a turning point: 'If it does not see the need for change, it will become irrelevant.' The equally vehement public criticisms of the press for its relentless pursuit of Diana inevitably received far less coverage.[40]

Diana's death was not the dramatic turning point in royal reporting that some had predicted. The more extravagant pledges against paparazzi photographs were soon quietly ignored, and only two years later the *Sun* provoked outrage by publishing a topless shot of Sophie Rhys-Jones, shortly before her marriage to Prince Edward. The *Sun's* immediate apology suggested, nevertheless, that it recognised the existence of a new, tougher mood concerning such gratuitous intrusions into the privacy of members of the royal family. The Palace's determination to preserve some level of privacy for Princes William and Harry, especially before they reached adulthood, was broadly accepted by the press, and there was some retreat from the excesses of the early 1990s. The coverage of Prince William's relationship with Kate Middleton severely tested the relationship between editors and the Palace but the tabloids usually responded, eventually, to the warnings from the PCC, lawyers and royal officials. Having learned from the Rhys-Jones furore, for example, the tabloids refused in 2012 to print topless pictures of Middleton (who had by then become the Duchess of Cambridge). This slightly less aggressive coverage went hand-in-hand with a rebuilding of the popularity of the monarchy, encouraged by fawning coverage of a string of ceremonial and commemorative events, such as Queen Elizabeth's Golden and Diamond Jubilee celebrations, Prince Charles's remarriage, and Prince William and Kate Middleton's wedding in 2011. The dark fears about the future of the monarchy voiced in the aftermath of Diana's death seemed preposterous a decade later.[41]

If slightly more measured in public, though, the intense pressure to deliver scoops about the royal family meant that in private journalists bent and broke both the PCC's code of conduct and, at times, the laws of the land. In 2007, Clive Goodman, the *News of the World's* Royal editor, pleaded guilty to illegally intercepting phone messages left for members of the royal family. Such phone hacking, it became clear, was only the tip of the iceberg; Goodman himself later admitted to hacking Kate Middleton's phone no fewer than 155 times. The routine monitoring of phone calls, combined with the ongoing scrutiny from crowds of photographers, underpinned an endless flow of stories about the activities and lifestyles of every member of the royal family. The ghost of Diana lingered on too, as certain papers – notably the *Express* – speculated about sinister forces behind her untimely death.

Both the press and the Palace had learnt lessons from the 1990s, however, and if the tabloids have stripped away some of the mystique of monarchy, they had no desire fatally to undermine it or remove its magic.[42]

Caution to the winds: Celebrity coverage in the 1980s and after

The changes that characterised the celebrity coverage of the 1980s were rooted in new editorial approaches to risk. The financial and reputational costs of libel actions had long acted as a significant restraint to speculative and unsupported stories, not least because the British libel laws were heavily weighted in favour of the plaintiff. For editors such as Kelvin MacKenzie, however, potential legal damages were an inevitable, and acceptable, consequence of the aggressive journalism required to stay ahead of the competition. Many of the most sensational, and editorially hazardous, stories were in the 'kiss-and-tell' genre, which became a staple of Sunday journalism in the 1970s and blossomed in the popular dailies during the following decade. Rather than collaborate with celebrities on 'confessional' articles, papers increasingly sought authentic, intimate revelations that would not ordinarily be volunteered. The testimonies of former lovers offered salacious tit-bits that could not be accessed by any other means, but were often subject to the distortions, exaggerations and fabrications of those with a grievance or a desire for money and publicity; by their nature, moreover, they could rarely be securely corroborated. From the mid-1980s, however, editors in pursuit of exclusives became increasingly likely to gamble on the veracity of such stories. In February 1987, the *Sun* accused popular singer Elton John of unlawful sexual activities, based entirely on the word of a gay prostitute with a drug addiction: 'Elton in Vice Boys Scandal' screamed the front page. Despite receiving a writ for libel, the *Sun* went on the offensive with a further headline, 'Elton's Kinky Kicks', and then rebuffed John's protests with a front-page editorial 'You're a Liar, Elton'. Further stories followed, including the fantastic claim that John's guard dogs had undergone surgery to stop them being able to bark. The original source for the stories had been dishonest, however, and eventually confessed his 'Sex Lies over Elton' to the *Mirror*. In December 1988 the *Sun* agreed a record £1 million settlement and made a grovelling front-page apology.[43]

The treatment of Elton John was only one example of a much broader tendency to run intrusive, and often speculative, stories about private lives. In 1987, the year of the initial John story, the *Sun* was censured no fewer than 15 times by the Press Council. Its stablemate, the *News of the World*, provoked controversy with revelations about the sex life of TV presenter Russell Harty; when he died eighteen months later, his friend Alan Bennett condemned the paper for outing Harty after 'trawling public life for sexual indiscretions'. At the same time, the *Daily Star* linked up with David Sullivan, who had built up a fortune in the pornography industry and had recently founded the soft-porn *Sunday Sport*, to develop a more explicitly sexualised approach. The paper's 'bonk journalism', full of titillating pictures and celebrity exposés, was too much for readers and advertisers, and was soon moderated; Sullivan instead set up a daily version of the *Sport*. If this episode demonstrated that there were limits to what the public would accept in a 'family newspaper', it also indicated the prevalence of the belief that the combination of sex and celebrity was the best way for tabloids to attract readers in a media environment dominated by television. In October 1988, Hugh Cudlipp, who had done so much to shape the character of the mid-century press, used a memorial speech for one of his colleagues to launch an excoriating attack on the depths to which tabloid journalism had plunged, arguing that 'nothing, however personal, was any longer secret or sacred and the basic human right to privacy was banished in the interest of public profit.' Newspapers now provided 'intrusive journalism for the prurient.'[44]

The Press Complaints Commission, established in 1990 as a result of the growing political and public concern about the excesses of the tabloid approach to celebrity and royalty, did little to rein in the competitive instincts of the press. Although it adopted and monitored a code of conduct, its continued lack of punitive sanctions left it unable to alter the culture of popular journalism. Labour's introduction in 1998 of the

Human Rights Act established for the first time in British law a right to privacy, which inevitably featured in suits between celebrities and the press – notably in the long-running dispute between the *Daily Mirror* and the supermodel Naomi Campbell. If privacy was a concept that was increasingly discussed and codified, though, journalists carried on much as before, merely updating their methods to take advantage of the possibilities offered by new technologies. There was a growing use of private detectives with expertise in exploiting online databases to trace addresses, phone numbers and car number plates; from the late 1990s, hacking into the messages on mobile phones became a widespread practice. These technologies enabled reporters to print stories whose source entirely mystified the celebrities in questions, and often led them unfairly accusing friends, family and employees for revealing secrets.

Over the same period, the traditional gossip column changed into a more explicitly celebrity and entertainment focused miscellany, as music, television and film stars finally displaced socialites and debutantes from the news pages. The *Sun's* launch of the *Bizarre* column in 1982 underlined the paper's focus on modern pop culture, and the feature's commercial importance was demonstrated by its ability to launch the careers of future *News of the World* and *Sun* editors, including Piers Morgan, Andy Coulson and Dominic Mohan. The *Mirror* eventually found a similarly successful brand with its '3am girls' gossip column. Both competed to provide the latest titbits, rumours and speculation. As pagination levels grew and the demand for stories intensified, so too did the celebrity galaxy expand. Reality television formats, such as Big Brother and X-Factor, provided 'ordinary' people with instant fame and made the prospect of achieving celebrity seem more realistic; for the tabloids, it provided endless opportunities to delve into contestants' pasts and to construct tantalising 'rise and fall' narratives.

As the celebrity cycle quickened with the rise of the internet, the press found themselves struggling to keep up, further encouraging the use of illegal means to keep ahead of the competition. The ever more insistent pursuit of the celebrity agenda has certainly kept some readers loyal, but only at the expense of heightening the distrust of journalists. The revelations of press misconduct revealed by the *Guardian*, and confirmed by the Leveson inquiry in 2012, led to the closure of the *News of the World*,

Britain's most popular paper and saw the reputation of tabloids sink further. Although it was the tabloid intrusion into the lives of 'ordinary' families, such as the Dowlers, that provoked the greatest public and political outrage, the testimony of certain stars, such as the singer Charlotte Church, detailing 'blackmail, illegal phone call interception, 24/7 surveillance and tracking, car chases, door stepping and blagging', and even breaking news of her pregnancy before she told her parents, painted a sobering picture of how far journalists were prepared to go in search of stories. Church observed that the coverage she endured was 'utterly horrifying at times' and 'devastating' to those around her.[45]

The tabloids have been impaled on the horns of a dilemma that has faced them since the 1960s. As the boundaries between public and private shifted, the press increasingly defined human interest in terms of revelations about private lives and, particularly, sexuality. Such material sold newspapers, but at a serious cost. As Lord Shawcross, the chairman of the Second Royal Commission on the Press, observed in the wake of the Profumo Scandal of 1963, 'although as individuals we may not be averse to wallowing vicariously in stories of sexual perversion and promiscuity, although we enjoy the spark of malice and listen curiously to the tongue of scandal, we do not approve of those who, for profit, purvey these things'. This reputational damage left the tabloids exposed as the media climate changed at the end of the century, and the internet brought new competitors who could provide celebrity content more quickly and with fewer constraints. The *Mail*, with its successful website *MailOnline*, recognised the potential of delivering celebrity content online, but it has proved difficult to combine such material with the traditional political and social commentary provided in the paper itself; on the internet, moreover, trust levels are lower, and attention spans shorter. As their scope narrows, tabloids risk being defined by the celebrity content, and losing the political and social presence that was so vital to their success across the twentieth century.[46]

Gender and Sexuality

The twentieth-century popular press conspicuously and self-consciously defined readers by their gender. The serious morning newspapers of the Victorian era had done this only implicitly: they tended to assume that their readership was male, and focused almost entirely on a public sphere dominated by men. The new popular papers, led by Northcliffe's *Daily Mail*, by contrast, actively sought to maximise their audience, and this meant reaching out in a very obvious way to women as well as men. Female readers did not just boost the overall circulation statistics, they also had a special economic importance to the newspaper business. Women were – or were perceived to be – the major spenders of the domestic budget, and hence they became the prime targets for advertisers looking to sell their products. As newspapers came to rely ever more heavily on the revenue from branded advertising, attracting female readers became a financial necessity. In a society in which men and women were still heavily segregated in both work and leisure, editors and journalists were confident that appealing to women meant providing a different sort of content from that aimed at men – the sort of content, in fact, that had fuelled the success of the burgeoning women's magazine sector throughout the nineteenth century.

Northcliffe encouraged his papers to provide material on fashion, housewifery and motherhood, and comparisons between the sexes became a staple of the feature pages. Northcliffe also believed that both men and women were interested in pictures of 'attractive ladies' and 'bathing belles'; this tendency, set alongside the propensity of branded advertising to display the female figure, ensured that newspapers were visually feminised in striking ways. In the early decades of the twentieth-century, therefore, the female reader moved from the margins to the centre of editorial calculations, ensuring that the definition of news was radically altered, that the boundary between public and private was redrawn, and that the visibility of women in public discourse was transformed. Much, though by no means all, of this content, was ultimately based on conservative gender stereotypes. Some women were frustrated at the lack of more challenging material directed at female readers, and the feminist movement often despaired at the difficulty of obtaining publicity for its campaigns. The *Mail* and the *Mirror* sought to secure female readers while opposing women having the vote: it was only during the First World War that Northcliffe was won over to the principle of women's suffrage.

The model established by Northcliffe and his imitators remained largely intact throughout the century. The basic assumption that men and women had different interests remained very resilient. In the middle decades of the century, the *Daily Mirror* increasingly injected a dose of sex into the traditional formula. The 'problem column', aimed primarily at women, became more prominent, and more space was given to journalists to write about personal relationships and sexuality. The belief that women were interested in celebrity and gossip encouraged the rise of those elements of the newspaper package. At the same time, the overtly sexualised pin-up emerged as a form of titillation for men, to be consumed before turning to the unlabelled 'men's pages', otherwise known as the sports section. The expectation that readers were conventionally heterosexual ensured that alternative sexualities were marginalised or ridiculed.

The concurrent rise from the late 1960s of Murdoch's *Sun* and a reinvigorated feminist movement exposed the tensions in this gendered editorial model. The topless 'Page 3 girl', a regular feature in the *Sun* from 1970, blatantly objectified the female body just at time when the women's movement was starting to put media sexism under closer scrutiny than ever before. More and more voices were raised against the crude stereotypes that littered popular journalism and denied the agency of women. The male dominance of the newsrooms was likewise exposed. By the end of the century, there were some significant shifts both in the gendered nature of reporting and the gender balance of the newsrooms. At the same time, some of the underlying assumptions of journalism remained unchanged, and tabloids still seek to appeal to the female audience primarily by offering a diet of lifestyle and celebrity journalism. The *Sun*'s continued defence of the 'page 3 girl', more than forty years after its first appearance, remains the most powerful symbol of the continuing inequalities.

The Northcliffe model

The *Daily Mail* reached out to the female audience from its very first issue on 4 May 1896. Northcliffe was determined that the traditional remit of the newspaper be broadened by including a page of features – heralded as the 'Daily Magazine, An Entirely New Idea In Morning Journalism', which would provide every week 'matter equivalent to a sixpenny monthly' – and he ensured that space was explicitly marked out for women's interests. 'A Note from the Editor' made a firm commitment to female readers:

> Movements in a woman's world – that is to say, changes in dress, toilet matters, cookery, and home matters generally – are as much entitled to receive attention as nine out of ten of the matters which are treated of in the ordinary daily paper. Therefore, two columns are set aside exclusively for ladies.[1]

The paper worked hard to convey the impression of metropolitan sophistication and expertise. It announced that the section 'will be under the direction of a lady who till recently occupied the editorial chair of a leading fashion weekly' (this was Mary Howarth):

> She will visit all the best shops in London in search of suggestions. Society weddings will be attended by her, and she will frequently make trips to Paris, Brussels, and all the other centres of fashion to gather material for her dress articles.

The aspirational tone of the column was immediately apparent: after all, few among the *Mail*'s target readership would be nipping across the Channel for fashion ideas. The paper was offering its suburban readers a taste of the glamour of high society. The seeds for the later flowering of celebrity culture were sown here. The admiration of wealth and status was further confirmed by a signed article by 'Lady Charlotte' on Christianity's contribution to civilisation, which promised readers a glimpse into the culture and wisdom of polite conversation in elite circles.[2]

Northcliffe himself displayed a genuine determination that the women's section should be treated as seriously as any other department. He ordered that recipes be checked by his own chef, and insisted that articles and stories were accurate and consistent. Those he suspected of being casual were, as one trusted journalist observed, 'flayed alive'. As time went on, Northcliffe carried out his own forms of market research to ensure that the women's page remained relevant and readable: he warned the editor that he had 'fifty women of all classes' giving their opinion of the features. He also reminded his staff that the material for women was an integral part of the wider operation. 'Don't be bluffed by journalists with only a men's outlook,' he told Tom Clarke, one of the *Mail*'s news editors. 'Read the woman's page every day.'[3]

The articles of the 'woman's realm' were not the only means by which the *Daily Mail* sought to attract the female audience. The first issue also contained the opening instalment of a fiction serial, directed above all at women. Northcliffe hoped it would encourage wives to remind husbands to bring their paper back home. More generally, a reorientation of news values allowed women and 'women's interests' to enter the main body of the paper. Northcliffe sent bulletins to his news editors reminding them to 'look out for feminine topics for the news columns'. Tom Clarke, recalled his proprietor's exhortations: 'Don't forget the women, Tom. Always have one "woman's story" at the top of all the main news pages.' Northcliffe urged journalists to consider the news from perspectives other than that of the metropolitan man: 'I think the *Daily Mail* might have had some reference to the great sale week,' he told the editor in July 1918, despite the limited space and the mass of war news to fit into the columns. 'The whole feminine population of the village where I am is *en route* for London this morning for the great day.' He praised the paper when it had a 'good wedding exclusive', for these were 'always very valuable to a newspaper so largely read by women'. Offering these different perspectives inevitably meant that female journalists and writers obtained new opportunities to contribute, and there was a steady rise of women in Fleet Street in these years, although they remained heavily concentrated in gender stereotyped roles.[4]

Emboldened by the success of his experiments in attracting female readers, Northcliffe went a step further and established a daily newspaper entirely written by and for women. The *Daily Mirror* was launched in November 1903 with an all-female staff under the original editor of the *Mail*'s women's columns, Mary Howarth. The first issue declared that it would not be 'a mere bulletin of fashion, but a reflection of women's interests, women's thought, women's work', covering 'the daily news of the world' and 'literature and art' as well as the 'sane and healthy occupations of domestic life'. Gendering sections within a newspaper was one thing: gendering the whole paper was another. The mainstream market was not yet ready for a women's daily newspaper, at least not in this form. The *Mirror* struggled to find a consistent tone and identity, and seemed caught between being a magazine and a newspaper. As its circulation plummeted, the *Mirror* was rescued only when Northcliffe removed the female staff, handed over the editorship to the experienced journalist Hamilton Fyfe, and turned it into an illustrated paper – as which it was a major success, becoming the first daily to rival the readership levels of the *Mail*. Yet if no longer written by women, or marketed exclusively for them, the *Mirror* maintained a distinctly 'feminine' identity, and it continued to attract a much higher percentage of female readers than any other paper until well into the 1930s.[5]

The *Mirror* experiment encapsulated the different aspects of Northcliffe's attitudes to women. His faith in the potential of the women's market led him to take extraordinary risks: he lost around £100,000 supporting the *Mirror* in its early months. At a time when women had barely gained a foothold in the world of journalism, he demonstrated his willingness to place a great deal of responsibility onto an inexperienced female editorial team, while simply by launching a 'women's newspaper' he continued to challenge assumptions about gender and popular publishing. Nor did the failure of the *Mirror* seem to alter his perceptions about the female audience. 'While we learnt there was no room in London for a women's daily paper,' recalled Kennedy Jones, 'we also discovered there was room in a daily paper for more letter press that directly appealed to women.' The *Mail* therefore increased its efforts in this area, even advertising itself as 'the woman's daily'. Tom Clarke noted that the setback to the *Mirror* did not undermine Northcliffe's 'faith that the future for popular newspapers and magazines depended on a big woman readership'.[6]

On the other hand, Northcliffe shared many of the conventional gender prejudices and stereotypes of his time. He continued to view women as being largely defined by their roles as wives and mothers, and the 'women's material' for his papers was produced on these terms. When he told staff to find 'feminine matter', he assumed that his meaning was self-evident: he wanted domestic articles, fashion tips, or society gossip. His forward-thinking with regard to the female market was tempered by what the new *Mirror* editor Hamilton Fyfe described as 'an old-fashioned doubt' as to whether women were 'really the equals of men'. Until the First World War, Northcliffe was sceptical about the need for female suffrage, and this was reflected in the *Mail*'s hostile comments about the activities of the suffragettes. The *Mirror* was rather more neutral, and indeed intermittently annoyed Northcliffe by giving publicity to the women's movement. 'Sorry to see the outburst of Suffragette pictures again' he complained to Alexander Kenealy, the editor of the *Mirror*, in 1912. 'I thought you had finished with them. Except in an extreme case, print no more of them.' It was only when women demonstrated their ability to serve the nation during the war that he changed his mind and became a proponent of women's suffrage.[7]

Northcliffe was equally conventional in his view of women as a form of social decoration. With photography becoming an increasingly important element of the competition between titles, he believed that pictures of beautiful women, in particular, were a way of making newspapers stand out in the market. 'A few attractive ladies would make the paper look better', he complained in a bulletin to the *Mail* office in August 1920. 'The public well know where to find these for they only appear in the *Daily Mirror* and the *Daily Sketch*.' He was concerned because a 'well-known public man' had recently told him that he had dropped 'the *Daily Mail* in order to get the *Daily Mirror* bathing pictures.' He believed that an eye for the female form was a prerequisite for a good journalist – he told Tom Clarke 'I have no use for a man who cannot appreciate a pretty ankle' – and was dismayed when his picture editor picked out photographs featuring 'common-looking ugly wenches'. Northcliffe was careful to impose limits on this aspect of newspaper competition, telling one of his editors in 1921 that he 'did not like the picture of Miss Noreena Feist, it is vulgar and inelegant. (Enough is as good as a feast)'. Nevertheless, by instilling the idea that popular newspapers should compete on their provision of female beauty and glamour, he planted the seeds of the later pin-up culture.[8]

Most of all, though, Northcliffe taught Fleet Street that gender difference, and especially changes in women's lives, provided an almost endlessly reliable talking point for features and opinion columns. In the decade after the First World War, in particular, the *Mail* helped to foster what was little less than a national obsession with the activities of 'flappers' or 'modern young women'. The popular press provided countless reports of women voting for the first time, moving into new public and professional roles, wearing short skirts, dancing, smoking and driving. 'If a future chronicler were to study the files of our newspapers,' speculated the novelist Rose Macaulay in 1925, 'he would get the impression that there had appeared at this time a strange new creature called woman who was receiving great attention from the public.' A good example of this press-generated controversy came when Donald Clark, a councillor from Tonbridge, Kent, declared in 1920 that mixed bathing on beaches was 'the worst public scandal of our so-called civilisation', and that 'much of the unrest in the country is due to the barbarous licence in women's dress'. Tom Clarke, suggested 'half-jestingly' to Northcliffe that the paper

> ought to commission the councillor to go round the seaside resorts and write his views of what the bathing costumes were and what he thought they should be. 'Capital', cried the Chief. 'Arrange it at once. Plan a tour and pay all his expenses. Send a first-class reporter with him to help him ... Send a photographer too ... It will be one of the best holiday-season features we have had for years.'[9]

The resulting series of articles were highly entertaining, but they had a more serious side in helping to focus public attention on changing notions of morality. By presenting Councillor Clark as a representative of Victorian propriety and then turning him into little more than a figure of ridicule, the *Mail* was helping both to undermine traditional standards and to clarify definitions of 'modern behaviour'. When some 'older school' *Mail* journalists complained that the feature was 'not only frivolous, but also getting near the pornographic', Northcliffe was unrepentant: 'Everybody is reading these articles … We must not become too respectable.' Many similar features about young women's fashions inevitably followed. More broadly, freelance journalists were advised that writing about gender differences was one of the best ways of getting an article published: 'A comparison between the sexes on practically every subject under the sun can be exploited … There is always something new happening to the sexes.' This guidance would resonate throughout the century.[10]

The sexualisation of the popular press: Problem pages

Northcliffe's populist tendencies were held in check by a profound concern for respectability. He wanted the *Daily Mail* to be a 'family newspaper' that middle-class readers would not hesitate to welcome into their house. Although he was keen for his papers to cover and debate personal and domestic issues – health, family, money and such like – he remained cautious about them delving too deeply into the private realm of sex and sexuality. This was partly to distinguish them from Sunday papers, such as the *News of the World*, which provided illicit titillation by reporting court cases involving sex offences and immoral behaviour. From the mid-1930s, however, a new generation of editors and journalists, inspired by a slightly freer public discussion of sexual issues, began to push back these boundaries and took different decisions about what was acceptable content. This can be seen most clearly in the emergence of what became two key tabloid formats: the problem page and the pin-up. After relatively restrained beginnings, popular newspapers, led by the *Daily Mirror* and the *Sunday Pictorial*, developed new ways of discussing and displaying sex, moving away from the traditional moralism of the courtroom to use self-consciously 'modern' languages of sexual welfare or sexual pleasure. Influenced both by the rise of psychological modes of thinking and the emergence of the sex survey, the press became more interested in scrutinising and debating 'ordinary' sexuality. Newspapers also engaged more actively with policy debates about 'social problems' such as prostitution and, in particular, homosexuality. By the 1950s – before the 'permissiveness' of the 1960s – the popular daily press had significantly redrawn the boundaries between public and private and its content had become much more overtly sexualised than in the early decades of the century.

Although there were some precursors in the 1920s, it was in the mid-1930s that the problem column became a central part of modern popular journalism. The prolific American agony aunt 'Dorothy Dix' (the pen-name of Elizabeth Meriweather Gilmer) was given a significant platform in the reinvented *Daily Mirror* from December 1935, while Ann Temple's 'Human Case-Book' was promoted heavily by the *Daily Mail* from its launch in 1936. Rivals soon followed suit with similar features of their own: 'everywhere problem columns appeared, disappeared, and reappeared', noted Temple. Indeed, the period from the mid-1930s to the 1970s can be seen as the 'golden age' of the newspaper problem column, when agony aunts such as Dix, Temple, Marje Proops and Claire Rayner were among the most highly paid and widely recognised journalists in Fleet Street, and significant amounts of money were invested by newspapers in responding to the hundreds of letters that poured in week by week.[11]

Newspaper problem columns and related features were regarded by many readers as an important source of advice and guidance on personal and sexual questions at a time when there were relatively few accessible sources of information about such matters. Ann Temple admitted that she was 'absolutely astounded' by the volume of post she received in response to her first column in 1936. In the 1970s, Marje Proops at the *Daily Mirror* received around 40,000 letters a year, and Claire Rayner at the *Sun* seems to have received anywhere between 250 and 1,500 letters a week. The *News of the World*'s John Hilton bureau – which addressed a broad range of consumer and citizenship issues as well as personal problems – received more than 100,000 a year. Such numbers suggest that a significant section of the readership viewed newspapers columnists as a trustworthy and convenient place to turn with their personal problems. Seemingly sympathetic figures with no direct power over readers' lives, these journalists offered many people an approachable alternative to intimidating and intrusive professional or local sources of advice.[12]

In the 1930s and 1940s, advice columns did little to challenge a sexual culture that emphasised privacy, respectability and female innocence. They consistently celebrated the virtues of sexual restraint outside marriage and defended the expectation that women (if not men) should be virgins when they wed. In the *Mirror*, Dorothy Dix repeatedly advised young women against any forms of physical intimacy with men that might put them in a compromising position. She declared bluntly in 1938, for example, that 'I don't believe in petting among boys and girls'. Ann Temple likewise espoused high moral standards based clearly on the Christian tradition, in which the individual should strive 'to keep the body in subjection to the mind'.[13]

Married readers, meanwhile, were warned about the disastrous repercussions of extra-marital affairs. A couple who had found love and happiness in each other's arms, despite both being married to other partners, were told by Dorothy Dix in 1938 to stop their affair immediately: 'There is something more worthwhile having in life than love, and that is the integrity of your own soul, and the knowledge that you had the strength to do your duty'. Dix advised wronged wives to 'make the best of a very bad job' and try to save their marriages. Ann Temple was similarly determined to protect the institution of marriage and expressed her concern that, due to the influence of Freudian psychology in the 1930s, 'the wholesome, imperative qualities of self-control, restraint and self-discipline were being interpreted as repressions'. She tried to make a stand against this creed of 'self-first' and the associated change 'from respect for marriage into the belief that love matters more than marriage'. During the Second World War newspapers believed that it was vital for popular morale that they defend relationships put under strain by military service and extended absences from home. Accordingly, adulterers were given even shorter shrift than usual, and columnists across Fleet Street warned women against consorting with American GIs. Columnists in this period prioritised the stability of marriage – deemed to be necessary for the stability of society as a whole – over individual happiness and fulfilment. Serious discussions of homosexuality, meanwhile, remained conspicuous by their absence.[14]

If newspaper morality often remained severe, the discussion of sexual matters in problem columns and related features was becoming less euphemistic. In 1942, with anxieties about public ill-health on the home front running high, the *Daily Mirror* ran an unprecedentedly explicit series on the dangers of venereal diseases, written by a specialist, and including answers to correspondents. These articles demonstrated the educational potential of newspaper problem pages. The survey organisation Mass-Observation suggested that the *Mirror* was helping to remedy significant gaps in public knowledge; some female respondents admitted they had never heard of the diseases until they read about them in the press. Another survey a year later, after a further series of VD information notices in the press organised by the Ministry of Health, found that those who were exposed to the material 'consistently showed more knowledge of the subject than those who had not.'[15]

The success of this series encouraged the press to give greater coverage to scientific studies of sexuality, particularly those, like Professor Alfred Kinsey's investigations in the United States, that were attempting to map the attitudes and behaviour of the 'ordinary' citizen. In 1949, the year after Kinsey's pioneering investigation of the habits of American men, the *Sunday Pictorial* commissioned Mass-Observation to conduct a survey into the British public's attitudes to sex. This was the 'first national random sample survey of sex' to be undertaken in Britain, and demonstrated that the popular press was using its money, motivation and cultural power not just to report on the new sexual science, but to set research questions and priorities. The results were published in a heavily advertised five-part series entitled 'The Private Life of John Bull'. The central theme of the report, identified in the first extract, was the existence of 'considerable individual confusion in a world of rapidly changing moral values.' 'Clear divisions of opinion' were evident both between churchgoers and non-churchgoers, and between men and women, while 'unconventional' attitudes could be found 'in every social group,' and were no longer restricted to 'progressive' or 'cosmopolitan' circles. Traditional Christian morality remained important, but Mass-Observation detected 'a move away from the Church's teachings towards greater sexual freedom.' This was the first of many surveys of sex and personal relationships that the popular press would commission or publicise over the coming decades as it fed the public's desire to learn ever more about the intimate lives of the national population.[16]

The news value of the sex survey was confirmed in 1953 when Kinsey's second study, *Sexual Behavior in the Human Female*, was greeted by a wave of articles in the British popular press. Newspapers emphasised how modern science was challenging conventional wisdom. 'Women, contrary to popular belief, are physically capable of responding sexually as quickly as men', noted the *Mirror* on the day of report's publication in August 1953: 'Female "frigidity" is a man-made situation ... They [men] go far too quickly and offer a variety of love-making that may mean little to a woman'. More broadly, individuals were invited as never before to think about the quality of their own sexual experience, to compare themselves to others, and to learn how to 'improve' their relationships.[17]

In the 1950s, moreover, problem columnists increasingly embraced the ideas of Freud and Kinsey, and played an important role in disseminating them to a broader audience. They now tended to portray sexuality – at least within marriage – less as a dangerous instinct to be restrained, and more as a positive and pleasurable force that needed to be expressed for personal well-being. So while columnists still warned against pre-marital and extra-marital affairs, they also became much more likely to encourage married readers, and women in particular, to lose their inhibitions and explore the possibilities of sexual pleasure. In 1951, for example, the *Mirror*'s Mary Brown invited husbands to 'air their grievances' about their wives and found that 'overwhelmingly' the most common complaint related to disappointing sex lives. Although Brown's traditionalism was evident in her assumption that men 'had stronger sexual urges than women', she insisted that sex had to take a 'happy and proportionate place in marriage' and called on women to be 'free and generous'; only when sex became a battlefield was it 'unpleasant and shameful'. In 1955, a contributor to the *News of the World* similarly emphasised the need for more 'generosity and joy' in the treatment of sex: 'Too many married people, especially women, think their duty is done if they refrain from casting their eyes beyond their marriage partner; or if they concede marital rights with patience'. Some of this material showed little understanding of the genuine reasons for women's anxieties about sex – fear of pregnancy, the thoughtlessness of their partners, an upbringing in social environments hostile to sexual expression – but space was also given to more sympathetic perspectives, such as those put forward by Kinsey himself.[18]

By the 1960s columnists increasingly acknowledged the sexual agency of women and supported their efforts to be self-reflective about sexual pleasure. In 1963 Marje Proops accepted that 'most girls have had some kind of sexual experience before marriage', but she told the 'recent bride' that after the wedding sex was more satisfying because the 'fear of pregnancy, guilt, [and] terror of being found out' disappeared. She encouraged newly-wed women to take the initiative in communicating their sexual desires. 'Tell him what you need and ask him about his needs'. Sex was a skill to be mastered gradually, with the appropriate assistance if necessary: 'You'll discover the art of sex by experiment, learning as you go. And if you find you are a bit slow on the uptake – or he is – buy a book'. Two months later, she wrote another column eulogising the power of sex to enrich lives: 'Without it (or without the best of it) life is arid, boring, wearying, unenticing, uneventful, uninspiring. With it (or the best of it) life is rewarding, exciting, moving, amusing, exhilarating and splendid. Those who maintain the myth that sex isn't everything have my profound pity'. Many journalists by the 1960s enthusiastically accepted the Freudian view that sex was central to individual identity and fulfilment.[19]

The growing appreciation of women's sexuality also encouraged columnists to be more sympathetic to those who admitted adultery. In 1966 Sara Robson in the *News of the World* was far more compassionate than Dorothy Dix would have been to a woman who had engaged in a brief one night affair after being frustrated by the sexual coldness of her husband. 'A normally passionate woman living with a husband she loves, but seldom makes love with, is dreadfully vulnerable to the temptation you fell for', Robson observed, adding that if the lack of sex was not addressed with expert help, 'similar incidents will happen again'. Such advice was typical of a wider shift among counsellors and psychologists in this period towards prioritising personal relationships over the stability of marriage. More broadly, some columnists sought to understand, rather than condemn, the mores of the young in an apparently more 'permissive' society. Marje Proops, in particular, caused controversy in the late 1960s when she advised boys to take their own contraceptives to parties, while in 1976 she accepted, with some reservations, that group sex was not inevitably harmful and could be pleasurable to some. Freed from the need to defend marriage as an institution, columnists took pragmatic decisions about 'alternative' sexual practices based on the available evidence.[20]

Problem columnists and feature writers did not restrict themselves to responding to individual cries for help. They increasingly used their positions to foster debate about 'social problems' and the laws governing sexual activity, helping to turn 'personal troubles' into 'public issues'. Anne Allen, a magistrate who became a prominent contributor to the popular press on welfare issues, was a persistent campaigner for more humane laws regulating divorce, homosexuality and abortion. Marje Proops was a vocal advocate of abortion law reform. In November 1964, she wrote a powerful column appealing to the Lord Chancellor 'on behalf of the 100,000 women who face up to the heartbreak and terror of the illegal abortion ever year, to bring the law into the twentieth century.' She also supported the decriminalisation of homosexuality and gave Leo Abse, the Labour MP, advice when he was drafting his homosexual law reform bills in the mid-1960s. Her position on this issue mean that she had to endure some unpleasant letters from homophobic readers, with one writing that 'You must be a lesbian yourself to want to make life easier for queers'. Campaigning organisations such as the Family Planning Association, the Abortion Law Reform Association and the National Council for the Unmarried Mother and Child (later One Parent Family) maintained contacts with problem columnists and found that being mentioned in their columns was one of the most effective ways of gaining national publicity. By encouraging a more positive, reflective and critical discussion of sex, problem columnists and feature writers made a significant contribution to the climate of reform in the 1950s and 1960s.[21]

The sexualisation of the popular press: Pin-ups

Advice columns and sexual welfare features comprised only one side of the sexualisation of the tabloid in mid-century, however: the other was the emergence of a more explicit and insistent pin-up culture. If agony aunts wrote largely for the female audience, pin-ups were regarded as a reliable way to titillate men. While Northcliffe, as we have seen, was fond of pictures of 'bathing beauties' and glamorous Society women, the emergence of a more overtly sexualised pin-up culture can be dated to the reinvention of the *Daily Mirror* in the mid-1930s. The new *Mirror* was seeking both to shake off its reputation as a 'women's paper', and also to target a working-class, rather than middle-class, market: saucy, cheeky, faintly unrespectable, photos, clearly aimed at a male gaze, provided one of the most effective means of demonstrating this editorial transformation. Picture editors tested the limits of acceptability, choosing shots that exposed more flesh and had an erotic allure. Well before the invention of the 'Page 3 girl', moreover, the audience's reaction to toplessness was tested. Photographs of bare-breasted black African women were justified as imperial reportage of exotic and less 'civilised' societies; such pictures had been included in respectable magazines such as *National Geographic* since the 1920s. In April 1938, the *Sunday Pictorial*, the *Mirror*'s sister paper, dared to publish what seems to have been the first photograph in a mainstream national newspaper of a topless white woman. This nude shot was a relatively tasteful picture of a 'spring nymph' reaching up to the blossom of an apple tree, but the model's exposed nipples were visible in the dappled sunlight. Hugh Cudlipp, the paper's young editor, was only allowed to publish this picture after personally obtaining the permission of the *Pictorial*'s chairman, John Cowley; the surprised Cowley seems to have been too embarrassed to refuse, to the great amusement of Cudlipp and director Cecil King. This experiment was not repeated, but it did embolden the editorial team to continue their practice of including revealing and overtly sexualised shots. Perhaps the most productive strategy, though, was to render nudity safer by transposing it into cartoon form. The 'Jane' strip, drawn by the artist Norman Pett, had been launched in December 1932 as a satire on a guileless 'bright young thing'; in the late-1930s it was transformed into a saucy feature in which the protagonist and her female companions contrived new ways of losing their clothing. During the Second World War, 'Jane' started brazenly displaying her breasts, becoming one of the forces' most popular pin-ups, and one of the central elements of the *Mirror*'s brand.[22]

This emerging pin-up culture was part of a classic tabloid editorial strategy to stratify the market, seeking to attract the target (male) working-class readers with an irreverent baiting of the respectable middle-classes. The *Mirror*'s editors welcomed criticism – as would *Sun* editors in later decades – because it merely served to confirm and publicise the paper's brash and risqué reputation. The *Daily Sketch*, previously the *Mirror*'s main competitor as a picture paper, walked straight into the trap by launching a 'Clean and Clever' campaign in 1938, denouncing the 'degradation' of journalism and pledging 'not to use the sensational, ribald and pornographic pictures which are making their appearance elsewhere'. The campaign did little more than advertise the illicit pleasures other papers were able to offer. A Mass-Observation survey of reading habits in December 1938 indicated the ways in which the market was becoming polarised around attitudes to sexual content. A female *Sketch* reader highlighted the disgust of those wedded to traditional morality when she described the *Daily Mirror* as 'the dirtiest little rag ever printed as a "daily" in this country'. She complained that its 'nefarious pages' contained 'many photos of half-naked females'. A male respondent, by contrast, admitted that the presence of daring 'sex photos' was one of his main reasons for taking the *Mirror*: 'I dislike the *Sketch*. It is not modern. I don't only want "All the news and pictures fit to print". I want the other side as well.' The former type of reader was already well catered for by the market; the latter, far less so. The triumph of the *Mirror* over the *Sketch* confirmed that there was, by the late 1930s, a substantial public appetite for unapologetically entertaining and titillating forms of sexual content. The reinvented *Mirror* appeared to many readers to be 'modern' and in tune with the times, unlike the moralistic and outdated *Sketch*.[23]

The pin-up culture grew during the Second World War – with photos often presented as a harmless source of pleasure for men defending the country – before flourishing throughout the popular press during the

1950s. This was part of a global phenomenon in which film stars such as Marilyn Monroe, Jayne Mansfield, Sophia Loren, and Brigitte Bardot were marketed more explicitly than ever before as 'sex symbols', glossy magazines such as *Playboy* (launched in 1953) brought nude shots to a wider audience, and consumer advertising became more eroticised. Tabloids endlessly photographed and interviewed the leading stars, and there was a constant stream of lesser models and actresses seeking to emulate these icons. The British media's appetite for female glamour in the 1950s led to the creation of arguably the first ever modern celebrity pin-up, famous only for her looks and not for any acting, dancing or singing abilities. Decades before the success of the glamour models Samantha Fox or Jordan, the press made the curvaceous Sabrina – real name Norma Sykes – into one of the biggest stars of the mid-1950s. Spotted by the comedian Arthur Askey, the young model was introduced into his television programme *Before Your Very Eyes* as a 'dumb blonde'. She was soon offered other television and film opportunities, but it was the feverish press interest – fed by Sabrina's wily agent Joe Matthews, who, in a typical publicity stunt, insured her breasts for £100,000 – that transformed her into a household name. The *Mirror*, for example, enthusiastically made front-page news out of an ITV ban on the 'daringly slinky black gown' Sabrina planned to wear during her debut on the Jack Johnson show, while the ups and downs of her relationship with Hollywood actor Steve Cochran were lavishly reported. In September 1957, the *Daily Mail* reported that Sabrina had been beaten only by Florence Nightingale and Joan of Arc in a poll of schoolboys to find their 'heroine': Jayne Mansfield, Brigitte Bardot and Diana Dors were all left trailing in her wake.[24]

As the endless innuendo about Sabrina's 'treasure chest' demonstrated, the press heavily eroticised breasts, making them the main signifier of sex in the public domain. Only days before Sabrina's poll success, Marje Proops had used her *Mirror* column to lament that the 'Cult of the Big Bosom' had 'reached idiotic proportions'. Her column was prompted by a letter from a twenty seven year-old mother of two, telling Proops that she was 'so self-conscious and unhappy' because she was 'only 33 inches round the bust', and was therefore considering spending £100 – a small fortune – on a breast enlargement operation. 'Every day', Proops revealed, 'letters arrive in this office, and every day thousands of girls and women all over this country stare at themselves despairingly in looking-glasses because their bust measurement is, they think, too small'. Proops argued that it was 'time we revolted against tape-measure dictatorship.' Proops received an 'amazing stack of letters' in response to her comments: 'Never have I had such overwhelming support ... from women of every age, shape and size. And from men too, believe it or not.' The following week, when film star Jayne Mansfield arrived in London flaunting her curvaceous figure, the *Mirror* even propelled the issue onto the front page. 'Has the Bust Had It?' asked the headline, as the paper considered whether the 'celebrity bosom' had become over-exposed. After reading hundreds of letters the showbiz reporter Donald Zec concluded that while readers had 'nothing against an attractive figure, displayed with taste', the 'outsize, over-exposed "Celebrity Bosom" HAS had it as far as most of you are concerned'.[25]

These gentle critiques of the pin-up culture helped to reassure female readers that their perspectives had not been completely forgotten, but ultimately they could do little to alter the customs of the boisterously male newsrooms, where the necessity of titillating readers remained an article of faith. Jack Nener, the *Mirror* editor between 1953 and 1961, agreed with Cudlipp that serious news needed to be lightened with glamour: he once demanded from his picture editor 'some tits to go with the rail strike'. Journalists continued to write unselfconsciously about the 'vital statistics' of the 'blondes' and 'beauties' that featured in the columns. Picture captions assumed the knowing complicity of male readers: 'Tear your eyes away from the picture for a second, chaps, and we'll tell you her name'. The continuing commitment to the pin-up was demonstrated when the experienced journalist Gerald Fairlie was sent to Ireland in 1961 to investigate the poor sales of the *News of the World*'s recently relaunched Irish edition. Fairlie concluded that the editors, conscious of previous problems with censors, were being too cautious, especially with the pictures. Fairlie emphasised, in particular, the importance of pin-ups: 'We must have bright pictures of pretty girls, freely sprinkled about the paper, and wherever possible on the top half of the front page ... lovely female forms are a necessity for our circulation. I stress this is a MUST.' The *News of the World* therefore started to include more daring content in its Irish edition. What was acceptable in Britain was not always suitable for the Catholic market, however, and for some years the paper retained an artist in its Manchester office to paint underwear on the more explicit shots before they went on sale in Ireland.[26]

The popular press and homosexuality

The entrenched gender stereotypes in Fleet Street were accompanied by similarly powerful assumptions about the 'normality' of heterosexuality. It was simply accepted that men should find pin-ups appealing, just as women should be intrigued by the trials and tribulations of heterosexual romance. In the first half of the century, editors tended to regard homosexuality as a distasteful topic that was unsuitable for a family audience, and most popular papers – with the exception of the *News of the World* – confined their coverage of the subject to the occasional court report (particularly cases featuring schoolmasters, vicars and others in positions of authority). As the historian Matt Houlbrook has noted, 'unless engaged with the apparatus of the law, queer lives remained hidden from readers.'[27]

Lesbianism was not a criminal offence, and so it received even less attention, emerging from the shadows only during intermittent moral crusades, such as in 1928 when the *Sunday Express* columnist James Douglas intemperately denounced Radclyffe Hall's novel, *The Well of Loneliness*, which described the life of a masculine lesbian, Stephen Gordon. 'I would rather give a healthy boy or a healthy girl a phial of prussic acid than this novel,' raged Douglas. 'Poison kills the body, but moral poison kills the soul'. Douglas's tirade is one of the most infamous pieces of twentieth-century popular journalism, and it produced immediate results: three days later the book was withdrawn by the publisher, Jonathan Cape, on the advice of the Home Secretary. In October, copies of the novel were seized and successfully prosecuted for obscenity. It was, however, an unusual and exceptional article in a period when the confused and imprecise journalism about sex mirrored the fluidity and uncertainty of popular sexual identities. As Houlbrook and others have demonstrated, men could have sex with other men while considering themselves to be 'normal'. Shrouded warnings about 'unnatural' sex were not enough to shape clear ideas about 'homosexuality' or to generate a well-defined binary opposition between heterosexuality and homosexuality.[28]

It was only in the 1950s, as the popular press extended and deepened its coverage of sexual issues, that this pattern altered significantly. A new generation of journalists responded to, and reinforced, a changing climate of opinion in which sexual knowledge was seen as both an essential part of citizenship in a modern welfare state, and a prerequisite for ensuring marital stability after the turmoil of wartime. The press became more open to, and interested in, scientific and psychological research into sexuality. Against this backdrop, homosexuality for the first time became a subject of sustained discussion and investigation in the popular press. But this more open debate did little to encourage toleration or understanding. Whether using traditional moral rhetoric, or deploying more recent knowledge about 'deviance' and psychological 'maladjustment', journalists generally maintained their traditional hostility to homosexuality. Crucial distinctions between relationships involving consenting adults, and those involving adults and children, were repeatedly obscured. In the process, the press whipped up a moral panic and urged tough action against the homosexual 'menace'.

The *Sunday Pictorial*'s three-part series 'Evil Men', printed in May–June 1952, exemplified these new tendencies. The self-declared intention of the series was to end the 'stupid, dangerous conspiracy of silence' that surrounded the subject of homosexuality. Douglas Warth, the author of the articles, argued that this silence, far from protecting the innocent, had 'enabled the evil to spread'. Most people thought that 'mincing, effeminate young men who call themselves "queers"' were 'freaks and rarities', but Warth warned that most underestimated the prevalence of homosexuals who were not 'obviously effeminate', and claimed that their numbers had 'grown steeply' since the Second World War. Warth drew on recent medical and psychological findings, but these were used selectively and remained subordinate to the moralising agenda. Warth admitted that there were a number of doctors who claimed that 'the problem could best be solved by making homosexuality legal between consenting adults', but he declared that this would be 'intolerable' and 'ineffective' because the danger of 'perverts' corrupting young people would remain: 'If homosexuality were tolerated here Britain would rapidly become decadent'. Science and psychology were used to put a modern, superficially progressive, spin on an old agenda of demonising homosexuals.[29]

The following year the arrests of a series of public figures for homosexual offences provoked several warnings from judges about the extent of the 'problem' and forced the issue up the press's agenda. It was, in particular, the arrest of, John Gielgud, the famous actor, in late October 1953 that opened the floodgates to a wave of newspaper comment. The *Sunday Express*'s uncompromising Scottish columnist John Gordon was the first to plunge in, criticising the lenience shown to Gielgud (he was fined £10 for importuning in a public lavatory). Behind the 'protective veil' of press reticence, Gordon claimed, a 'rot has flourished ... until it is now a widespread disease. It has penetrated every phase of life. It infects politics, literature, the stage, the Church, and the youth movements.' He called for homosexual men to receive 'sharp and severe punishment' and be treated as 'social lepers'. Around Fleet Street, editors felt under pressure to address the issue – indeed, the press covered more cases involving homosexual offences in 1954 than any year before or since. This press excitement reached its peak with the sensational trial of the Hampshire aristocrat Lord Montagu and the *Daily Mail* journalist Peter Wildeblood in March 1954, which became the most prominent case of its kind since the Wilde trials in 1895. Gay men certainly felt the change in the climate: 'We thought we were all going to be arrested and there was going to be a big swoop', recalled one. 'The newspapers were full of it. I got so frightened I burnt all my love letters'. The government was moved to act, and established the Wolfenden Committee to examine the twin 'problems' of prostitution and homosexuality. The Committee's report, published in September 1957, called for the decriminalisation of consenting adult homosexuality, and laid the groundwork for eventual law reform in 1967.[30]

In the decade after the Wolfenden Report, the press debate about homosexuality became more nuanced, and many sections of the popular press were gradually won over to the case for decriminalisation. The *Daily*

Mirror declared its support for the Wolfenden proposals as soon as they were released – despite conducting a poll showing that a majority of the paper's readers disagreed – and throughout the 1960s influential popular journalists and commentators, including Bernard Levin, Monica Furlong, Anne Sharpley and Marje Proops, argued for greater understanding of gay men. It was widely argued that legal sanctions merely encouraged secrecy and blackmail. When Leo Abse's Sexual Offences Bill reached its final stages in July 1967, the *Daily Express* was alone among the London popular dailies in voicing its disapproval. The paper maintained that the legislation had been sought only by 'a small minority', and that it would result in 'unnatural practices' becoming 'more easily indulged'. The *News of the World* similarly made clear its dislike of the Act, and there was some opposition in Scotland, with papers expressing their relief that the measure did not apply north of the border.[31]

Yet if most popular newspapers were prepared to accept the legal toleration of an 'unfortunate' minority, gay men and women continued to be patronised, sneered at, or regarded with suspicion. They were out of the ordinary, and therefore acceptable targets of ridicule and contempt. The *Mirror* columnist Cassandra's innuendo-laden assault on the popular American entertainer Liberace – he was described as 'the summit of sex – the pinnacle of masculine, feminine and neuter ... [a] deadly, winking, sniggering, snuggling, chromium-plated, scent-impregnated, luminous, quivering, giggling, fruit-flavoured, mincing, ice-covered heap of mother love' – cost the paper over £8,000 in damages after a libel trial in 1959. In April 1963, meanwhile, the *Sunday Mirror* offered a guide 'How to Spot a Potential Homo'. This 'short course on how to pick a pervert' warned readers to be suspicious of the middle-aged man with 'an unnaturally strong affection for his mother', the man with 'a consuming interest in youth', the 'fussy dresser', the 'over-clean man', and the 'man who is adored by older women'. Such stereotypes remained very resilient, as did the image of the lesbian as mannish, butch, and psychologically abnormal.[32]

From the early 1970s, a vocal gay rights movement sought to counter these cultural attitudes and develop 'gay pride', but it found the tabloids to be a fairly obdurate opponent, suspicious of minorities asserting themselves and claiming rights and pleasures. Openly gay individuals frequently received vitriolic treatment. Margaret Colquhoun, the Labour MP for Northampton North, was outed by the *Daily Mail* in 1976, and faced widespread mockery in the press. Jean Rook, the *Daily Express* columnist, wrote such a blistering attack on her that a group of what Rook described as 'hefty, hairy-legged lesbian ladies' stormed into the *Express* office to protest. The editor, Derek Jameson, defused the situation by promising to print an open letter from Colquhoun in response, but Rook was unrepentant, describing the letter as an 'embarrassment' and continuing to use her columns to criticise gay rights activists of both sexes. In 1983, Peter Tatchell, the Labour candidate in the Bermondsey by-election, found the tabloids to be equally aggressive, with journalists fixated on his sexuality at the expense of his policies, even searching his rubbish for evidence to use against him. He was portrayed as a self-obsessed, effeminate, 'gay rights extremist' who was out of step with his potential constituents: 'His pouting lower lip hardens if anyone dares argue with him', sneered the *Sunday Mirror*. Such treatment drove him away from parliamentary politics, although ironically, Simon Hughes, the victorious Liberal candidate, would later be outed himself.[33]

The tabloid response to the emergence of HIV/AIDS in the early 1980s vividly exposed remaining prejudices and checked any momentum towards growing toleration. Repeatedly described as a 'gay plague', AIDS was firmly associated with homosexual promiscuity and became a way of justifying and reviving suspicion of gay men. In December 1986, for example, the *Sun* praised the outspoken comments of James Anderton, the Chief Constable of Greater Manchester, and drew clear distinctions between 'decent' citizens and 'perverts':

> He accuses homosexuals of spreading the deadly virus through their obnoxious sexual practices ... Their defiling of the act of love is not only unnatural. In today's AIDS-hit world it is LETHAL ... What Britain needs is more men like James Anderton – and fewer gay terrorists holding the decent members of society to ransom.

The tabloids reflected and fostered a wider political climate opposed to the assertion of gay rights, and offered support for the Thatcher government's introduction of Section 28 of the Local Government Act 1988 which banned schools from promoting the 'acceptability of homosexuality as a pretended family relationship'. The *Sun*, at its most aggressively heterosexual under the editorship of Kelvin MacKenzie in the 1980s, brazenly rejected the Press Council's criticism of the paper for its liberal use of the word 'poof'. 'Readers of *The Sun* know and speak and write words like poof and poofter', it argued. 'What is good enough for them is good enough for us.' The *Daily Star* used similarly derogatory terms, headlining an article about gay soldiers 'Poofters on Parade'. Both the assertive masculinity of the populist tabloids, and the outraged moralising of the *Mail* and the *Express*, served to focus hostility on gay men and women.[34]

In the 1990s and 2000s, however, a more tolerant and open-minded climate gradually emerged, encouraged both by the better understanding and treatment of HIV, and by the New Labour government's programme of legislative reforms to improve the position of gay men and women. Openly gay Labour MPs such as Stephen Twigg and Ben Bradshaw received relatively sympathetic press coverage, and when the *Sun* ran a front-page story in 1998 headlined 'Is Britain run by a Gay mafia?', the storm of criticism led editor David Yelland to apologise and promise not to 'out' public figures without some pressing public interest. This pledge was not kept, and tabloids continued to pursue 'gay scandal' stories with some relish, as MPs such as Clive Betts, Mark Oaten and Simon Hughes found to their cost, but the unapologetically hostile coverage of the past became increasingly rare. 'Respectable' and openly gay men and women could now flourish in public life, even if tabloids remained suspicious of those who either remained closeted or 'flaunted' their sexuality in public. The *Sun* and the *Mail* expressed reservations about some of the moves to legislative equality, particularly the Coalition government's introduction of gay marriage in 2014, and equal treatment in the press still remains some way off, but the distance travelled in recent decades in the acceptance of alternative sexualities would have seemed remarkable to the men hounded by the sensational press coverage of the 1950s.[35]

The popular press and the 'permissive society'

The popular press's mid-century brand of titillation, relationships advice, court reporting and social investigation – smiling pin-ups who did not expose too much flesh, and reporting which eventually dissolved into euphemism – was a formula for success in a society in which censorship remained strict and moral judgements severe. The tabloid press was generally more risqué and had more sexual content that most of the rest of mainstream, family-oriented popular culture. During the 1960s, this situation changed radically. With the rapid decensorship of literature after the Lady Chatterley trial of 1960, the liberalisation of cinema and television content, the abolition of the Lord Chamberlain's oversight of the theatre, the rise of a more provocative and youth-oriented music culture, and the emergence of a flourishing genre of soft-porn magazines such as *Penthouse* and *Men Only*, British culture became far more sexualised. Nudity, swearing and explicit sexual description became increasingly common, especially from the late 1960s. The press's traditional sexual content very quickly risked seeming stale and old-fashioned; editors struggled to know how much more daring they could afford to be in the new climate.

Rupert Murdoch, who in 1969 bought the faltering *Sun* from IPC, and Larry Lamb, poached from his job as the northern editor of the *Daily Mail* to be the relaunched *Sun*'s first editor, grasped the opportunity with both hands. They developed a hedonistic and consumerist language of (heterosexual) sex, focusing on sexual pleasure and the creation of a liberated lifestyle – of which the 'Page 3 girl' became the central visual image. The paper tended to assume a certain level of sexual knowledge and experience of its readers, but offered advice on how to improve sexual technique and develop an understanding of the opposite sex. Some more basic educational material remained, as did moralising condemnations of those who deviated from the paper's sexual norms, but there was a clear shift in emphasis towards fun and fantasy.

The paper's pleasure agenda – for both women and men – was evident in the first week of the relaunch in November 1969. 'We Enjoy Life and

We Want You to Enjoy it with Us' declared the first Pacesetters section for
women. The sexual dimension of this enjoyment was clear in early articles
which provided advice on 'Undies For Undressing', asked 'does beefcake
turn you on?', and offered a quiz to 'Test Your Sex IQ'. Readers were also
enticed with the first instalment of a week-long serialisation of 'The Book
Every Woman Wants to Read' – Jacqueline Susann's erotic bestseller *The
Love Machine*. The second issue included the first topless pin-up, and two
days later the paper led the front-page with the headline 'Men are better
lovers in the morning – Official'. The paper was unapologetically providing
entertainment, information, and guidance for a young, sexually informed
target audience. 'The *Sun* is on the side of youth' declared an editorial at
the end of the first week, and the paper sought to establish its liberal, permissive credentials by insisting that it would 'never think that what is prim
must be proper', because 'the only real crime is to hurt people'.[36]

Symbolic of this new approach was the *Sun's* serialisation in October
1970 of *The Sensuous Woman*, a sex manual written by the American author
Joan Garrity. Garrity claimed to be able to show all women how to 'attract
a man worth your attention, drive him wild with pleasure, and keep him
coming back for more' by improving self-awareness and honing sensuality through a series of 'sexercises'. Hers was a post-Christian view of sex in
which the key requirements were physical preparation and proper technique: women should 'train like an athlete for the act of love' and be able
to move their 'pelvis and bottom as if they were loaded with ball-bearings'.
The underlying implication was that women who failed to master these
techniques could not complain if unsatisfied partners sought a better
experience elsewhere. Inadequacy could not be tolerated in the sexually
demanding 1970s: 'If you are going to stop him from straying, you must
give him the variety and adventure of love at home that he might find,
and easily, elsewhere ... Married or not, loving you as he does, he will
not stop looking and maybe sampling another woman'. Women were
told to be equally demanding: even if a partner was 'ideal' in every way
except that 'he doesn't turn you on as a lover', he should be ditched. Great
sex, it seemed, was now a required part of the modern lifestyle. With its
emphasis on pleasure, physical technique, and the realisation of fantasy,
the feature was an accurate guide to the way in which the press coverage

of sex was moving, and the *Sun* produced a number of similar features in subsequent years.[37]

The 'Page 3 girl' itself was likewise an attempt to update the newspaper pin-up for an era when nudity was increasingly common. The first 'proper' page three girl – a staged photograph, advertised on the front page, and insouciantly captioned – was printed on 17 November 1970, the first anniversary of the paper's relaunch: '*The Sun*, like most of its readers, likes pretty girls. And if they're as pretty as today's Birthday Suit girl, 20-year-old Stephanie Rahn of Munich, who cares whether they're dressed or not?'. Over the next few years, the 'page 3 girl' became a regular, institutionalised feature that was central to the paper's brand identity. The paper unapologetically flaunted this aspect of its appeal – 'The *Sun* is always best for nudes' was a frequently used tagline – and welcomed the associated controversy: 'The more the critics jumped up and down, the more popular the feature became', recalled Larry Lamb in later years. It also became a lucrative marketing opportunity as 'page 3' calendars and playing cards rapidly sold out. The *Sun* consistently argued that it was doing no more than responding to changes in contemporary culture. 'The Permissive Society is a fact, not an opinion,' the paper observed on its first anniversary, in an editorial piece directly opposite the topless Stephanie Rahn. 'We have reflected the fact where others have preferred to turn blind eyes.' It portrayed itself as a fun, cheeky, freewheeling publication in tune with the spirit of the time, 'Britain's brightest, most irreverent, most unpredictable paper'.[38]

By embracing 'permissiveness' and modern notions of sex, Lamb and his team were able to justify nudity. Yet just as the moral opposition to nudity was crumbling, a powerful critique emerged from a different quarter: the resurgent feminist movement, attacking the sexualisation and commodification of the female body. Women had been complaining about pin-ups for years, but now they were imbued with a fresh confidence that their feelings were shared, and offered a new intellectual framework within which to understand their feelings and formulate their complaints.

The *Sun*'s editorial team hoped that female readers who did not approve of the 'page 3 girl' would still be enticed by the other material in the paper. The ultimate goal, though, was to attract women as well as men with 'page 3'. Attractive, 'liberated' and glorying in their sensuality, the 'page 3 girls' were presented as aspirational figures; the paper missed few opportunities to emphasise how many young models sought to appear in its pages. Lamb maintained a female perspective on the feature by seeking the advice of the Pacesetters team on the models used, and by using one of them, Patsy Chapman, to write the captions; he himself was adamant that 'they had to be nice girls'. Further balance was achieved by the regular inclusion of male pin-ups, complete with captions conducting a knowing dialogue with female readers. By the mid-1970s a 'Daily Male' pin-up was frequently found in the *Sun*. Other papers followed suit, appropriating the language of equality to explain such features. The *Mirror* commemorated the Sex Discrimination and Equal Pay Acts becoming law in December 1975 with a front-page pin-up of 'hunky' singer Malcolm Roberts, and the headline 'Girls, it's your turn now'. When a female reader complained that the picture of Roberts was 'in no way equal to the girl on Page Five as she was virtually naked and he had his trousers on', and demanded instead 'a (nearly) nude every day', the *Mirror* responded with a more revealing image of actor Patrick Mower in briefs.[39]

For most of the 1970s, the *Sun* remained relatively cautious in its development of the 'page 3' feature: it did not push back the boundaries of acceptability too far – in the early 1970s most 'page 3' photographs fitted either into the naturist tradition, or sought to convey a saucy humour – it crafted a plausible form of words to justify the feature, and it worked hard to win over female readers in other ways. Over time, however, as the paper's circulation continued to rise and 'page 3' became better established, some of this caution was gradually lost. The launch of the *Daily Star* in 1978 meant that the *Sun* for the first time faced a competitor unafraid to compete in the pin-up market ('No newspaper in history lost sales by projecting beautiful birds', the *Star*'s editor, Derek Jameson, told his staff, as he introduced the first full-colour topless pin-ups, the 'Starbirds'). Kelvin MacKenzie, who became the *Sun*'s editor in 1981 with a remit to see off the *Star*'s challenge, was far more combative than Lamb, and combined a reinvigorated 'page 3' with an unapologetically Thatcherite agenda. 'Page 3' photography increasingly borrowed the props and poses of soft-pornography, and popular models such as Samantha Fox and Linda Lusardi were transformed into national celebrities.[40]

The feminist campaign against 'page 3' only really took off in the mid-1980s when the Labour MP Clare Short tried to introduce legislation banning 'sexually provocative' photographs in the press. She received thousands of letters from women uneasy and often angry at the way the *Sun*'s pin-ups shaped attitudes to women. Polls by *Woman* magazine and the *Star* newspaper found a clear majority of women opposed to the feature. The *Sun* responded by viciously attacking Short, but there were former insiders who were concerned at the direction 'page 3' had taken. Larry Lamb admitted in 1989 'that there is an element of sexploitation involved' and confessed that he was uncomfortable with the realisation that he had contributed to 'the current fiercely competitive situation in which the girls in some of our national newspapers get younger and younger and more and more top-heavy and less and less like the girl next door.' 'Page 3' became so heavily promoted and so central to the *Sun*'s brand that it increasingly overwhelmed the other images of women in the paper. The values of 'page 3', for example, were imported into the problem pages. Kelvin MacKenzie was frustrated at the seriousness of the paper's 'Dear Deirdre' column, and instructed staff to 'Tell her to put a dirty letter in here'. (This trend was not confined to the *Sun*: in the late 1980s, Claire Rayner felt obliged to resign from the *Sunday Mirror* after editorial demands for 'sexier letters'). The subordination of the problem columns to the wider agenda of sexualised entertainment became even clearer with the introduction of regular photo strips featuring scantily clad models; websites soon offered lurid video equivalents.[41]

Originally a symbol of permissive modernity, though, by the early twenty-first century 'page 3' was starting to look as dated as the mid-twentieth-century pin-up, notwithstanding the introduction of 'page 3.com' and '360 degree' pin-up images. Executives feared that dropping it would threaten the paper's identity in a declining market and risk leaving it without a point of difference from its rivals; the *Sun*'s first female editor, Rebekah Brooks, retained the feature on her appointment in 2003, despite previously have criticised it. Concerted feminist campaigning, particularly the 'No More Page 3 campaign' launched by the writer Lucy-Ann Holmes in 2012, has once more raised the profile of the arguments against the sexualisation of the female body, and has prompted the first signs of a lack of editorial confidence in 'page 3'. The *Sun on Sunday*, launched in February 2012 and deliberately seeking to court female readers after the controversy of the phone-hacking scandal, has not included topless pin-ups, while in August 2013, the Irish edition of *The Sun* dropped 'page 3'. As the *Sun* reaches out for readers in a declining market, it seems likely that 'page 3' will become the place for celebrity photographs rather than posed glamour shots.

Feminism, post-feminism and the appeal to women

The success of the *Sun*'s sexual agenda further polarised the popular press between papers placing a heavy emphasis on sexual titillation (notably the *Sun*, the *News of the World*, the *Star* and later the *Sport*), and papers such as the *Mail* and the *Express* which retained a preference for the traditional Northcliffe model. Whichever editorial strategy was adopted, though, attracting female readers remained essential, and this required updating the appeal to women to keep pace with social change and rising expectations. The relaunched *Sun*'s women's section was entitled 'Pacesetters' to underline the dynamism of its intended audience, and the introductory message from Joyce Hopkirk, its first editor, emphasised that it was 'for women who believe there is more to life than washing up': 'We plan to make your life more lively. The *Sun* will always remember that half its readers are women'. Larry Lamb argued that these pages were in tune with a 'new mood of feminine feminism, as opposed to militant feminism', expressed by modern women who were in control of their lives but were suspicious of the women's movement.[42]

At the same time the *Mail* revitalised its women's section by placing it under the charge of Shirley Conran and rebranding as 'Femail'. These changes were consolidated in 1971 when Vere Harmsworth (who had recently taken over as Chairman of Associated Newspapers), and new editor David English, relaunched the *Mail* as a tabloid. Harmsworth captured the spirit of Northcliffe when he insisted that 'We have to direct ourselves to women', providing 'a news coverage that women want to read'. English and his successor, Paul Dacre, followed this advice closely, and invested heavily in feature pages aimed primarily at the female audience. The subjects that dominated the 'Femail' section and its various competitors – fashion, body management, relationships, celebrity, cooking and careers – were strikingly similar to those that filled women's pages decades earlier, although they were now increasingly presented in a 'post-feminist' language which more readily acknowledged women's agency, earning power and dislike of being patronised by men.[43] Support and sympathy was offered to women trying to cope with the conflicting demands of modern femininity – 'Quick-change wives' in the words of the *Mirror* Woman section, leading a tiring double life at work and home – but the emphasis remained on personal changes that could be made rather than campaigns for structural reforms. 'Fight Back' by getting regular exercise and asking for more help from the family, advised the *Mirror* weakly.[44]

These modernised women's sections were accompanied by the rise of the outspoken female columnist. Jean Rook, presented by the *Daily Express* as the 'first lady of Fleet Street' from the launch of her column in 1972, pioneered the role. In tune with the times as a strong, straight-talking, often deliberately controversial, commentator, Rook nevertheless espoused a conservative, commonsensical view of the world that was profoundly sceptical of organised feminism. She viewed Margaret Thatcher as a kindred spirit, and proudly claimed to have been the first in Fleet Street to spot her potential. Lynda Lee-Potter, who took over the Rook's column at the *Mail* when she defected across to the *Express*, performed a similar job, and attracted acclaim and derision in equal measure. In recent years, Allison Pearson and Liz Jones, both writing for the *Mail*, have led a shift to a more confessional and intimate form of writing aimed at women, recording their body-image problems and the frustrations of their personal relationships.[45]

While frequently celebrating strong, independent-minded women, the tabloids consistently stereotyped or marginalised organised feminism. When a group of protestors disrupted the 1970 Miss World contest, being televised live on the BBC from London's Albert Hall, the *Mail* dismissed them as 'yelling harpies' and asked what was 'degrading about celebrating the beauty of the human body?' A mocking cartoon portrayed a frumpy, bespectacled woman wearing a sash with 'Miss Women's Liberation Movement 1970' as a male spectator yelled 'Moo'. A *Sunday Express* cartoon was similarly derisive, depicting an ageing, unattractive woman telling her young and shapely female companion that 'I'm all for Women's Liberation. I'm sick and tired of being nothing more than a sex symbol'. These representations of feminists as extreme, ugly, and sexually frustrated were very resilient, and were repeatedly mobilised, for example, in the coverage of female peace campaigners at Greenham Common during the 1980s. A study of the *Daily Mail*'s coverage in 2008 found that 37 per cent of the articles on the women's movement were critical, including scathing attacks on 'Feminism Gone Mad' and 'po-faced feminists' in editorials and columns by writers such as Peter Hitchens. At the same time, the tabloid defence of 'family values' often bled into a critical approach to women trying to combine motherhood with a career, and sexually adventurous women found themselves being judged far more harshly than like-minded men. The entry of more and women into journalism, and the associated rise of the most talented, such as Wendy Henry and Rebekah Brooks, to positions of editorial authority, certainly helped to moderate some of the worst excesses of tabloid sexism, and even led to campaigns applauded by the women's movement, such as the *Sun*'s series on domestic violence. The basic editorial attitudes and assumptions entrenched by years of male dominance will, nevertheless, take a long time to erode.[46]

The scrutiny and judgement of the female body, meanwhile, has arguably intensified in recent years, and imperfections continue to be cruelly highlighted and mocked. A characteristic article in the *Mail* in March 2003, for example, revealed the 'swimsuit age' of stars snapped on the beach. 30-year-old pop star Mariah Carey was given a 'swimsuit age' of 45 because she had 'let herself go' and displayed 'chunky thighs'. Sailor Ellen MacArthur, meanwhile, 'may be fit but her body is chunky. She hasn't had children yet, but already looks rather matronly.' The *News of the World*'s obsession with pert breasts, meanwhile, led it to sneer at those who failed to measure up. Under the headline 'Jodie's sunken treasure chest', the paper in May 2004 showed how the model Jodie Marsh's 'biggest assets have taken a dive' and appeared 'to sag a bit'. When twenty-four-year-old glamour models were unable to sustain the physical expectations laid down by the tabloid press, it is unsurprising that many women complained that the media stimulated anxieties about body image. The *Daily Mail* sparked outrage in July 2014 when it was similarly judgemental about the female politicians entering the cabinet in a high-profile feature describing the 'Downing Street Catwalk'.[47]

The 'post-feminist' language of the tabloid women's sections, the sexual explicitness of modern journalism, and the growing acceptance of alternative sexualities, cannot entirely disguise the continuities in the popular press's treatment of gender and sexuality. Powerful assumptions about the different interests and capabilities of men and women remained evident in the newspapers of the early twenty-first century, and attractive women were routinely held up for the male gaze just as they had been in Northcliffe's time – just now wearing fewer clothes. Although 'permissiveness' has been broadly accepted, ideas about appropriate behaviour remain deeply entrenched, family values are still celebrated, and 'promiscuous' women or gay men, in particular, still face intense scrutiny. If the amount of sexual content in the press has changed out of all recognition, the basic underlying impulses – to use it to titillate or to moralise – remain very much in place.

CHAPTER 5

Class

Few items signify an individual's class and social status more quickly and concisely than the newspaper he or she reads, and it is no surprise that novelists and social commentators alike have long delighted in labelling people by their choice of reading matter. In Britain's heavily stratified society, the newspaper market has always been structured by class, and editorial judgements about appropriate content, layout and language have been powerfully shaped by social judgements about the target reader. In the eighteenth century, newspapers were aimed mainly at the urban middle-classes, and as the market expanded different papers catered for different social and regional niches. The unstamped press of the early nineteenth century developed a radical, populist rhetoric in order to attract disenfranchised working men, while in later decades Sunday papers sought to articulate class much more through the prisms of escapism, sensation and melodrama. Northcliffe's *Daily Mail*, and its imitators, were aimed at the expanding lower-middle classes, the office clerks and shop workers commuting from the suburban homes shooting up outside major cities. The intense commercial competition of the 1930s, and the emergence of the tabloid proper, was the consequence of the desire to spread the daily newspaper reading habit throughout the working-classes, while the later success of the *Sun* was intimately connected with its ability to voice the concerns of a more consumerist and mobile blue collar workforce. Elite papers responded by reinforcing their distance from their popular counterparts: in the late 1950s *The Times* famously – and unsuccessfully – advertised itself as the paper for 'top people'.[1]

Class based appeals had to be deployed carefully, however. Although editors and journalists had clear ideas about the social characteristics of their core readership, they did not want to alienate too many potential readers who might be tempted to try the paper, especially given that many people, in mid-century particularly, read more than one title. Newspapers were, after all, passed around and shared – on average, every purchased copy was read by three people. In the late 1950s, for example, far more people in social category AB – the 'top people' – read the *Daily Mirror* (860,000) than *The Times* (560,000), even though they made up just 6 per cent of the *Mirror*'s total readership, against half of *The Times*'s. Indeed, no fewer than 38 per cent of these 'top people' regularly read the *Daily Express*, which was more than the *Daily Telegraph* and *The Times* combined. *The Times*, for its part, had some 166,000 readers in the unskilled working-class category DE, and the *Telegraph* 248,000. In previous centuries, illiteracy and high prices had imposed very real restrictions on the circulation of newspapers; in the more educated and affluent mass market of the twentieth century, such barriers largely fell, and class-based rhetoric that was too overt and explicit could be commercially counter-productive. As a result, leader-writers and columnists tended to invoke 'the public', 'ordinary citizens' or 'hard-working people', rather than specific classes, and newspapers offered wide-ranging and miscellaneous content to connect with as diverse an audience as possible.[2]

Class, too, was by no means a static category. If the classless society that many commentators – and newspapers – predicted with tiresome frequency from the late-1950s never arrived, greater affluence did reduce the chasms that separated the classes in the first half of the century, and social identities became more fluid. At the start of the twentieth century, a significant section of the working-classes lacked the vote, the trade union movement had limited power, and politics and public life were saturated with the elitist attitudes incubated by private schools and Oxbridge. By the end of the century, elitism and inequality remained stubbornly persistent, but it was much more difficult to express openly the class-based condescension that pre-war generations would have taken for granted. Such shifts inevitably affected the tone and content of newspapers, and perhaps the hardest editorial challenge was not so much to create a bond with a particular readership, but to move with it as times changed. Many of the most successful papers gradually lost touch with their core constituency: by the 1930s, the *Daily Mail*'s social pessimism and political extremism alienated its readership, just as the *Express*'s imperial outlook seemed increasingly old-fashioned after the 1960s, and the *Mirror*'s working-class collectivism failed to connect with more consumerist and individualistic generations. As circulations declined, moreover, maintaining a coherent social identity became harder and harder.

Reaching the suburban middle classes

On its launch, the *Daily Mail* appealed to its lower middle class market by astutely combining brightness, value and accessibility with respectability, social aspiration and an acquisitive individualism. It sold at a halfpenny, half the price of its main competitors, but it flattered its readers that 'the mere halfpenny saved each day is of no consequence to most of us', and emphasised that its value lay more in its 'conciseness and compactness'. The large number of readers for whom the halfpenny saving was indeed of significance could persuade themselves that the purchase of the paper was justified by its status as the 'busy man's paper'. 'The size of the paper has been selected with a view to the convenience of travelling readers', the *Mail* noted in a nod to its target suburban commuters, but was 'within a fraction of that of *The Times*', the measure of newspaper authority, and was 'identical in quality to the best paper used by other morning sheets'. The investment in the latest printing and typesetting machinery explained the lower price – 'that is the whole explanation of what would otherwise appear a mystery' the paper insisted defensively – but there would be no concessions in terms of news provision or the standard of writing. Readers could rest assured they were not settling for a second-class service.[3]

The *Mail*'s language, layout and content all sought to reassure readers that this was a solid, conventional enterprise that was not defined by crude populism. Despite experimenting in dummy issues with news on the front page, Northcliffe eventually decided to follow tradition and place advertising there instead. There was a deliberate avoidance of slang and colloquialism in the writing, as can be seen in the careful and pedestrian style of the opening editorial: 'Two points strike one in the report of the Highways Committee of the London County Council on the tramways scheme, a full and early abstract of which appears in our news columns'. A society column respectfully recorded the movements of the royal family and landed elites, observing, for example, that 'Princess Victoria of Wales has a very smart French poodle who is clipped and curled, ringed and tufted in the approved modern fashion.' Two 'fashionable marriages' were described. 'Today's Dinner', as suggested in the women's columns, was white soup, followed by cold lamb, mint sauce, asparagus and mashed potatoes, and finished with marmalade pudding. The recommendation of lamb was made 'presuming that your Sunday joint was a roast shoulder of lamb'. There was, however, a concession regarding the asparagus: 'If this vegetable is too expensive, substitute a salad in its place ... or it may be omitted altogether.' Either way, it was hardly simple working-class fare.[4]

This editorial strategy – deployed, with minor variations, in the subsequent launches of the *Daily Express*, *Daily Mirror* and *Daily Sketch* – was based on a series of insights and assumptions that Northcliffe endlessly reiterated to his staff, and which gradually became Fleet Street's accepted wisdom. 'Everybody likes reading about people in better circumstances than his or her own,' Northcliffe told Tom Clarke, one of the *Mail's* news editors: 'Write and seek news with at least the £1000 a year man in mind' (a salary which denoted the prosperous middle classes). The 'Chief' was acutely sensitive to any material that would threaten the carefully cultivated air of respectability and gentility. In an angry letter to Pomeroy Burton, the General Manager of Associated Newspapers, in 1912, Northcliffe complained that the social standing of his papers was decreasing 'by reason of the low tone of the advertising department'. In this era before the existence of accurate and authenticated readership surveys, some of the *Mail's* 'low class advertisements' were being used by rivals as 'evidence of the low class of our readers', thus threatening accounts with motor car firms and 'high class drapers, such as Debenham and Freebody'. The fault lay with the company's advertising men, who were not, Northcliffe lamented, of the social calibre to understand the situation: 'They measure up entirely by amount of money, not by class. They forget that a lot of cheap vulgar advertisements all over the paper can just as effectively lower its tone as cheap vulgar articles.'[5]

Northcliffe was equally attentive to 'cheap vulgar articles' that gave ammunition to the many critics of the *Mail* and *Mirror*'s populism. In 1911 he wrote despairingly to Alexander Kenealy, the editor of the *Mirror*, that his paper frequently contained 'news which is below the intelligence of the average fourth housemaid', adding that 'You can imagine what educated readers think of it.' Photographs and illustrations were required to be tasteful and aspirational. A *Daily Mail* picture of a 'man-monkey' in January 1914 led to Northcliffe demanding that the person responsible for its insertion be 'very severely reprimanded'. 'A well-known doctor has complained of it,' he explained, 'and a lady of high distinction has written to me personally about it.' In July 1920, meanwhile, he was disappointed that the *Mail*'s photo page was dominated by 'life among the lower orders', adding 'that is not what we want so much of.' He was even sensitive to the balance of addresses in the letters column. In February 1921, Lewis Macleod, the letters editor, received a censorious missive noting that 'The Chief says that everyone admires the dexterity with which you print letters from the East End, the less responsible suburbs, Catford, Chevening Road, and the rest of them. This naturally misleads the public as to the class of people who read the Paper'.[6]

In the pages of the new daily papers, working-class men and women often appeared as distant, unknown and potentially sinister figures, requiring investigation, scrutiny and perhaps control. In June 1900, for example, the *Daily Express* offered 'a few facts' about the docker, penned by an 'ex-docker'. An accurate picture of these men was not readily available without such an insider, the paper claimed, because 'one must work, eat, drink, and sleep with a dock labourer many months before one can understand the man and his devious ways'. The portrayal nevertheless pandered to every middle-class stereotype of the dissolute worker:

> Ninety per cent of the genus docker are the merest dregs of bibulous humanity, who, when not working in the docks, spend their time in loafing around the street corners and public houses. These are hard words, but, unfortunately, absolutely correct ... Give the average dock labourer the chance of a permanent position at £1 per week,

and the chances are ten to one that he does not avail himself of the opportunity
to shake himself clear of the docks ... Candidly, the docker does not like to work.[7]

Newspapers frequently played to contemporary concerns – fed by the
publicity given to the poor physical quality of army recruits during the
Boer War – that the squalor of urban life was leading the 'deterioration'
of the race. In 1904 the *Mirror* noted the 'feeble and undersized physique',
a 'weedy, chestless look', that characterised many in the working classes.
'There can be no doubt,' the article observed, 'that the contrast between
the well-fed, well-exercised upper and middle class and the ill-nourished,
undeveloped working class has become painfully striking' because 'the
"classes" are encouraged to develop their bodies and the "masses" are not.'
These feeble workers were encouraged to wrestle and box. Other *Mirror*
reports identified alcohol and 'sheer bodily filthiness' as key factors explaining 'impaired physique'. The paper publicised a *Lancet* report arguing that

> With possible exceptions in the cases of Tibet and Lapland we are compelled to
> admit that the English working classes are probably the dirtiest bipeds in the world,
> alike in their clothes and in their persons. They display themselves in public, and
> even travel by public conveyances, in conditions which would not be tolerated in
> any other civilized country.

Poor parenting was also condemned, as in a *Mirror* report bluntly headlined 'The Incredible Ignorance of the Working Class Mother', detailing
the death of a two-year-old child after being fed nuts:

> The wonder of this is that the babies of the poor grow up at all, for not one woman in
> a hundred feeds her children properly. This is not through want of heart, but through
> crass ignorance. Directly the baby is born, it is given bread-and-milk sop to stop its
> first wails, and the solidity of its wonderful diet increases day by day, until by the
> time it is six months old it will cheerfully eat tinned salmon and pickled cucumber,
> apple dumpling, and bread and cheese, and wash the whole down with a draught
> of its mother's dinner beer.

Only by middle-class intervention through borough councils, the paper
suggested, was there any likelihood that 'better ways may be taught to the
poor'.[8]

The unthreatening 'deserving poor', by contrast, were often given sentimental treatment, evoking pity and even encouraging charitable giving, but almost invariably failing to examine the political or economic structures underlying poverty. A *Mirror* report from August 1904, headlined 'Too Old to Work – Touching Story of a Tragedy of Age', offers an example of the typical combination of maudlin writing and class condescension:

> The homely tragedy of working-class life was painfully brought out yesterday at Brentford. After lingering between life and death since the early part of July, John Edward Blawchamp, seventy-five, a cooper of Isleworth, tottered feebly into the dock to answer a charge of attempting suicide. With his snow-white hair, his bent shoulders, and his utterly hopeless look, Blawchamp presented a most pathetic figure, his feeble form shaking with suppressed sobs while the story of his rash attempt to end his life was related. In a voice choking with emotion the aged wife told the magistrate that her husband was terribly upset because he was losing his eyesight, and he feared he was getting too old to work. He was 'a good, dear husband,' she said pleadingly, and he had never been in a police court before.

With the heart-warming ending suitable for such melodrama, the magistrate asked that Mr Blawchamp be taken to the infirmary in a cab and looked after for a week. When reduced in this fashion to an individual narrative stripped of social context, journalists could afford to be generous. When political reformers and trade unionists pushed for more collective solution, scepticism and hostility quickly emerged, as we saw in Chapter 2.[9]

The *Daily Herald* emerged as the labour movement's attempt to counter the demonisation and stereotyping of the working class. It launched in April 1912 as the sinking of the *Titanic*, one of the biggest stories of the century, unfolded. Its coverage demonstrated its difference from other papers, with fiery condemnations of the higher death rates among poorer, steerage class passengers – 'Women and Children Last' ran one bitter headline. It immediately made clear its preparedness to support industrial action of all kinds, with the second issue sympathetically reporting on strikes at the Earls Court Exhibition and on the Great Northern Railway, even though the latter was not backed by the relevant union. As the paper's historian Huw Richards has observed, 'the early headline "Strike and Strike Hard" might have served as the paper's motto.' Perhaps the most eye-catching feature of

the early *Herald*, though, was the series of searing cartoons contributed by
the young radical Australian cartoonist Will Dyson. Dyson turned the class
imagery of the other popular dailies on its head: the capitalists were the
selfish and grotesque figures, desperately seeking to keep the manly, determined workers in their place. Politicians participating in the 'Westminster
shallowdrama' were not to be trusted, and even apparently progressive state
welfare measures such as health insurance were criticised for being weighted
unfavourably against working families. Lack of investment and advertising
revenue ensured that the *Herald* had to focus on survival rather than on
competing with the better-funded dailies, but it did provide an important
space for a different articulation of class politics.[10]

This class politics was at its sharpest in the decade after the First World
War, and the overwhelming dominance of the right-wing middle-class press
ultimately put the labour movement on the defensive. The war had enabled
a significant growth in the membership and authority of the trade unions,
and the splits in the Liberal Party after 1916 opened the door for Labour
to become the second major party at Westminster. The 1917 Bolshevik
Revolution in Russia raised the spectre of proletarian uprisings around the
globe, and led to considerable anxiety about the activities of Communist
activists and sympathisers. The 1918 enfranchisement of all working men,
the promises of homes 'fit for heroes' and the short-lived post-war inflation-
ary boom, suggested to some that the political and economic dominance
of the middle-classes was being undermined. These fears were articulated
in the *Mail*'s prominent campaign defending the taxpaying middle classes,
dubbed the 'New Poor'. The 'New Poor', argued the *Mail* in October 1919,
was 'a vast silent and increasing section of the community' who were 'trying
to keep up the appearance of living in middle-class comfort and actually
living in penury, scraping and saving to make both ends meet.' They were
suffering at having to sustain the burden of a much expanded state, while
Labour was 'being looked after by a tame Government apprehensive of
its power'. 'Every day shows how rates, taxes and other financial burdens'
were 'widening the circle' of the New Poor. Northcliffe urged his journalists to pursue the matter to 'try and do something for an inarticulate class
who are getting hammered all round.' The Middle Class Union, an extra-
parliamentary organisation established in March 1919 which soon had a

significant suburban membership, sent its 'heartfelt thanks' to Northcliffe for the 'unsolicited fashion in which his newspapers are championing the cause of the middle classes'.[11]

The New Poor campaign fed into a broader crusade in the right-wing press against Government waste, commonly denounced as 'squandermania'. Rothermere used the *Daily Mirror* to publicise his Anti-Waste League which sought to mobilise opinion against 'excessive' government spending. When 'Anti-Waste' candidates won by-elections at Dover and Westminster in January and June 1921 respectively, the Lloyd George government decided to act, and appointed the Geddes committee to identify severe cost-cutting measures. Over the course of 1920–21, the post-war boom fizzled out, and the government shifted to a deflationary regime that prioritised financial institutions and middle-class savers over industry and its workers, and which scaled back promises of social reconstruction. The vocal discontent of the right-wing popular press had helped to shape a political and economic settlement that was decisively in favour of the middle-classes, and which would be overseen by a dominant Conservative Party until 1940.[12]

As the 1920s progressed, the economic difficulties besetting Britain's heavy industries – coal, iron and steel, textiles and shipbuilding – became ever clearer, and unemployment rates rose significantly in areas where such industries dominated, such as northern England, the central belt of Scotland, and South Wales. London, the South East and the Midlands, by contrast, were far more prosperous, as light consumer industries, such as car manufacturing, thrived and extensive suburban house-building programmes were undertaken. The popular press, powerfully shaped by its metropolitan middle-class perspective, and reliant for survival on an ethos of consumerism that attracted big advertisers, gave far more space and attention to the flourishing south. Newspapers endlessly debated the fashions and behaviour of the 'flappers', modern young women who almost always had a certain amount of money to sustain their lifestyle. The *Daily Mail*'s Ideal Home Exhibition, a hugely popular and lucrative event in this period, generated numerous articles setting out the latest in domestic design and labour-saving technology, and continued to set the tone for the women's pages. The gossip columns expanded and offered colourful descriptions of the pleasure-seeking activities of the wealthy 'Bright Young Things', satirised at the end of the decade by Evelyn Waugh's *Scoop* (1930). Luxury spending was praised for sustaining trade and employment. Under the headline 'The Value of "Luxuries" – A Dreary World Without Them', for example, a commentator in the *Mail* justified the money spent by women in sustaining their decorative role, arguing that 'If they had no beautiful clothes to show off women would not travel and spend money' – so 'where would be ... the expensive hotels, and the great shops?' The complacent assumption was that elite prosperity would eventually trickle down to improve the lot of the masses.[13]

At the same time, the efforts of trade unionists to defend their position by industrial action were frequently portrayed as illegitimate assaults on the nation. The *Mail* and the *Mirror*, in particular fomented numerous 'red scares' during the 1920s (see Chapter 2), drawing attention to outspoken comments of the most radical figures and implying that the 'agitators' and 'militants' would inevitably corrupt, mislead or overpower the moderate mainstream. The General Strike of May 1926, called by the TUC in support of the miners' action to maintain their wages and conditions, was presented as a case in point. It was, in the stark words of the *Mirror*, 'the most formidable weapon ever presented at the head of a democratic Government by its own nationals.' The paper's stance was quite clear: 'The Government cannot capitulate. It represents the nation and must refuse to be intimidated into surrender. In protecting the national interests the Government can count upon the support of the people at large.' The 'nation' and the 'people' were silently conflated with the respectable middle classes, and opposed to the trade unions, a sectional and selfish interest group out to defend their own interests. When the strike was called off, the *Mirror* declared 'The Nation Has Won': the unions had failed 'in their attempt to substitute Government by force for Government by law.' 'We can already see,' the paper observed gravely, 'in diminished employment, in the suffering of workers, in the waste of millions, the hideous results of the action of a group of fanatics who have posed as the friends of working men and women.' Such was 'the inevitable evil of industrial war'. The conservative press continually reinforced the argument that interests of the economy, as an abstract ideal, embodied the nation's best interests.[14]

Winning over the working classes

The polarised class language characteristic of the first quarter of the twentieth century started to soften as the newspaper market matured and the political environment shifted. By the end of the 1920s, daily newspaper readership was widespread among the lower middle-class audience, and the prospect of major circulation gains rested on tapping the working-class market. The *Express* and the *Mirror*, in particular, spotted opportunities to reach out to a broader audience, while the *Herald*, bolstered by the commercial muscle of Odhams Press, sought to widen its circulation beyond its core audience of politicised skilled workers and urban intellectuals. At the same time, Labour's victory in the 1929 general election demonstrated conclusively that it had replaced the Liberals as the second main political party, and the failure of the General Strike further encouraged the labour movement to turn away from industrial action to a parliamentary strategy. Although the Labour Party would be riven by splits in the economic crisis of 1931, and heavily defeated in the general election of that year, former leader Ramsey MacDonald's tenure as Prime Minister of the National Government between 1931 and 1935, and the moderate course pursued by the opposition, made the hyperbolic 'red scares' of the 1920s increasingly implausible. Despite the inevitable social tensions caused by the economic depression, George Orwell noted in 1937 that 'class-hatred' seemed to be diminishing because 'it tends not to get into print, partly owing to the mealy-mouthed habits of our time, partly because newspapers and even books now have to appeal to a working-class public'. As the public sphere became more inclusive, class feelings were best studied in private conversations.[15]

The *Daily Herald*'s relaunch in 1930 saw the paper combining a moderate trade unionist perspective with a more commercial and consumerist outlook. It sought to downplay its reputation as the radical organ of the militant working-class. In the 1920s its scathing critiques of capitalism had severely restricted its advertising revenue. Poyser, the *Herald*'s advertising manager, had frequently despaired that attracting commercial interest in the paper was almost impossible. 'I should be glad if you would discourage editorial attacks on known advertisers', he requested in 1926 after the paper had censured Boots the Chemists: 'they make our task harder and the securing of advertisements for the *Daily Herald*, even in the best of times, is far from easy.' Before the 1930 relaunch, his laments went unheeded. Afterwards, by contrast, the *Herald* increasingly absorbed the materialistic ethos of the rest of the daily press. It encouraged readers to pay attention to advertising columns and have faith that 'good advertisements in the *Daily Herald* mean good goods'. A huge increase in advertising enabled the number of pages to be doubled to twenty, and when the 1 million circulation mark was reached in April 1930, the paper proclaimed its success as an advertising medium:

> Advertisers have been quick to realise that the new and enlarged *Daily Herald* has enabled them to display their products before an army of readers who have been largely neglected in the past. Readers in their turn have not been slow to appreciate that the firms which advertise most freely are the firms whose products are the best.[16]

The advance of consumerism was clearest in the women's pages, where the previous emphasis on careful economy was gradually eroded. 'It Pays to Keep a Well-Filled Store Cupboard', announced an article in August 1931, during the depths of the depression. Features championed the virtues of kitchen gadgets from Moulinette mincing machines to icing syringes. In 1936 Sylvia Pankhurst, the left-wing political activist and former suffragette, complained to Walter Citrine, the General Secretary of the TUC, that the *Herald*'s women's pages were 'designed to please advertisers because, either openly or covertly, they "puff" various commodities':

> Neither in the *Herald* nor anywhere else have I ever seen dress notes or cookery notes written from the point of view of a working woman of small means with a large family to cater for, giving her a practical idea of where the cheapest and best wearing materials are to be obtained, how to lay out her money most economically in the matter of food so as to give her children an appetising meal with the most possible of essential food values.

Pankhurst's criticism was by no means exceptional. In February 1937, the secretary of a local Labour Party wrote in to express the frustrations of his female members: 'How you expect working women to follow in any degree some of the advice given on their page beats them. Some of the writers are simply giving the impression they represent the firms advertising in your columns.' The example of the *Herald* underlined how the market insistently pressurised papers to be aspirational and materialistic in tone, rather than being content to cater for the everyday lives of readers.[17]

At the same time, the *Daily Herald* used its editorial columns to champion the labour movement and defend the working classes from the misrepresentations of the right-wing press. As unemployment worsened in the early 1930s and many working-class communities found themselves under severe pressure, the *Herald* took pains to counter the residual Victorian assumption that joblessness was the result of individual failings of the workers themselves, insisting instead that it was the inevitable consequence of an economic system which was inefficient as well as hostile to the interests of the working classes. 'There has been a tendency in some circles to regard every benefit receiver as a malefactor,' the paper noted in August 1931:

> The view has been spread that the unemployed do not want employment. In some minds the facts that men have fought for work in the docks, that hundreds apply where one vacancy is advertised, have not been able to shake that view. For the fair-minded, a different view is inescapable – the view that the unemployed man or woman is out of work through no personal fault, but because a disorganized industry has no use for them.

The *Herald* channelled working-class fear and resentment at the household 'means test', which assessed the level of benefits that families were eligible to receive. Veteran columnist Hannen Swaffer denounced the test as a 'degrading inquisition' which treated the unemployed 'not only as paupers, but almost like criminals': it was a 'form of mental torture' imposed on 'poor workless folks, the victims of capitalism, replaced by machinery, displaced by rationalisation'. More than any other paper, the *Herald* remained attentive to the details of benefit policies and the conditions of the unemployed, seeking always to protect the dignity of the working classes.[18]

A class-based editorial perspective was by no means the only way to appeal to the *Herald*'s core readership, however. The working-class passion for sports was fully exploited in the back pages, and this was enough to attract some men. One survey briskly summed up the preferences of one *Herald* reader: 'Likes best and spends most time on the racing and sports page. Considers the other stuff a lot of tripe.' Another reader 'doesn't like its politics, but says it is best for sports.' Many socialists had long opposed the provision of racing tips in the paper as encouraging the vice of gambling, but the *Herald* recognised, even before the reinvention of 1930, that these were essential for keeping its target audience.[19]

The working-class market had always been the *Herald*'s prime focus, but during the 1930s papers previously targeted at the lower middle classes tried more diligently to broaden the base of their circulation. The *Express*, under the editorship of Arthur Christiansen, was an optimistic, aspirational and visually appealing production that sought to appeal to the people on the 'back streets of Derby' or 'on the Rhyl promenade'. Christiansen was keen to discard the 'stuffy pomposities' that lingered on in Fleet Street, aiming to present the news in way 'that everyone could understand'. Snappy writing and headlines made the paper more accessible than its more pedestrian rival the *Mail*, which made far less effort to reach working-class readers ('The *Daily Herald* are welcome to all the sale they can pick up in the mining districts of the country,' sneered Rothermere, the *Mail*'s owner, to Beaverbrook in 1933). Readership surveys found that working-class consumers valued the *Express* for being 'easy to read'; they also admired its 'cheerfulness', even in the late 1930s, as war approached (in stark contrast to the almost unremitting gloom of *Mail*). Although the *Express* was sceptical of the labour movement, Beaverbrook's belief in the economic importance of stimulating domestic demand led to the paper campaigning for higher wages for workers, and he maintained his faith that ordinary people would strive to better themselves. 'The world is increasing, improving and developing through the years,' he told one of his editors in 1931. 'The *Daily Express* is a paper of progress, and is convinced that the human race is bettering its position'. Three years later he told his son, Peter, that he should try 'to promote trade; to make more employment; to bring better times; to add to the prosperity of the world; to create more happiness for people'. This positive, consumerist thinking permeated the paper and proved appealing to men and women of all classes; the *Express* readership was more evenly distributed across social groups than any other paper.[20]

It was the *Daily Mirror*, however, that would make the biggest shift in its class appeal as it sought to reposition itself in the mid-1930s from a declining picture paper taken primarily by middle-class women in the South – mocked by incoming features editor Hugh Cudlipp as the 'Daily Sedative' – to an outspoken tabloid seeking to combine an Americanised commercial populism with the attitudes and perspectives of British proletarian culture. This was a gradual process, remaining incomplete until the Second World War, but it was clearly underway in the mid-1930s, with the introduction of strip cartoons (very much an American import), the 'Live Letters' column, which gave space to the concerns of ordinary readers in suitably demotic language, the increasingly sexualised pin-ups, with their hint of the saucy seaside postcard, the punchy sports writing of Peter Wilson, and, perhaps most significantly, in the columns of Cassandra (William Connor). Cassandra provided an abrasive, politicised commentary that railed against inequality, social rigidity and unthinking traditionalism. He employed a potent language of class that drew on, but modernised, an older populist radicalism, and which focused insistently on the remoteness, selfishness and insensitivity of the political and social elites.

Cassandra's analysis of the 1936 Abdication crisis (see Chapter 3), for example, was based on the view that those opposing the king's marriage formed a hypocritical class-based clique featuring 'the Church, the West End of London and the aristocracy'. 'There is more corruption, there is more spiritual rottenness in the West End of London than in any other place in the country,' he decried, while the aristocracy was the source of a 'sorry pageant of adultery and divorce'. Cassandra tapped into the 'Us' and 'Them' dichotomy that frequently shaped the working-class worldview in order to protest against the attempts to stitch up a constitutional settlement through 'a few hasty telephone conversations among politicians'; he demanded that 'the people themselves have to be consulted'. Such appeals had little effect, but Cassandra maintained a long-lasting guerrilla campaign against privilege. In June 1938, for example, he highlighted the sorry case of 33-year-old William Challis, who had been convicted, for a second time, of embezzling small amounts of money from his employer. His easy, conversational tone was laced with bitterness about inequalities of class, wealth and power:

It makes me sick! The sanctity of property in this country! You can rot your guts out in some landlord's slum and all the rigorous mechanism of the law will see that you pay your rent for that privilege. And if you try to sneak seven and six and get caught – then God help you! When I think of the vast frauds put over on this country by crooks in the City of London who go unscathed, and when I hear of poor devils like Challis who get three months hard for grabbing a handful of change it makes me proud to be an Englishman. Does it hell![21]

Cassandra also used a class perspective in his increasingly frequent discussions of the deteriorating international scene in the late 1930s. He presented the Spanish Civil war as 'a class struggle', observing that the Spanish peasants were trying to 'throw off the yoke' of 'unparalleled misery and poverty'. The Chamberlain government's policy of appeasing Nazi Germany, meanwhile, was repeatedly associated with decadent and out-of-touch social elites. It was, Cassandra proclaimed in September 1938, 'a rich clique, born and bred in the selfish cradle of the ruling classes' who were happy to sacrifice the Sudeten territories; similarly, in April 1939, it was the leisured classes, represented by *The Times*, the Cliveden Set and those who 'fish and play golf' who were celebrating Franco's victory in April 1939. While remaining detached from, and indeed often critical of, the official policies of Labour and the trade unions, Cassandra offered an appealing and persuasive class-based commentary on the reader's world.[22]

Cassandra's columns added some substance and seriousness to a paper that was, at the same time, appealing to working-class readers by taking the practices of the Northcliffe revolution to the next level – increasingly jettisoning the concern to adhere to the norms of middle-class respectability and 'proper' language use in favour of more direct and controversial articles with colloquial headlines and prose. In December 1936, for example, the *Mirror* sent Alice Hines Randall, their 'factory girl contributor', to investigate scandalous rumours about lorry-drivers enjoying the services of a network of sexually promiscuous young women. 'I Became a Lorry-Girl!' screamed the headline, as Hines described how the stories prompted her to find out more: 'So I says to myself, "Wot about it?"'. 'After my own experience', she eventually concluded, 'I'll say it's all bolony!' Such titillating, slang-strewn pieces would have been instantly rejected by Northcliffe, but became an increasing presence in the *Mirror* as it sought to draw attention to its new editorial direction. In July 1938, an article advised 'unattached' women how to 'find your man' on holiday. The main advice was 'for the first day or so stay alone': 'Your brother, sister and mother are all jealous of you. If they saw the slightest chance of your getting off with a desirable male they would do their best to kybosh it at once'. Such cheeky, informal writing marked out the *Mirror* from its competitors and attracted a steadily growing readership from young working-class men and women. By the outbreak of the war, the paper was starting to ruffle the feathers of the social elites: the exclusive Marlborough Club in London so disliked the paper's combination of outspoken politics and brash entertainment that it banned the paper as a 'red and pornographic rag'.[23]

The *Mirror* cemented its working-class credentials during the Second World War, presenting itself as the paper for ordinary servicemen and women and acting as a channel for popular frustration with bureaucratic inefficiency and military traditionalism (see Chapter 1). Cassandra's crusade against 'Army foolery' struck a chord because readers could see how they were crushed by hierarchy and protocol in their everyday lives. Leader-writer Richard Jennings similarly denounced Britain's military leadership in class-laden terms, dismissing officers as 'bone-heads' and 'out of touch toffs'. An 'us versus them' consciousness pervaded the advice and commentary the *Mirror* provided for soldiers and industrial workers alike. From an early stage, too, the *Mirror* made clear that the purpose of the war was to win a better future for ordinary people: new housing, urban reconstruction, and a welfare state built on the principles laid down by the Beveridge plan would redistribute wealth, opportunity and security to the working classes. Within days of the war ending, the *Mirror* adopted the slogan 'Forward with the People' and used a class-based appeal to campaign for the defeat of the Conservative Party in the forthcoming general election. A typical Zec cartoon from June 1945 depicted a working man, representing the public, lying on his back and tied with ropes, being harangued by a morning-suited toff representing the Tories: tickets attached to the ropes explained how the unfortunate and exploited citizen was 'Forced to pay high prices for goods to make profits for the price rings'; 'Forced by necessity to make the children leave school in order to earn some money'; 'Forced to live in slums'; 'Forced to stand in dole queues'; and 'Forced into a cheap and shoddy existence by an out-of-date economy'. Political and social reconstruction, led by a Labour government, promised to put an end to such miseries.[24]

The 1945 election campaign represented an important staging post in the ongoing reinvention of the *Mirror*. Having thoroughly transformed its editorial identity and market position since the mid-1930s, the paper's political voice grew in confidence and authority after Labour's landslide election victory, and Cassandra's acerbic columns were supplemented by a range of other left-of-centre contributors. The *Mirror* never approached the *Herald*'s dutiful commitment to the Labour Party – and even the less to the trade unions – but it became an important critical friend, and senior editorial figures such as Cecil King and Hugh Cudlipp mixed regularly with party leaders. In the second half of the 1950s, indeed, Richard Crossman, the prominent Labour MP, became a columnist for the paper. The paper continued to offer powerful class-based critiques of the ineptitude and complacency of social elites. In 1955 the *Mirror* roundly condemned the 'monstrous stupidity' of the 'chaps at the Foreign Office' – the 'Old School Tie brigade, long-haired experts and the people-who-know-the-best-people' – after they failed to spot the treachery of Soviet spies Guy Burgess and Donald Maclean. Burgess and Maclean evaded proper scrutiny, it was suggested, because they fitted comfortably into the public school and Oxbridge ethos of the diplomatic service; their colleagues, observed the disgusted columnist Keith Waterhouse, were the 'slap-happiest bunch of incompetents who ever disgraced a government department.' Cassandra and Waterhouse repeatedly attacked the 'farce of the Honours List' and the aristocratic insularity of the Royal Circle, while, particularly at election time, the *Mirror* highlighted the continuation of poverty and urban squalor despite Conservative protestations that most people had 'never had it so good'. In 1957, too, the *Mirror* introduced Reg Smythe's cartoon character Andy Capp, who would become an enduringly popular personification of northern working-class culture. Smythe portrayed, and affectionately mocked, Capp's enclosed world of flat caps, pigeon racing, pub sports, drinking, and arguments with his long-suffering wife, Flo. This was a world that many readers both recognised and enjoyed, even if they knew it was being gradually eroded by affluence and technology.[25]

During the 1940s, notes the historian Ross McKibbin, there was a redistribution of social esteem in favour of the working classes, as a result of the 'People's War', the Labour Party's consecutive electoral victories in 1945 and 1950, the construction of a welfare state, and the narrowing of economic differentials. The *Daily Mirror* and the *Daily Herald*, selling 4.5 million and 2 million copies respectively by the end of the 1940s, significantly reinforced this process by giving greater visibility to working-class lives and viewpoints at a time when most aspects of British mainstream national culture – the BBC, theatre, cinema – remained dominated by middle-class voices. These papers contributed to the rise of social democratic reformism, and encouraged politicians to prioritise the avoidance of the unemployment and poverty that scarred working-class life in the 1930s. At the same time, both papers' class rhetoric remained relatively moderate, and they accepted much conventional thinking in terms of the state and civil society – continuing to support, for example, the monarchy, empire, the maintenance of great power status, as well as the capitalist market and associated consumerism from which they both profited. If the *Mirror* and *Herald* gave expression to many working-class frustrations and discontents against a society stacked against them, their radicalism remained contained and they did little to trouble fundamentally the underlying power structures.[26]

Rewriting class in an age of affluence

The optimistic consumerism and the blithe downplaying of international turmoil that had served the *Express* so well in the 1930s became impossible to sustain amidst the warfare and austerity of the 1940s. Newspapers shrunk in size as a result of newsprint rationing, and much of the remaining space was inevitably consumed by serious reports of war, Cold War, and political debate. Amidst an unfavourable political climate, the post-war *Express* articulated the annoyance and anxiety of the middle-class families unable to enjoy their previous standards of living, and sniped at the Attlee government for its excessive intervention in the economy. 'Nothing like prosperity and happiness can reign in Britain until taxes are savagely cut', the paper complained. William Barkley, the chief Parliamentary reporter, argued that Labour's attempts to create social equality would only produce stagnation, because 'inequality means progress'; regarding the rich with envy was 'wicked', at least 'where the wealth has been accumulated by successful exertion'. In a striking echo of the *Mail* a generation earlier, the *Express* in 1953 lamented the middle-class 'New Poor', struggling to keep up appearances under such as burdensome taxation regime.[27]

In such constrained and uncertain times there were frequent discussions in the newsrooms about how to pitch the consumer advice that papers offered. Writing to Beaverbrook about the contents of the *Sunday Express* as he stepped down as editor in 1952, the veteran Scottish journalist John Gordon feared that the paper gave female readers 'fancy fashions instead of keeping our fashion news keyed on the shops that ordinary women patronise':

> This week black lampshades – how that must thrill Wigan. And in other recent weeks how to use garlic – a cookery item abhorred in Britain and never kept in any normal British home. And how to cook peppers – a vegetable few British housewives have ever heard about. We are, in fact, keeping our women's page to that small class of people who adopt the pose that a chicken's leg cooked in France must always be better than any hot-pot cooked in Lancashire.

Yet there were similar dangers in only offering the mundane. Two years later, Beaverbrook asked about a feature on ski clothes on the *Express*'s women's page. His son, overseeing the paper, accepted that 'in relation to our total sale the number of women interested in ski clothes must be small', but argued that the author, Anne Scott-James, was 'right sometimes but not too often, to lift her sights to the caviar-and-foie-gras level, rather than always on boiled beef and carrots'. Even in straightened times, the *Express* believed it important to encourage aspiration.[28]

From the mid-1950s, however, as rationing ended, affluence spread and numerous commentators started to speculate about the *embourgeoisement* of the working classes, it became easier for the *Express*, and its right-wing rivals, to champion consumption and material improvement. As pagina-tion returned to pre-war levels and advertisers obtained more space to display their wares, there was a renewed confidence in the commercial ethos, leading to enthusiastic reporting of the products and appliances that marked the modern lifestyle, such as cars, television sets and washing machines. As Hugh Cudlipp observed in 1962, the *Express* was 'tailor-made for The Affluent Age' because it was 'fundamentally materialist', the '"I'm all right, Jack" newspaper ... a distillation of Dale Carnegie and Samuel Smiles, preaching that hard work and application can enable every ambitious reader to make his pile like Lord Beaverbrook.' Yet with the national press facing daunting new competition for advertising revenue in the shape of ITV – launched in 1955 – papers with an older and less afflu-ent readership struggled. The *News Chronicle*, a liberal paper that suffered with the demise of its political party, merged in 1960 with the *Daily Mail*. The following year, the *Daily Herald*, finding its ageing, working-class and predominantly male readership increasingly unprofitable, was bought by IPC, the owner of the *Daily Mirror*, with the aim of relaunching it. The class-based appeal and dutiful Labour support that had succeeded in the 1930s was no longer commercially successful in the new social and political circumstances of the 1950s and 1960s.[29]

The relaunch of the *Daily Herald* as the *Sun* in September 1964 gave an insight into the new attitudes to class that were becoming the accepted wisdom in Fleet Street. The new editorial strategy owed much to market research commissioned by IPC. Mark Abrams, Britain's foremost com-mercial pollster, was asked to 'bring together in perspective sociological data from many sources, and in the light of today's trends to predict the nature of our society tomorrow.' His report argued that class identities were becoming less important and would continue to weaken. In the post-war world 'class barriers have tended to lose their clarity and become confused,' he argued, and 'under conditions of increasing general prosperity the social study of society in class terms is less and less illuminating'. The defining role of class was being replaced 'by differences related to age and to stages in the family life cycle', with the rise of youth culture accentuating the dispari-ties between the younger unmarried, and older married, generations. 'The middle-class teenager', he asserted, 'probably has more in common with a

working-class teenager than he has with middle-aged middle-class people.'
The needs of the under-35s, better educated than ever before, were increasingly 'determining the general climate of British society'. Their political
approach was 'secular and critical rather than ideological and undiscrimi-
nating, and women enjoyed a much higher status than ever before. In a
post-industrial society, moreover 'consumer politics displace ideological
politics'. Traditional party labels were falling into disuse.[30]

The new paper accordingly downplayed class and emphasised its
modernity and progressivism. The *Sun* was 'born of the age we live in', and
welcomed 'the age of automation, electronics, computers'. Trying to counter
the perception that it was tied to the Labour Party, it declared itself to be
'politically free', pledging instead to 'campaign for the rapid modernisation
of Britain – regardless of the vested interests of managements or workers.'
If the rhetoric of 'modernisation' was one favoured by Harold Wilson's
recently elected Labour government, the equal prominence given to the
'vested interests' of management and workers indicated a paper edging
away from its relentless championing of the trade unions. The pledges to
support 'progressive ideas', fight injustice and expose 'cruelty and exploitation' similarly avoided the language of class. There was an overt appeal to
female readers – many of whom had regarded the *Herald*, like the unions,
as a masculine environment – with the declaration that the 'present role
of British women is the most significant and fruitful change in our social
life', now that women had been 'released from household drudgery by
labour-saving devices, gadgets and intelligent home-planning'. 'Women
are the pacesetters now,' the paper noted with a nod to the title of its new
women's pages, 'and there is no country with a higher sense of fashion, coif-
fure and chic'. The editorial strategy was clear, but it was both misguided
and poorly executed. Abrams had correctly identified that class identities
were shifting under the pressure of economic and social change, but these
were slow and gradual changes. Class was far more resilient than many of
the optimistic commentators of the period realised. At the same time, the
Sun itself suffered from both a poor news service and a lack of the self-
confident irreverence that had enabled the *Mirror* to win over so many
readers. The paper was issued in an odd, not quite tabloid size, suggesting
an editorial uncertainty in its popular mission. While the paper picked up

some readers in its first year, circulation soon declined again: the 'newspaper readers of tomorrow' remained elusive.[31]

The new thinking about class could also be traced in the *Mirror*. After Labour's third successive general election defeat in 1959, which prompted debate about whether affluence was eroding the party's core working-class support, the *Mirror* dropped its 'Forward with the People' slogan and declared its growing interest in the new culture that was growing up around young people. 'The accent is on youth,' announced an editorial: 'The accent is on gaiety'. Throughout the 1960s the *Mirror*'s underlying assumption was that its working-class audience was becoming wealthier, better educated and more aspirational. 'There is the intelligent grammar schoolboy on the horizon,' noted Cudlipp in 1962, 'seeking something more helpful to his career than the bosoms of film stars and the adventures of Romeo Brown [a detective cartoon published daily in the *Mirror*]'. 'Less that is trivial, and more that is informed comment, will appear in the popular newspapers,' he argued. No editor, 'except at his peril', will 'ignore the significance of the growing seriousness of interest among readers'. The *Mirror* tried to cater for this trend, particularly with its thrice-weekly Mirrorscope insert, introduced in 1962, which put the spotlight on serious issues of current affairs, science or culture. As well as entertain, the *Mirror* increasingly sought to foster the ethos of working-class self-improvement.[32]

But it was Rupert Murdoch's *Sun*, bought from IPC and relaunched in November 1969 under the editorship of Larry Lamb, that eventually hit the commercial jackpot with an earthier, more pleasure-focused and consumerist appeal to the working-class audience. In some respects, the paper looked back to the past by adopting the *Mirror*'s old slogan, 'Forward with the People', and trying to imitate the brash outspokenness that had proved so effective in the 1940s. At the same time, the paper was far more convincingly 'modern' than its IPC predecessor. Rather than focus on the rather abstract social trends of affluence and new technology, the *Sun* hitched its fortunes to 'permissiveness'. It presented itself as 'the lusty young *Sun*', and argued that 'People who pretend that yesterday's standards are today's, let alone tomorrow's, are living a lie'. The casual acceptance of top-lessness in its pages gave a very visible sign of its permissive intent, as did the insistent reporting of stories with a sexual angle, and the serialisation of sex manuals and 'bonkbuster' novels (see Chapter 4). It drew further attention to its stance by mocking those who had been 'whipped into a froth of anxiety' by its contents, updating the conventional working-class 'us-them' dichotomy into a contrast between the cheerfully vulgar and the respectable do-gooders. It combined this with extensive coverage of the most popular working-class leisure activity of all – television-watching – as well as pages of football, horse- and greyhound-racing news. 'We acknowledged what many journalists were at that time anxious to forget,' recalled Lamb: 'that the basic interests of the human race are not in philosophy, economics or brass-rubbing, but in things like food and money and sex and crime, football and TV.'[33]

As the cultural studies scholar Patricia Holland observed in 1983, the *Sun* addressed a 'working class defined by its modes of consumption rather than its place in production', and unified its readers 'in terms of their forms of entertainment, by cultural attitudes rather than by class solidarity.' 'Middle-class bureaucrats, social workers and cultural moralists' were the paper's chief enemies. A typical example of this approach was the attack on the 'Silly Burghers of Sowerby Bridge', prompted by local councillors from the Yorkshire town removing the *Sun* from the reading room of the public library. The *Sun* fought back, gleefully mocking the town as a 'glum pimple on the face of the Pennines', and offering a competition to win a free weekend there – with the second prize being a whole week. A cash alternative was eventually offered to the winner. Underneath the fun and games was a shrewd, and commercially effective, strategy to portray the *Sun* as the populist champion of down-to-earth pleasure-seekers, as opposed to the humourless intellectuals, do-gooders and officials who sought to intervene in and disrupt the lives of ordinary working-class readers. Whereas IPC's serious-minded and self-improving *Sun* was a flop, Murdoch and Lamb's brash and boisterous creation went from strength to strength. By 1978 the *Sun* had replaced the *Daily Mirror* as Britain's most popular daily, with just under four million sales a day. The 'soaraway' *Sun* seemed unstoppable.[34]

The decline of the industrial working class

Despite its well-defined editorial strategy, Murdoch's *Sun* initially lacked a clear political identity. Support for Labour in the 1970 general election, and the miners in their strike in 1972, shifted to a lukewarm backing of Edward Heath's Conservatives in February 1974, while the following October a despairing paper called for an all-party coalition. At this stage, too, the paper welcomed Britain's entry into Europe. In the late 1970s, however, the paper was gradually won over to Margaret Thatcher's Conservative populism. Chief leader writer Ronnie Spark and political correspondent Trevor Kavanagh translated new right messages into demotic language, alleging that Britain suffered from excessive taxation, welfare scrounging, declining school standards, threats to law and order and social disintegration caused by immigration. Despite popular support for institutions such as the NHS, it was not difficult to portray the state in negative terms, given its extensive intervention in the economy and its role in setting prices and wages. As Stuart Hall, one of the earliest and most penetrating critics of Thatcherism observed in 1979, ordinary working people increasingly saw the state as 'a powerful, bureaucratic imposition' rather than something that defended and protected their interests. The prudish councillors intervening to prevent simple working-class pleasures could easily be rhetorically aligned with the state officials interfering with the economy and individuals' pay packets.[35]

This aggressively right-wing political stance became far more prominent when Kelvin MacKenzie assumed the editorship in 1981. MacKenzie himself came from a middle-class south London background – his parents were both journalists – but he became known for his abrasive populism and confrontational style. He had a clear idea of the *Sun*'s readership, once telling his staff that many of them were like 'the bloke you see in the pub – a right old fascist, wants to send the wogs back, buy his poxy council house, he's afraid of the unions, afraid of the Russians, hates the queers and weirdoes and drug dealers'. He believed that his target audience were determined to enjoy their life and pleasures free from the intervention of outsiders, wanted to spend their own money rather than hand it to the state, and were hostile to people who threatened their freedom or prosperity: immigrants, benefits cheats, striking union members and tax dodgers. The *Sun* highlighted social divisions and championed ordinary workers as individuals, rather than in collective terms or as members of a labour movement.[36]

The interventions the *Sun* made on behalf of employed workers were highly selective and often contained an anti-union agenda. In 1982, for example, the paper supported nurses' claims for higher wages. These were essential, and deserving, workers able to win extensive public sympathy, and, crucially, they stopped short of going on strike in support of their claim for higher wages:

WE'RE MARCHING WITH THE ANGELS

They'll wear our badge at rally for a fair deal. YOUR caring *Sun* is going on the march with Britain's angry angels in London on Sunday. We have made thousands of special badges for the nurses to wear with pride in their mass rally for a fair pay deal. The badges bear the *Sun* masthead and the slogan: 'Give 'em the money Maggie' ... The *Sun*'s plan was welcomed yesterday by the Royal College of Nursing, which is organising the rally.

Here were all the typical elements of a *Sun* crusade: emotive appeals ('angels', 'caring *Sun*'), the invocation of 'justice' ('fair deal'), colloquial rhetoric ('Give 'em the money Maggie'), and, with the badges and slogans, the techniques of commercial advertising. When the Royal College of Nursing accepted a pay increase of 7.5 per cent in the summer, the *Sun* could claim victory for these ordinary 'angels'.[37]

In other industrial disputes, the defence of workers' rights often depended explicitly on an anti-union agenda. On the same day as it campaigned for nurses, the *Sun* celebrated the case of four 'Fired Dinner Mums' who got their jobs back after being unfairly dismissed by Walsall council for their 'principled' refusal to join a union, and thereby 'landed their bosses in the soup'. The following day, in a 'world exclusive', the paper offered a platform for the discontent of 'two angry locomen' who exposed 'An amazing dossier of fiddles among British Rail drivers and guards'. Under the headline 'Sometimes a Driver Gets Double Time for Lying in Bed', the paper claimed that 'thousands of pounds a week' were wasted in overtime payments for work not done. When rail workers hit back by refusing to handle train deliveries of the *Sun*, journalists posed as champions of free speech and defenders of a disgruntled public. The *Sun* was the 'Paper They Can't Gag', and declared that 'YOU back US in the Great Rail Debate', because letters ran 12 to 1 in favour of the *Sun*'s stance. The complexities of industrial relations were repeatedly reduced to simple binaries, with the *Sun* invariably standing for the 'ordinary public' against the vested interests of selfish unions or short-sighted bosses. At the 1982 Labour Party conference the Labour MP Frank Allaun condemned the *Sun* as 'the most reactionary, jingoistic and anti-working class paper of them all', but the paper brushed aside his criticism: 'Our readers will see right through this hysterical charge that the *Sun* is anti-working class. No newspaper has a better record in defending the real interests of working class men and women'.[38]

The *Sun*'s attempts to create and dramatise an opposition between the interests of the 'ordinary workers' and the labour movement was most evident during the miners' strike of 1984–85. The miners were emblematic of a traditional industrial working class culture, with an associated sense of community and defiant independence, that was becoming increasingly isolated and even endangered in modern Britain. Reporting the miners' strike was not, therefore, simply a matter of relating the events of the day or even taking sides in a political-industrial dispute, but rather a process of aligning with some of the central symbolism of working-class readers. The *Sun*'s unwavering support for the Conservative government and the police, and its inability to understand the miners' determination to protect their way of life, demonstrated its distance from an audience that had been so assiduously targeted by its predecessor, the *Daily Herald*. The *Sun* had no specific labour correspondent, and few reliable contacts in the union movement, and it showed little sensitivity to union history or labour culture. It sought to circumvent the NUM's structures by calling on miners to respond to a ballot conducted by the *Sun* – 'Miners! Tell Us What You Think' implored front-page headlines – and attempted to demystify the symbolic power of the picket line. 'A picket line is not some cross between Holy Writ and a witch doctor's spell', argued an editorial in March 1984.

'There is nothing magical or democratic about it ... The *Sun*'s message to all sensible miners is: Cross that line!'[39]

In rhetoric reminiscent of the 1920s, the *Sun* portrayed the unions as fighting an outdated 'class war', with links to hostile foreign powers (notably the Soviet Union and other communist nations). Picketers were described as a 'Red Rent-A-Mob' looking for 'aggro', and the paper denounced Arthur Scargill's 'Marxist vision'. Even more controversially, the *Sun* in May 1984 attempted to run the front page headline 'Mine Fuhrer' above a picture of Scargill apparently making a Nazi salute. The paper's production chapels refused to run the picture or headline, and the issue was published without either. By repeatedly questioning the legitimacy, lawfulness and patriotism of the union movement, though, the *Sun* supported the Thatcherite model of society in which the central relationship was that between the individual and the market. Accepting that economic logic of the argument to close the pits, the paper argued that rational and clear-headed miners should return to work or take the generous redundancy package on offer. The *Sun* mobilised women as representatives of the family and its consumerist ambitions, using their anguish to show how the strike was inhibiting the material acquisitiveness of the 'ordinary' working family. A miner's loyalty, it was clear, should be to his family not to the community or union. According to this view, the strike was quickly, routinely and insistently translated into a law-and-order issue. The violence of the picket line was nothing more than thuggery which needed to be punished; the police were valorised, and picketing elided with other forms of criminality. People 'have seen ordinary bobbies struggling to hold back packs of mindless thugs who belong in some zoological freak show rather than in the midst of an otherwise decent society', observed an editorial in April 1984: 'When a sparkling Margaret Thatcher said on TV that the police were superb, she spoke for the whole nation.'[40]

The *Daily Mirror*, the *Sun*'s main competitor in the working-class market, was, by contrast, far more sensitive to the pain experienced by industrial communities. The paper had an industrial relations specialist, Geoffrey Goodman, who had both a deep knowledge of, and considerable access to, the main unions. He made clear his 'profound sympathy for the miners' plight'. He led the *Mirror*'s efforts to explain why the miners had been forced into action, and tried to humanise them. 'Miners do the toughest, most thankless job in Britain,' he wrote: 'Yet I know of no people who are more gentle at heart, more human in their responses and grasp of realities.' Those disturbed by their anger and even the occasional violence on the picket lines should recognise that 'No community has had to suffer such wholesale decimation as the miners in recent years'. Indeed, it was a surprise that there had not been 'more violence as our great industries have been reduced to limp shadows': 'if people and their work become the victims of ruthless policies, they may become brutalised themselves.'[41]

Yet despite the *Mirror*'s left-of-centre politics and its understanding of the motivations for the strike, it could not condone it. The keynote of the paper's coverage was sadness at the inexorable and inevitable decline of the industrial working class, and a recognition that the decline could be managed, but not prevented. The miners' desire to fight was natural, perhaps even admirable, but history was against them, and the *Mirror* despaired at the sight of Thatcher exposing and exploiting the fractures within the working class: 'A national strike would only lead to humiliating defeat', the paper argued in March 1984. It accepted that 'Fighting to save jobs may be the right battle,' but insisted that 'it comes at the wrong time.' Rather than support the strike, the *Mirror* appealed for the miners to retain their decency, reported the difficulties of the mining communities, and focused its ire on the 'militancy' and aggression of the supposedly neutral Thatcher government.[42]

The reporting of the miners' strike exposed the political, social and market positioning of the two main working-class papers in particularly vivid terms. The *Sun* represented the voice and views of new blue collar workers who bought into the Thatcher project. Individualistic, pleasure-seeking and consumerist, they wanted to participate in the 'property-owning democracy', and were fearful of threats to their economic security – whether they came from trade unions, welfare scroungers or immigrants. Although the *Mirror* had never been tied to the union movement in the way the *Herald* had been, it was far more deeply embedded than the *Sun* in traditional working-class industrial communities, and represented an older and more nostalgic readership supportive of collective bargaining and the welfare state. It acted as a channel for anxieties about the disruption and loss of industrial Britain, but its powerlessness in the face of the defeat of the miners' strike, and the consolidation of Thatcherism in subsequent years, only added to its sense of despair and disillusionment, just as the *Sun* was emboldened by the belief that it accurately represented the new, modern and aspirational working people.

By the late 1980s, as it reached its commercial and circulation peak, the *Sun* had mastered the working-class market with its right-wing populism. Its demotic appeal, broad humour and exploitation of popular pleasures ensured that many saw no contradiction between its political agenda and its class positioning. Surveys from this period made clear that, despite the pro-Conservative and anti-union political content, *Sun* readers perceived themselves and their paper as distinctively 'working class'; contrasts were frequently made with 'people of a higher class' or 'professionals' who would shun the paper. 'Recently I stayed in a very nice three star hotel in Shrewsbury', observed one reader, 'and I was the only person that asked for the *Sun* ... I think people [there] don't like to be seen to be as a *Sun* reader.' As trade unionism and traditional working-class collectivism continued to decline, there were few challenges to *Sun's* commercial position. The paper retained its ability to identify and represent popular constituencies – proudly championing the 'White Van Man' at the turn of the century, for example, and running a regular column interviewing van drivers on issues of the day – while also periodically channelling public anger at elite targets, from selfish bankers to 'toff' Tories. The *Sun's* bitter attack on Andrew Mitchell, the Conservative Chief Whip, in September 2012, for allegedly referring to a police officer as a 'pleb', showed the paper's continued investment in class-based outrage. There remained few better ways for a paper to burnish its populist credentials than by exposing and denouncing the private snobberies of those holding power.[43]

At the same time, the *Sun* broadly supported Conservative attempts to divide the nation between the 'workers' and 'shirkers', and to demonise the 'undeserving poor'. In August 2010, for example, the paper launched a high profile campaign to 'Stop Benefit Scroungers' in order to 'slash the £5billion wasted in Britain's out-of-control handouts culture'. Readers were encouraged to phone and email with information about 'benefits cheats' in their area, and they 'bombarded' the *Sun's* office with calls. 'Our campaign has the backing of Prime Minister David Cameron', the paper declared proudly, 'and together we are determined to tackle those who fraudulently drain Britain's resources'. The *Sun* relentlessly spotlighted individuals making unusually large claims on the benefits system or obtaining expensive accommodation to house large families. While inequality was growing, the anger and frustration of *Sun* readers was directed far more often at the bottom, rather than the top, of society.[44]

Defending 'middle England'

If the *Sun* became the defining symbol of the Thatcherite working classes, by the end of the century the *Daily Mail* had reclaimed its earlier position as the voice of the conservative middle classes. As newspaper circulations steadily declined, the *Mail* outperformed the market, overtaking the *Mirror* in 1999 and, by 2013, even outselling the *Sun* on Saturdays. Commercial success brought cultural prominence as the *Mail* was increasingly seen, by politicians, policymakers and social commentators alike, as a reliable guide to the anxieties and aspirations of 'middle England'; it was equally often lambasted by liberal critics as one of the main obstacles to progressive change.[45]

The *Mail*'s success owed much to the way in which two long-serving editors – David English (1971–1992) and Paul Dacre (1992–) gave the paper a coherent political and social identity. The imagined reader is captured by Dacre's description of the inhabitants of Arnos Grove, the north London suburb in which he grew up: 'frugal, reticent, utterly self-reliant and immensely aspirational. They were also suspicious of progressive values, vulgarity of any kind, self-indulgence, pretentiousness, and people who know best.' If the *Sun* matched its right-wing values with a brash hedonism and cheeky humour, the *Mail*'s conservatism was underpinned by a defence of the family, marriage, respectability and traditional virtues. Leader-writers and high-profile columnists such as Lynda Lee-Potter, Simon Heffer, Jan Moir and Richard Littlejohn (who joined the paper, twice, from the *Sun*) repeatedly castigated 'progressive' opinion, 'political correctness' and the failure to enforce law and order, frequently invoking an image of a golden past from which Britain had sadly fallen. Feminism and gay rights activism were consistently attacked for undermining the family, and the paper maintained a high-profile campaign against David Cameron's plans to introduce gay marriage. 'It Isn't Those Who Oppose Gay Marriage Who Are The Bigots – It Is The Liberals Who Demonise Them,' ran a typical headline over Stephen Glover's column in February 2013. Liberal judges failing to hand down punitive sentences or enforcing human rights legislation were another favourite target: 'End This Human Rights Insanity' screamed a front-page headline in February 2011, supporting David Cameron's declaration of war on 'unelected judges' after they 'put the human rights of paedophiles and rapists above public safety'. The paper regularly inflamed law-and-order anxieties with its lurid coverage of crime and the threat posed by immigration. The paper was a notable supporter of Tony Martin, the Norfolk farmer jailed in 1999 for shooting a burglar, despite his claims of self-defence.[46]

Yet this often angry and gloomy news agenda was balanced by a deft appeal to middle-class aspirationalism and the insistent pursuit of celebrity and human-interest stories of interest to its target readership. The *Mail* took full advantage of the greater pagination enabled by computerisation and the move from Wapping, adding feature pages which offered detailed guidance for leisure and consumption opportunities. The *Femail* section reflected and fed the growing middle-class preoccupation with health, diet and fitness ('Are Your Neighbours Middle-Class Cocaine Addicts Like Me?' asked one feature article in May 2012), while offering advice about fashion and furnishing remarkably similar in style and tone to the early decades of the twentieth century. More broadly, the paper aligned itself with the interests of the property-owning classes, almost obsessively tracing the rise (and occasional fall) of house prices, and championing economic policies that supported 'hard-working' families. Governments were attacked if they sought to squeeze the middle class. In February 2011, for example, the paper criticised Nick Clegg, the Deputy Prime Minister, for his suggestion that middle class households would 'barely notice' being moved into the higher income tax band: such an attitude showed 'contempt' for 3 million families.

In December 2012, similarly, the *Mail* denounced Coalition plans to raise the cap on payments for residential care in old age as a 'Middle Class Care Bill Fiasco'. 'Only the Rich Can Afford to Be Middle Class Now' lamented another headline in May 2013. The echoes of the 'new poor' of the 1920s and 1940s rang loud and clear in the *Mail*'s austerity Britain.[47]

The striking continuities between the *Mail* at the start of the twentieth and twenty-first centuries demonstrated how central class remained to British society, despite the dramatic social and economic shifts of the intervening decades. Certainly, Dacre's *Mail* operated in a very different media environment. The rise of newspapers catering for a working-class market – the *Herald*, the *Mirror* and the *Sun* – posed a significant challenge to the elitism and stuffiness of British society and culture, and gave far greater visibility to the voices and opinions of ordinary working people. In the middle decades of the century, in particular, the *Herald* and the *Mirror* gave powerful support to social democratic reformism and the construction of a welfare state. For all their intermittent rhetorical attacks on privilege and elite, though, the popular press rarely offered radical, systematic critiques of the institutions and social practices that enabled the persistence of inequality, and the commercial preoccupation with human interest, sport, celebrity and consumption did little to politicise or mobilise readers. From the 1980s, the tabloids increasingly fed public fascination with the luxurious lifestyles and properties of celebrities, while denouncing 'welfare scroungers' and 'benefits cheats'. They reinforced an individualistic culture in which collectivism seemed both dated and dangerous, appealing on the one hand to readers' aspirations, and on the other to their fears about losing what they had to a rapacious state or the undeserving poor. All the while, the calcification of Britain's social structure faded from view.

CHAPTER 6

Race and Nation

Popular newspapers have played a central role in shaping public understandings of the nation – or, in the political theorist Benedict Anderson's famous formulation, in establishing the nation as an 'imagined community'. When the *Daily Mail*, the *Daily Express* and the *Daily Mirror* were launched at the turn of the twentieth century, the reading public predominantly consumed local or regional newspapers, and urban and provincial identities remained very strong throughout Britain. Essential to the success of the new titles was their ability to reach readers around the country, and to do that, they needed to place the nation – its politics, culture and identity – at the forefront. They benefited from both a favourable intellectual climate and a conducive international situation. The late nineteenth century had seen the rise of racial and Social Darwinist thinking, which understood the world to comprise a hierarchy of competing races battling for pre-eminence; with their vast global Empire, the British confidently assumed their own racial superiority. Popular culture was awash with judgements and generalisations about different peoples and races. At the same time increasingly tense geopolitical rivalries between the great imperial powers (Britain, France, Russia, Austro-Hungary) and rising nations such as Germany, the United States and Japan, encouraged the rise of popular nationalism. Imperial skirmishes, diplomatic stand-offs, rumours of foreign spies and predictions of war all tended to lead to a patriotic rallying to King and Country.[1]

Newspapers created and sustained a sense of nation in three main ways. First, they reported and celebrated British achievement abroad. In the first half of the century, this often entailed a focus on the Empire as an expression of British greatness, and on the heroism of British troops in defending and maintaining it. Military victory was viewed as a reflection of national virtue and a confirmation of racial qualities. In the second half of the century, national competitiveness was increasingly articulated in other arenas, such as popular culture and, particularly, sport. Second, reporters described foreign lands with an eye to their exoticism and difference. Whether travelling in nearby European countries or visiting more distant parts of empire, journalists made confident judgements about national character and racial cultures, implicitly or explicitly contrasting them with the settled virtues of the British. Third, newspapers highlighted the threat posed to an idealised white British population by the arrival and settlement of other national and ethnic groups. Immigrants, whether Jews fleeing the Russian empire in the early years of the twentieth century, West Indian or Asian families seeking new lives in the post-Second World War decades, or Eastern European workers taking advantage of the accession of their states into the European Union, have consistently been portrayed as a source of crime, a burden to national welfare systems and a cause of social tension.

There were, of course, significant shifts in the nature and tone of this rhetoric across the century. As Britain gradually dismantled its empire and lost its great power status, many of the older certainties about British superiority were challenged. As foreign travel came within the reach of ordinary Britons, and readers obtained first-hand knowledge of different places and peoples, sensational reports of foreign customs and self-confident generalisations about other populations became harder to sustain. In the second half of the century, too, overtly racialised language became increasingly less acceptable, and many derogatory epithets fell out of use. Beneath the surface, though, there were equally striking continuities. Tabloids continued to find the language of race and nation to be one of the best ways of rallying and uniting their diverse mass readerships which crossed boundaries of class, gender, age and region. The jingoistic coverage of the Falklands War, the denunciations of the European Union, the hostility shown to Islam and the stereotyping of immigrants all demonstrated the commercial and cultural potency of strident warnings about 'outsiders' and external enemies. These tendencies were only reinforced by the striking under-representation of ethnic minorities in the newsroom. In the mid-1970s there were fewer than a dozen black and Asian journalists working on mainstream newspapers and magazines, and although numbers gradually increased into the twenty-first century, very few held positions of editorial authority. Although claiming to speak for the British nation, the tabloids time and again betrayed a white metropolitan English outlook.

Britain ruling the waves

Britain's political, economic and cultural life at the start of the twentieth century was profoundly shaped by its position as the centre of the world's most extensive empire. The new popular press, led by the *Mail*, dedicated plenty of space to Empire, and particularly imperial conflict, in a deliberate strategy to tap into a perceived public hunger for information (see Chapter 1). Newspapers were peppered with reports of imperial activity, debates about imperial policy, and advertisements displaying imperial commodities. Imperial success was widely accepted as proof of British racial superiority, the efficacy of Britain's governing institutions, and the moral virtue of its people. A *Daily Mirror* editorial in April 1904, for example, breezily accepted involvement in colonial skirmishes in Tibet, Nigeria, and Somaliland, against the backdrop of increasing tensions with Germany, as proof of English virility: 'That England is always at war shows an amount of energy and superabundant spirits that go a long way to demonstrate that we are not a decaying race. Three little wars going on, and the prospect of a large one looming before us, we take quite as a matter of course.' Similarly self-congratulatory was the *Mirror*'s report – headlined 'Why Englishmen Succeed' – of the speech of Lord George Hamilton, a Conservative MP who had served as Secretary of State for India, at the opening of the Indian Empire Exhibition at the Whitechapel Art Gallery in the same year. Hamilton, the paper reported, 'spoke of the creation and maintenance of the Indian Empire, and remarked that he had often wondered how it was that Englishmen had such a happy knack of administering alien troops. He believed that success was due to the characteristic upon which Englishmen prided themselves – of having a sense of fair play.' Time and again, the press complacently held up 'fair play' as the defining trait of the English/ British, conveniently obscuring the ruthlessness and brutality that was an inevitable feature of imperial expansion.[2] Newspapers actively sought to reinforce this imperial spirit. In November 1904 the *Daily Mail* established a weekly overseas edition to 'strengthen the bonds of empire' and serve as a message from the 'home-stayers' to those who were 'bearing the White Man's burden across the seas'. The paper also ran an Overseas Club pledged to defend the 'greatest Empire in the world'. Able-bodied men were encouraged to learn how to bear arms; the final lines of the club's motto implored members to 'Pray God our greatness may not fail through craven fears of being great.' From 1903, the *Mail* and the *Express* also gave considerable support and publicity to Empire Day, an annual celebration of the imperial project held on 24 May, Queen Victoria's birthday. Papers invested significant sums in constructing a network of correspondents to provide the latest news from around the Empire, supplementing the detailed content received from the news agencies. By 1900, the *Mail* had its own reporters in Calcutta, Bombay, Simla and Columbo, providing several Indian news items per day.[3]

Imperial reportage emphasised the difference and otherness of colonial peoples by highlighting exotic customs, practices and lifestyles, and pointing out what were deemed to be lower levels of 'civilisation' or the lack of respectability. The Indian caste system was held up as a backward curiosity, while sati rituals, involving the self-immolation of recently widowed women, were deemed by many to demonstrate a barbaric failure to protect the 'gentle sex'. Beyond the more serious political and social issues, countless human-interest stories were produced – the *Mail* reported in 1904, for example, that there were some 23,000 fatal snake bites per year in India, and a similar number of criminals sentenced to be whipped. The material wealth, colourful habits and multiple wives of Eastern princes and rulers were described in typical Orientalist fashion: one reporter noted that when facing the Amir of Afghanistan on the cricket pitch 'it is not etiquette, certainly not good policy' to get him out 'too quickly, nor to send him "tricky balls" difficult to hit to the boundary'. Colonial peoples, readers were repeatedly informed, lacked the notable British quality of honest 'fair play'.[4]

Reports of the exotic other were by no means confined to the Empire. If anything, even more alarming and outrageous activities could be found in areas that did not benefit from the steady hand of British rule. In April 1900, for example, the *Daily Express* offered readers sensational stories of 'Vaudoux [Voodoo] Worship and Human Sacrifice' from 'the almost unknown republic' of Haiti, a sinister island 'Where Black Rules White'. In the same year, coverage of the aftermath of the Boxer rebellion in China dwelt on the uncivilised savagery that characterised the punishment of troublemakers. 'Execution is a fine art in China,' the paper recounted with gruesome relish:

First, the criminal is BOUND TO A CROSS and, as the wretch with bulging eyeballs looks upon the scene with horror, the gentlemen upon whom devolves the principal work advances with drawn sword. Possibly the offence was a light one, or it may be that the wretch has obtained partial remission, in which case he will have the felicity of being killed with eight strokes instead of twenty-four – or possibly seventy-two. At the first stroke, the executioner nimbly whisks off one of the eyebrows – so neatly as to scarcely draw blood. Hey, Presto! off comes the other ... After that all that remains is to decapitate the lifeless and maybe still quivering body, and the execution is complete.

Such coverage, like crime reporting, combined overt moral disapprobation with a barely disguised fascination with the transgression of the boundaries of respectable (British) life. It also fed popular contemporary narratives of the 'yellow peril' based on the perceived threat posed by rapidly growing East Asian societies to western civilisation.[5]

Descriptions of foreign societies could provide vicarious thrills, but reports of immigration into Britain were often designed to provoke anger and resentment. In the late nineteenth and early twentieth century, most immigration into Britain came from Ireland and from Jewish communities in Eastern Europe. This latter movement – some 120,000 Jews entered Britain between 1880 and 1914, with the vast majority settling in East London – provoked the fiercest response from the national and local press. Journalists issued frequent warnings about the threat these 'aliens'

posed to the British way of life. 'Nobody has a word to say for the unre-
stricted admission of this rubbish, except a few amiable people who have no
knowledge of the modern immigrant alien' lamented the *Daily Express* in
November 1901:

> The East End of London and other crowded districts are filled with people who
> naturally have no British patriotism, and who only feel contempt instead of gratitude
> towards the country that admits them. A vast proportion of the foreign immigrants
> to this country could never be of the slightest use to us. On the contrary, they have
> become an intolerable nuisance.[6]

Court reports and letters fleshed out in very human terms the abstract
concerns about immigration. In May 1904 a *Daily Mirror* report from
an inquest, dramatically headlined 'Ruined by Aliens', described how a
Bethnal Green marble mason had committed suicide because 'he had been
depressed through his business falling off', as a result of 'coloured marble
coming from abroad and the foreign Jews cutting things so fine that they
have ruined the trade'. Later in the same year, the paper uncritically repeated
an anecdote about tensions between Jews and Christians in the East End
descending into violence after a trivial incident in which a Jewish man was
alleged to have 'smacked a Christian boy's ear':

> the Jews rushed out of their overcrowded dens in scores and attacked the Christians
> with sticks and stones. The Christians got reinforcements, and soon there was a
> battle royal between them, about 200 each side, and only the timely arrival of police
> prevented a serious riot. This will show how easily the embers of revolution which
> are smouldering would, with the slightest puff, spread into a serious conflagration.

'More Alien Hordes' ran a *Mirror* headline nine days later: 'Fresh Army of
Russian Jews Descending on England – Organised Invasion'. The frequent
use of the militaristic rhetoric of violence and 'invasion', with its images
of uncivilised armies and 'hordes' descending upon pure English shores,
helped to create a climate of suspicion and hostility that led to the passage of the Aliens Act 1905, the first modern piece of legislation restrict-
ing immigration into Britain. This legislation was not enough to stop the
headlines or cure the anxieties, however: 'Alien Horde for Great Britain',

reported the *Express* in April 1906: '80,000 Foreigners Ready To Land This Year'. Even in the first decade of the century, it was evident that the British state would struggle to meet the popular press's demands to keep the world at bay.[7]

War, Empire and the rewriting of patriotism

The First World War intensified and extended the assertive patriotism and imperialism that characterised much of Edwardian Britain. The press happily undertook its propagandist duties and sought to rally the public around the defence of the nation and empire, deploying increasingly crude stereotypes of enemy populations in the process. The Germans became the 'Huns' or the 'Boche', a savage race capable of indescribable atrocities, and those residing in Britain were immediately regarded with suspicion, not least because it was widely assumed that there were, in the words of the *Express*, 'a large number of German spies in England.' Northcliffe, who had led the 'scaremongering' about Germany before 1914, was adamant that the *Mail* should maintain an unremittingly hostile line to all things German. In 1915, he wrote to one of his managers concerned by the suggestion that the newspaper was using printing moulds from Germany: 'If there is any truth in this statement,' he warned, 'I shall be obliged to ask for your resignation'. If Kaiser Wilhelm II was the personification of the German war machine and the chief target of British anger, journalists deemed his subjects to be fully complicit in German crimes. In May 1915, for example, when German submarines sunk the RMS *Lusitania* on its journey from New York to Liverpool, with the loss of over 1000 lives, the whole nation was held responsible. 'Germans are rejoicing with the high glee of fiends over their infamy,' reported the *Mail*: 'The whole German nation, men and women, have shown that they approve of the deed'.[8]

Anti-German sentiment reached its highest pitch during the election campaign that followed soon after the Armistice of November 1918.

Northcliffe relentlessly encouraged the *Mail* to pressurise Prime Minister Lloyd George into pledging to seek a severe peace settlement with punitive reparations being made to Britain. 'Lloyd George is under suspicion of forgiving the Germans and forgetting the war too quickly', wrote Thomas Marlowe, the *Mail*'s editor, to Northcliffe at the end of November 1918: 'He is acting on the belief that Englishmen like to shake hands after a fight: so they do, but not this time. They don't regard the Hun as a clean fighter and they don't want to shake hands with him.' An editorial days later made the *Mail*'s position crystal clear, demanding 'Full Indemnity from Germany', the 'Expulsion of Huns' and 'Rigid new immigration laws to keep out undesirables':

> The people should realise that if the Germans are not made to pay, then the employers and workers of this country will be put under bondage for a century in order that we may become debt free. If the interned Germans are let loose we shall have centres of unrest created by them wherever they settle. If the disbanded German and Austrian armies are allowed to trickle into England ... then we shall have wages reduced to the German scale all round.

The paper insisted that it was doing no more than voicing the righteous anger of the British public expressed at election meetings around the country: 'Reports from all quarters establish that whatever heckling is indulged in has reference to three questions: Will the Kaiser be surrendered and tried? Will Germany be made to pay up? Will the Huns be sent out and kept out?' This pressure from the *Mail* and rest of the right-wing press certainly seems to have encouraged Lloyd George to harden his rhetoric on peace-making, and he travelled to Paris the following year well aware that any concessions to the Germans would be severely criticised. When Lloyd George 'is vigorous in fighting Germany I support him,' Northcliffe told Marlowe: 'when he sings his "Be kind to poor little Germany" song I oppose him.'[9]

The aggrieved patriotism of the immediate post-war period was inflamed by the tensions produced by the extended and divisive process of demobilisation. Britain had relied heavily on men from across the Empire to sustain its military effort and maintain the capacity of the merchant navy, but black and Asian men often experienced suspicion and hostility rather than gratitude in British port cities and towns. In Liverpool, Cardiff and London, a number of clashes with local workers and residents in 1919 received extensive coverage and lurid headlines. Central to the reporting was an anxiety about the sexual threat black and Asian men posed to white women. 'It is naturally offensive to us that coloured men should consort with even the lowest of white women,' wrote the *Sunday Express*, voicing contemporary hierarchies of race and class: 'Racial antipathy is always present, the sex jealousy inflames it to a violent, unreasoning wave of emotion'. The *Sunday Chronicle* sent a 'special correspondent' to travel through Limehouse in London ('Chinatown'), and his dramatic article insisted that 'even the most unobservant visitor' could not help but be struck 'by the number of white women who lounge in the doorways, nurse their children on the steps, or wait in the small general shops which abound'. These women, the paper explained, were the 'wives – often, indeed, the devoted slaves – of far from prepossessing Orientals': 'The fact is that Asiatics have some deep, irresistible influence over the women they marry. Their wives become insensible to the degradation into which they sink, and unquestionably fulfil the behest of their masters.' The reporter expressed, moreover, 'a deep pity for the offspring of these ill-assorted unions', repeating the claim that 'the half-caste inherits the worst characteristics of both parents'. Using the languages of eugenics, he warned that 'the boy in whose blood surges the twin tides of Orientalism and Occidentalism has impulses only the slow process of western civilisation has kept in leash'. The only way to protect white women and preserve 'western civilisation', he concluded, was to impose restrictions on the mixing of different races. Such journalism inevitably served to encourage and legitimise those seeking to limit the movement and opportunities of 'outsiders'.[10]

Yet if in the short-term the First World War encouraged a belligerent nationalism and fostered suspicion of foreigners, the scale and brutality of the events on the Western Front ultimately caused severe damage to the late-Victorian and Edwardian notions of patriotism and imperial masculinity. There was widespread disillusionment with the grand rhetoric of war and Empire as it became clear that the huge sacrifices of 1914 to 1918 had not secured a lasting peace. This was symbolically captured by cartoonists increasingly repudiating the traditional aggressively masculine figure of

'John Bull', and preferring instead more domesticated and unassuming figures to represent the nation and its public. Poy's 'John Citizen' in the *Mail*, and Strube's 'Little Man' in the *Express* both sought a quiet life undisturbed by the demands of the state'; David Low's 'Colonel Blimp', by contrast, satirised the bluff imperial manliness of an earlier generation of heroes. It is similarly striking how little the supposedly virile leadership of Oswald Mosley and the active patriotism of the British Union of Fascists appealed to the wider public. Rothermere's encouragement of this form of 'national regeneration' does not seem to have resonated much with the *Mail*'s readership (see Chapter 2).[11]

In the inter-war period the popular press retained its support for the imperial ideal, but accepted a less muscular and interventionist imperialism. Celebrating Empire Day in 1929, the *Express* maintained that the occasion was a 'reminder of where the strength, the greatness, and the mission of this country really lie'. At the same time, it remained conscious that imperialism had been tarnished by the bloodshed of the past, and attempted to give it a modern appeal: 'If ever there was a time when the Empire was associated with ideas of greed and aggression, of conquest and aggrandisement, that time is long since passed. First and foremost the Empire is a co-partnership of peace.' The goal of Empire, the paper declared, was to 'continue spreading British ideas of law, society, government, and liberty'. The faith in the essential superiority of British customs and institutions remained unchallenged, but it was now restrained by a greater realism about the limits of British power and a genuine desire to avoid the warfare that had cost so many millions of British lives. Nor was Empire buttressed by Christian rhetoric in quite such an uncomplicated way as before 1914. In May 1937 the *Mirror* reported a sermon delivered by the Archbishop of York which attempted the 'rather difficult task of reconciling Christianity with Imperialism'. The paper accepted Archbishop Temple's argument that the two could be reconciled if the Empire was regarded 'as a great fellowship', rather than 'a "self-assertive" machine for imposing one nation's will upon others', although not without observing that the 'real thing in the past has not be quite so Christian.' Nation and empire remained potent rallying cries, but they had to be used more judiciously to a more critical and weary public.[12]

The result of these political and cultural shifts was that Fleet Street approached the outbreak of war very differently in the late 1930s than it had twenty-five years earlier. Whereas the most popular paper of 1914, the *Mail*, had been full of belligerent warnings about the German threat, the market leader in 1939, the *Express*, retained its faith in appeasement and declared its confidence, as late as August, that there would be 'No War This Year'. The idealism of 1914 was conspicuously absent, and aggressive posturing seemed unsuitable. When the Labour MP George Buchanan wrote to Gerald Barry, the editor of the *News Chronicle*, asking to contribute an article on the preparations for war, he noted that there had been little of the 'flamboyancy' that marked the previous conflict: the mobilisation 'is not yet covered with a horrid glamour or Rule-Britannia-ism'. Indeed, on the left there was a particular determination that support for a campaign against Hitler should not be corrupted by militarism or jingoism. Colonel T. A. Lowe, writing in the *Herald*, emphasised that the modern soldier was not just a blindly patriotic 'tough guy' but a 'hard-working artisan, a skilled craftsman and a self-respecting citizen' simply carrying out his duty to protect Europe from dictatorship. Similarly, Walter Layton, the *News Chronicle*'s editorial director, insisted at a policy conference in July 1939 that the paper 'should give as much space as possible to interesting stories of the new militia, etcetera, but should avoid any implied glorification of war'. The goal was to emphasise 'the idea of service to the nation and the necessity of ultimately forming some plan for achieving peace.'[13]

Instead, commentators celebrated the good-natured, if rather cynical, sense of humour supposedly shared by the British public. Sent out to test the atmosphere of the crowds in London towards the end of August 1939, the *Express* reporter Hilde Marchant declared 'You Can't Stop Those Cockney Wisecracks': 'The Londoner is crisis hardened ... no war will stop a Cockney from wisecracking ... It's grand to be in London.' Strube's cartoons reinforced this image of a calm nation: one depicted his famous 'Little Man' very deliberately lighting a cigarette while being shot at from all sides by 'Propaganda', 'Rumours', 'Scares', and 'Tension'. Such were the qualities of a nation 'united by the love of liberty and not marshalled by force and oppression'. The *Mirror* provided similar reports of an undaunted population, describing how 'cheerfulness was the keynote of Britain's people in the hours of crisis yesterday'. The paper called on its readers to draw heart from this resolute mood: after all, it declared, in the past 'we've always come smilin' through'. The *News Chronicle*, meanwhile, offered five shillings for each comic anecdote from mobilising servicemen, and boasted that even floods 'have not dampened the humour of the men in camp'. If the First World War and its aftermath destroyed the high ideals of its participants – 'the Great War was meant ... to make the world safe for democracy, and it established dictatorships throughout Europe', noted the *Express* bitterly – the cynical humour and restrained patriotism of 1939 offered a defence against similar disillusionment.[14]

War itself inevitably saw a resurgence of patriotic rhetoric and the return of derogatory stereotypes and epithets for enemy peoples, even if the tone remained different from 1914. After Churchill replaced Chamberlain as prime minister in May 1940, for example, the *Mirror* sought to rally the nation with some stirring language:

> Pride of your race is plainer today than it was yesterday. A direct challenge will always induce the happy-go-lucky Britisher to take off his coat and fight. Today all of us are stripped for action. The spirit of Britain flashes as vividly as summer lightning.
>
> We expect no quarter – and will give none to the Teutonic Barbarian. Our only regret is that we ever allowed the monster to rise after the licking we gave him in the last struggle.[15]

Hitler, and Nazism more broadly, provided easy targets to demonise, although the traditional language of 'Huns' was resurrected too. Racial language was more evident in the coverage of the Japanese, particularly during the fall of Hong Kong in 1942, where the anxieties about the contamination of white women emerged strongly. 'Hundreds of Our Girls are in Jap Hands' screamed the *Mirror*'s front-page headline on 11 March 1942, highlighting the typically British pluck of the 'nurses, ARP telephonists, code-and-cipher girls and official secretaries' who 'knew what unspeakable horrors they faced, but declined to desert their posts'. The paper was clear that an honourable death was preferable to being left in the hands of barbaric racial enemies:

Knowing what to expect from the Japanese infidels, a band of British nurses in Hong Kong carried loaded revolvers in their handbags. The women, all under thirty, planned to die rather than be outraged by Japanese. And last night their mothers in England had one fervent hope – a hope that their girls had time to take their lives before the yellow men found them.

Headlines declaring 'Our Hong Kong Girls Raped and Murdered' were designed to outrage and inflame the population at home, and further reinforced beliefs about the inhuman 'Oriental' and the 'yellow peril' that had pervaded popular culture since the nineteenth century.[16]

As the tide of the war turned in favour of the Allies, the press developed a powerful narrative about the pluck, fortitude and defiance of the British people sustaining them through the dark days of Dunkirk and the Blitz to a long journey towards eventual victory. 'We know our men are fighting with hearts of lions,' declared the *Sunday Pictorial* in July 1943: 'They are proud sons of a nation that has never flinched to face superhuman odds like these.' By 1945, the portrayal of the war as a triumph of British spirit and unity, these qualities enabling a defiant nation to 'stand alone' as other European countries fell under the sway of the Nazi regime, was well established, and it would be further elaborated in print and in the cinema in future decades. This potent mythology of the 'finest hour' had significant consequences for post-war politics and culture. It made it harder for the public to understand, and come to terms with, Britain's loss of great power status over the coming decades; the financial and diplomatic cost of victory was not immediately transparent to citizens understandably preoccupied with the return of peace. At the same time, the endless replaying of war stories, with their gallery of brutal Germans, villainous Italians and treacherous French, did little to foster the spirit of European amity that would underpin any moves to European integration. Despite the important role played, once again, by imperial troops, moreover, wartime success was typically portrayed as that of a white nation; it would be easy for subsequent critics of post-war immigration to claim that the entry of black and Asian men and women had somehow diluted the shared national virtues that had underpinned wartime victory.[17]

Immigration and the emergence of multi-cultural Britain

Most initial newspaper reports of post-war immigration from the West Indies were relatively respectful and benevolent, if a little patronising, as a nation that saw itself as tolerant welcomed workers needed to tackle a labour shortage. In June 1948, for example, the *Daily Express* applauded Oswald Denilson, described as 'the first of 430 job-hunting Jamaicans to land at Tilbury yesterday morning from the trooper *Empire Windrush*', for taking up a £4-a-week job as a night watchman in Clapham. Denilson got his job, the paper recorded, 'after making a speech of thanks to government officials. He called for three cheers for the Ministry of Labour and raised his Anthony Eden hat. Others clapped. Panamas, blue, pink and biscuit trilbys, and one bowler hat were waved.' Such diligent and deferential workers seemed to pose little threat to a nation rebuilding after the traumas of war, although there were some concerns expressed even at this stage about potential economic instabilities caused if too many men and women from the colonies sought to settle in Britain.[18]

As journalists were sent to investigate immigrant communities and consider what impact they were having on local areas, however, anxieties generated by racial stereotypes repeatedly came to the surface. The concerns about cross-racial sexual relationships that had been voiced after 1918 now became even more prominent. Under the sensational headline 'Pat Roller Looks for Trouble In "Stepney's Shameless Harlem"', for example, the *Daily Record* in August 1953 explained that Stepney's Cable Street was known as 'the worst street in Britain'. If deprivation was not quite at the levels of some areas of Glasgow, Roller observed, 'Cable Street poses a problem Glasgow just doesn't have: the problem of coloured men and white women living together in hovels which would disgrace the worst slums I know in the Gorbals'. Black men were presented as possessing an irresistible and dangerous sexual allure: 'Women come to black Stepney and parts of Bow from all over Britain', and ended up 'fighting and brawling over some of the men'. Prostitution spread its tentacles. 'Blowzy, frowsy, middle-aged harlots have left the West End to cash in on the traffic down in the East End,' Roller reported: 'Brothels have sprung up all over the place.' One welfare worker told Roller that her organisation 'had rescued "quite a lot" of girls from black Stepney and brought them back into the family fold', but that it was 'not easy' to do so. Such articles, with their motifs of decadence, corruption and attempted rescue, updated the nineteenth-century tradition of scare stories about the 'white slave trade'. But the issue of inter-racial sex was not just related to the broader problem of urban poverty, it was presented as a wider question about which everyone should have an opinion. In 1954 the popular magazine *Picture Post* bluntly asked 'Would You Let Your Daughter Marry A Negro?' Two years later, George Gale wrote a series of articles for the *Daily Express* under a similar headline, 'Would You Let Your Daughter Marry a Black Man?' Gale insisted that the honest answer was 'no', explaining that the gulf between West Indian men and white Britons was too large to easily bridge, and that 'mixed-race' children suffered because of the inferiority of West Indian culture. These features consolidated the widespread belief that black men were sexual menaces who could threaten any family.[19]

The outbreak of rioting in Nottingham and Notting Hill in 1958 – sparked off, according to some accounts, by sexual jealousies – raised immigration to the top of the political agenda, and generated numerous stories associating immigrants with violence, crime and social tension. Reports implied that the sheer scale of immigration made trouble inevitable, and used alarmist language that emphasised the lack of control. The *Express* blamed the rioting on the 'postwar flood of immigrants from Britain's territories overseas', while the *Mirror* noted that 'Britain is the only Commonwealth country which allows immigrants to pour in without restriction.' In subsequent years, there was widespread press backing for legislative measures to limit immigration, although rarely did these legal restrictions seem to do enough to assuage fears about the problems of integration. Shortly after the passage of the 1962 Immigration Act, for example, the *Express* highlighted the difficulties 'problem children' lacking a command of English were causing to schools in certain areas of the country. In the following years, reporters tendentiously highlighted schools 'Where

8-In-10 Are Immigrants', suggested that local authorities were pleading to stop a 'flood' of immigrant children into schools, and offered the 'facts' about 'Your Child's School and the Immigrant'. As with the concern about inter-racial sexual relationships, reporters dramatised social problems by linking them to potential threats to readers' families.[20]

There were, nevertheless, some significant attempts in Fleet Street both to challenge negative representations of immigrants and to identify white racism as the root cause of the much-discussed social problems. The *Daily Mirror*, in particular, consistently campaigned against the 'colour bar' and used some of its most prominent contributors to combat racist stereotypes. In March 1954, for example, Keith Waterhouse wrote a three-part series, based on a fortnight's travel around the country, exposing the 'Blind Black Hate' that '60,000 bitterly persecuted coloured folk suffer here today'. He cast an unforgiving spotlight on the actions of white Britons whose 'contempt and ignorance and jealousy' often made the lives of immigrants a misery: 'What happens in the heart of a coloured man when you call him a wog?' he asked. He denounced Birmingham as 'Jim Crow city of violent colour hate and segregation', and peeled back the polite facades that hid the realities of racism: 'No coloured man in this city will go after a flat where "respectable" tenants are asked for – because respectable means white. Or after a job where "experienced" hands are needed – because experienced means white. Or into a cafe where only "regular" customers are served – because regular means white.' Waterhouse's series was by no means an isolated intervention. The *Mirror* commissioned him to write another major set of articles shortly after the Notting Hill disturbances of 1958, because 'white citizens must know the facts about the coloured men and women in our midst'. Waterhouse patiently addressed recurring anxieties about stealing women, houses and jobs, and soberly pointed out the very real difficulties that black workers faced: 'Jamaicans today are in steel, coal, Lancashire cotton and public transport. Colour bar or no, there are still few jobs that employers will give to coloured people if they can get white workers instead.'[21]

The *Mirror*'s campaigning continued into the 1960s. The paper denounced the 1962 Commonwealth Immigration Act as a shameful 'Race Law', supported the Labour's Governments Race Relations legislation, and continued to expose examples of racism. John Pilger took up Waterhouse's crusading mantle. In a notable two-part series in 1967, entitled 'Black Britons', Pilger directly challenged the widely held view that black and Asian individuals were not properly British. His first article featured black Liverpudlian Edward Bedford, who was described as being 'as English as chips and chimney pots'; only discrimination and ignorance, Pilger argued, prevented Bedford from feeling a sense of belonging. For all its admirable determination to educate the public about immigration, however, it is striking how rarely black and Asian commentators were able to discuss their own situation; on the *Mirror*, and elsewhere in Fleet Street, white 'experts' were allowed to interpret and explain the experiences of immigrant communities. At moments of high tension and controversy, moreover, the *Mirror* did sometimes compromise its position. In the immediate aftermath of the Notting Hill riots, the paper accepted that 'some of the coloured people who have settled here are no-goods', and supported immigration restrictions: Commonwealth citizens 'should not be allowed to enter Britain as immigrants unless they have a job and a home to come to.' In 1968, too, the *Mirror* backed the government's measures to limit the entry of Kenyan Asians, occasionally resorting to the rhetoric of 'flooding' more usually used by right-wing papers. These concessions partly reflected the editorial team's awareness that despite their attempts to calm fears, many of the *Mirror*'s readers remained deeply concerned about the impact of immigration.[22]

The popular press helped to intensify the immigration debate still further by giving extensive coverage to Enoch Powell's deliberately inflammatory 'Rivers of Blood' speech in April 1968. The historian Matthew Young has persuasively argued that the popular press 'played an important role in constructing, reinforcing and disseminating the concepts and ideals which gave Powell's speech its resonance'. Columnists such as the *Express*'s Robert Pitman had for some years expounded Powellite themes of the country being overrun by materialistic immigrants. 'While thousands of our own workers are being thrown, out of jobs,' wrote Pitman in October 1966, 'immigrants – with full permission from Mr. Jenkins [the Labour Home Secretary] – are still flooding into Britain at the rate of 60,000 a year. They are not fleeing from persecution like the pre-war refugees. They are simply coming (who can blame them) in search of a better life with full welfare benefits.' In 1967, the *Sunday Express* gave Powell himself a platform to discuss his views on the subject. Foreshadowing his later words, he predicted that Britain's 'coloured population' would reach five million by the end of the century and claimed that the failures of immigration legislation had landed Britain with 'a race problem of near-American dimensions.'[23]

The 'Rivers of Blood' speech, with its apocalyptic rhetoric and memorable anecdotes, was perfectly pitched to grab Fleet Street's attention, and dominated front pages for several days. While most editorials condemned Powell's language – the *Mirror* denounced it as 'inflammatory, bigoted and irresponsible' – the *Daily* and *Sunday Express* offered him support, and the *News of the World*, while not endorsing all aspects of the speech, concluded that 'We can take no more coloured people. To do so, as Mr Powell says, is madness'. Other papers gave space to readers or commentators to outline their fears about the impact of immigration. Editors were well aware of the strength of feeling on the topic, with opinion polls suggesting that over 70 per cent of the population shared Powell's views, and the *Mirror* admitting that its heavy post-bag of readers' letters was 40–1 in favour of Powell. Powell's speech became a reference point in all future press debates about immigration, and his warnings of violent discord cast a shadow over the lives of minority communities. The *Express*, in particular, started fanning concern about the scale of illegal immigration with headlines such as '800,000 People Who Shouldn't Be Here' and 'Visitors Who Never Go Home'. Few issues had the same power to unite a readership in indignation, and as politics became increasingly divisive in the 1970s, the right-wing tabloids returned to it again and again.[24]

By the 1980s, newspapers tended to distance themselves from Powell's anti-immigration positions, even if they continued to give them considerable publicity. In September 1985 Powell suggested that the government should pay black people to be repatriated, and was widely criticised by the tabloids. Under the headline 'You're talking rubbish, Enoch', for example, the *Sun* offered details of a poll of its readers showing almost three-quarters opposed to Powell's suggestion. The *Daily Mail* denied that Powell was a racist, but declared his proposals 'impractical'. At the same time, the right-wing press's support of Thatcher's law-and-order agenda provided plenty of opportunities for the expression of fears about the impact of immigration. Verbatim reporting without editorial intervention enabled papers to give space to controversial views, and to present opinion as fact. Under the headline 'City Riots on Way, Says MP', the *Sun* quoted the view of backbench Conservative MP Harvey Proctor that 'a rise in the number of blacks will lead to strife – and bring troops on to the streets': "'What we saw in Brixton was a U trailer for an X-certificate film.'" The paper likewise quoted 'furious Tory MP Terry Dicks' when he called for the Notting Hill Carnival to be banned: "'The blacks don't deserve to have a carnival – they do not know how to behave any more'". A roster of political contacts could be relied upon to provide outraged comments on any immigration-related news story.[25]

Another common tabloid strategy was to criticise, trivialise or misrepresent the 'political correctness' agenda. *Sun* reports on the use of racist language sometimes repeated the offending terms – 'Panto Pals Tell Race Joker Stan To Pak It In' – or displayed a tone of levity that betrayed a belief that the accusers lacked a sense of humour or proportion:

> Bingo Fan Blacked in 'Golly' Rumpus – Bingo fan Dave Hale faces the boot from his social club – for shouting 'Golly, Golly' every time he gets a winning line. Furious black members claim Dave's delighted cry is 'racial abuse.' They want him to yell, 'Housey, Housey' like everyone else – or be banned from the club where he has played three nights a week for the last ten years.

In its own reports, too, the *Sun* frequently employed derogatory labels such as 'Jap' and 'Nip', blithely ignoring sensitivities around such terms. The paper called for the abolition of the Commission for Racial Equality, arguing that it had 'failed' to combat discrimination and served 'no useful purpose'. By demanding special treatment for ethnic minorities,' argued an editorial, 'it causes resentment among the white majority', while 'by promoting positive discrimination in employment, it gives blacks the impression they don't have to try too hard'. Those demanding rights for ethnic minorities were aligned with other 'fanatics' of the 'loony left', a muddle-headed group who were portrayed as lacking the straightforward common-sense of the ordinary reader. The rights agenda was implicitly presented as a threat to the hard-won status of the *Sun*'s core white, male, working-class constituency.[26]

The *Sun* used British participation in war to develop its aggressively patriotic rhetoric. The paper's reporting of the Falklands campaign in 1982 was spiced throughout with attacks on the 'Argies' (see Chapter 1), and reports on the military engagements often betrayed the imperialist assumption that the Argentinians troops somehow lacked the manliness and bravery demonstrated by the British. 'Commandos with fixed bayonets gave the Argentines a taste of cold steel in a ferocious hand-to-hand battle on the outskirts of Port Stanley,' ran a typical report: 'The Argies had no stomach for the close-quarters combat … and crumbled before the Task Force's full-blooded assault at the weekend.' At the start of the 1991 Gulf War, the paper devoted its entire front page to a Union Flag, encouraging readers to 'Support Our Boys and Put this Flag in Your Window'. Two days later, the paper displayed its outrage under the headline 'Firm bans Sun flags as Muslims start moaning':

> True Brits at a factory were ordered to RIP DOWN their Sun Union Jacks yesterday – after Muslims complained. Patriotic workers had plastered their walls with our front page of a soldier's face on the British flag to show our support for squaddies in the Gulf. But bosses at machete-makers Ralph Martindale's in Newtown, Birmingham, banned the flags after Asians in the 200-strong workforce complained.

With its dichotomies between 'true Brits' and 'Muslims', 'patriotic workers' and 'Asians', the paper reinforced the Powellite assumption that immigrants could not be integrated into the national community. The following day, the *Sun*'s controversial columnist Richard Littlejohn called on the government to 'Kick Out Fanatic Muslims'. In language reminiscent of the First World War panic about enemy aliens, Littlejohn claimed that in 'Mosques all over Britain, Muslims prayed for an Iraqi victory. Some welcomed the prospect that there could be terrorist attacks here.' While admitting that the opponents of the British war effort 'by no means' represented all Muslims, he declared them to be 'a vocal and powerful minority' who were nothing less than 'the enemy within'. He concluded that 'those with British passports should be interned for the duration while the Government seeks ways of revoking their citizenship', and those without British passports 'must be deported without delay'. More than forty years after the arrival of the *Empire Windrush*, many press commentators still found it difficult to view black and Asian men and women as 'true Brits'.[27]

Keeping Europe at bay?

If victory in the Second World War, and the successful development of an atomic bomb, had reinforced Britain's sense of itself as a 'great power', by the late 1950s, after the Suez debacle had exposed British reliance on the United States, such illusions were increasingly difficult to maintain (see Chapter 1). With decolonisation happening apace, the global significance that had underpinned British identity for so long was rapidly diminishing, and Britain was faced with finding a new 'role' in the world. One potential solution was to participate in the European project, launched with great fanfare in 1957 as six European nations signed the Treaty of Rome in 1957 and established the European Economic Community (EEC). The popular press was divided about the merits of joining the EEC. The *Daily Mirror* viewed it as a necessary modernising step, and in June 1961 started campaigning in favour of entry. The fiercest opposition campaign from the *Daily Express*, whose ageing proprietor, Lord Beaverbrook, remained committed to his lifelong cause of Empire. Even into the late 1950s, the *Express* gave extensive coverage to the annual Empire Day celebrations, distributing free Union Flags through newsagents at a considerable cost. Internal memoranda also debated whether or not the term 'Commonwealth' should be used in place of 'Empire' ('Personally, I think it is a lost cause that may as well be abandoned', Arthur Christiansen bravely told Beaverbrook). When Conservative Prime Minister Harold Macmillan announced in 1961 that Britain would apply to join the EEC, the *Express* led a full-blown crusade in opposition.[28]

Central to the *Express*'s 'Commonwealth not Common Market' campaign were fears about the loss of the traditional sources of national identity, as Rene MacColl's article in January 1962 made clear: 'Loss of identity is a disturbing condition in an individual. Cause for lively alarm. How much worse for a nation!' MacColl argued that Britain would find 'itself being elbowed out of its own way of doing things' by 'hidden persuaders inspired by Bonn, Paris and Rome'. George Gale, writing in the *Express* later that year, agreed that Britain had a way of life and a set of institutions which were fundamentally incompatible with those in Europe. Joining the EEC would lead to the loss of what had made Britain great, to the detriment of the whole world:

> Britain is required to lose itself in Continental Europe the spirit of whose laws and temper of whose political institutions are radically different from and inferior to our own ... The identity of this country is infinitely too valuable a possession to ourselves and our children, to Europe, to the Western Alliance, to the world, for it to become lost in the Continental land-mass.

The *Express* greeted French President General de Gaulle's veto of Britain's application in ecstatic terms: 'Glory, glory, Hallelujah! It's all over; Britain's Europe bid is dead. This is not a day of misery at all. It is a day of rejoicing, a day when Britain has failed to cut her throat'. The *Express* had given the most strident articulation since the Second World War of a particular vision of Britain as being vitally connected to its imperial roots and traditions, and as being able to stand alone if required, and the paper milked this temporary success for all it was worth. Politically it may ultimately have been a Pyrrhic victory, but culturally it helped to sustain a vision of Britain that would remain influential.[29]

By the early 1970s, when Edward Heath finally negotiated Britain's successful entry to the EEC, the popular press had broadly been won over to the merits of the European project, not least because few now believed that Britain's economy was strong enough to sustain itself outside the Common Market. The *Express* maintained a lone opposition to entry in 1973, but when a referendum to confirm Britain's membership was held in June 1975, it too fell in alongside the rest of Fleet Street in support of the Yes campaign. For the *Mirror*, referendum day was 'The Most Important Day Since the War' and it called on readers to make 'A Vote for The Future'. The *Sun* agreed that Britain needed a 'future together', rather than a 'future alone'. The sizeable 'Yes' majority suggested that Fleet Street's united front had a significant impact on voters.[30]

Yet the referendum was to prove the high point for popular Europeanism. During the 1980s the right-wing tabloids fed off Margaret Thatcher's increasing Euroscepticism, with the *Sun*, in particular, updating the *Express*'s old anti-European rhetoric with its own brand of belligerent patriotism and aggressive humour. During the 'lamb war' of 1984, for example, the *Sun* ran a 'Hop off, you Frogs' campaign, offering free badges and awarding prizes for the best anti-French jokes submitted by readers. Jacques Delors, the President of the European Commission from 1985 to 1995, became a tabloid hate-figure, and he was repeatedly attacked when he expressed his federalising ambitions. On 1 November 1990, the *Sun*'s ran a front-page headline 'Up Yours, Delors!' above a photograph of a hand appearing out of a union flag and displaying the internationally recognised 'V-sign'. *Sun* readers opposed to plans for a single currency were encouraged to 'tell the French fool where to stuff his ecu' by turning towards France at midday and telling him to 'Frog Off'. This was part of a wider crusade against European interventionism, featuring a range of frequently confected stories – such as those detailing plans to harmonise food products such as sausages and rhubarb ('Save our Sizzlers', 'Rhu Must Be Barmy – British Rhubarb has to be Straight, say EU Chiefs'). The *Daily Mail* joined the crusade, running a 'Red Tape Alert' feature documenting 'bizarre red tape nightmares' imposed by Brussels. During the 1990s, Prime Minister John Major, who signed the 1992 Maastricht Treaty which set in train further measures of integration, was castigated by the press for his perceived failure to protect British sovereignty, and the tabloids fomented much of the in-fighting that severely weakened the Conservatives' credibility as a ruling party.[31]

The Euroscepticism of the political columns was reinforced by the tabloids' increasingly chauvinistic feature writing and sport journalism. In April 1987, under a headline blurring military and football successes ('Victorious ... In 1918 ... In 1945 ... In 1966 ... And Now'), the *Sun* declared that it was 'invading' Germany. This stunt was nominally in response to critical comments made by the German *Bild* newspaper about British

tourists in Majorca, but it betrayed the continuing hold of the Second
World War on British popular culture:

> It's war folks! Your patriotic *Sun* was last night assembling a Wapping task force to
> invade Germany – and give those lout Krauts a lesson to remember. We sprung into
> action after a blitzkrieg attack on YOU by the vicious, heartless barons of Germany's
> gutter press ... [We will] Seek unconditional guarantees that the Germans desist
> from their dawn raids to capture deckchairs and sun-beds ... It's not going to be
> fun, being a Hun.

The belligerently jocular tone was typical of Kelvin MacKenzie's *Sun*,
masking the paper's reliance on tired or offensive cultural reference points
rather than finding new ones. At a time when hooliganism marred numerous international sporting events involving British teams, the paper was
accused of pandering to a dark and potentially violent strain of popular
nationalism.[32]

Football reporting itself also increasingly drew upon historical references and nationalistic stereotypes to wage metaphorical war against traditional enemies. The coverage of the 1996 European Championships, held
in England, exemplified this tendency. England's victory against the Dutch
enabled the *Sun* to contrast the muscular and hard-working English players with the effete overseas sophistication of the Dutch, as well as indulg-
ing in familiar historical comparisons. Under the headline 'Shearer Clogs
'Em – Ecstatic England trample through the tulips', the paper described
how the Dutch side 'was dismantled like a cronky, condemned windmill',
before noting that 'By coincidence yesterday was the 181st anniversary of
the Battle of Waterloo.' When England met Germany in the semi-final, the
Daily Mirror, edited by Piers Morgan, who had recently joined the paper
after a career with the *Sun* and *News of the World*, sought to match the
chauvinistic bravado of his old employers. 'ACHTUNG! SURRENDER'
declared the front page, 'For you Fritz, ze Euro 96 Championship is over.'
English players Stuart Pearce and Paul Gascoigne were pictured wearing Second World War tin helmets, while a smaller headline announced
that the '*Mirror* declares football war on Germany'. The Press Complaints
Commission received more than 300 complaints about the coverage but did

not uphold any, ruling that the issue was one of taste rather than articulating discrimination or incitement to hatred. Several commentators expressed their disappointment that the *Mirror*, with its proud tradition of questioning jingoism in the Suez and Falklands crises, seemed intent on imitating the belligerence of the *Sun*.[33]

Race and nation in the twenty-first century

The *Mirror*'s 'Achtung! Surrender' front page was, in some respects, the last hurrah of a tabloid culture that was changing. The outspoken chauvinism of Kelvin MacKenzie's *Sun* was gradually moderated after he stepped down in 1994, and Piers Morgan quickly repented his paper's Euro 1996 headline, eventually returning the *Mirror* to its left-wing traditions. With the election of the New Labour government in 1997, the debates about Europe became less intense, and the press gradually recognised that the construction of the Channel Tunnel and the introduction of cheap airline flights were making the British population more outward looking and cosmopolitan. Tabloid opposition to race relations organisations receded, and the use of derogatory epithets became increasingly unusual. The *Sun* drew praise from the Commission for Racial Equality for its response to the terrorist attacks of 11 September 2001, with the paper at pains to highlight that Al-Qaeda did not represent the true face of Islam. The *Sun* condemned the twenty-first century heirs of Enoch Powell, the British National Party, denouncing them in 2004 as the 'Bloody Nasty People', a 'collection of evil, hate-filled moronic thugs.' In October 2014, meanwhile, the *Sun* devoted a front page to a picture of a young Muslim woman wearing a Union Flag headscarf in support of the 'Making a Stand' campaign against Islamic State extremism. 'We must not give way to Islamophobia,' insisted an editorial: 'Most British Muslims are proud to belong to both a nationality and a religion which value peace, tolerance and the sanctity of life.' At such moments, the crude racialised rhetoric of earlier decades seemed a distant memory.[34]

Yet if there was a greater acceptance of, and sensitivity to, Britain's diverse ethnic population, there remained many striking continuities with earlier anxieties about outsiders seeking to enter Britain. In August 2001, the United Nations High Commissioner for Refugees condemned the British tabloids for vilifying asylum seekers, noting that they 'are continually branded a problem, statistics are being twisted and negative stories are being endlessly highlighted.' Such warnings had little effect. In 2003, the *Daily Express* ran 22 front-page stories about asylum-seekers and refugees in a 31-day period, with sensational headlines such as 'Asylum War Criminals on Our Streets', and 'Asylum: Tidal Wave of Crime'. The terrorist attacks on London in July 2005 enabled the press to link refugees to violence: 'Bombers Are All Spongeing Asylum Seekers' announced the *Express* in one particularly tendentious headline. The expansion of the European Union, enabling the free movement of individuals from eastern Europe into Britain, brought a wave of hostile articles about Poles and later Romanians: 'Polish Migrants Take £1bn out of the UK Economy' claimed the *Mail* in July 2007. Tabloids accused the government of being unable to police its borders. 'Immigration: What A Mess' declared the *Mail's* front page in October 2014, as the paper argued that 'Britain's immigration shambles is rapidly getting worse'. A cartoon inside pictured a middle-aged white man feebly placing a finger in a small crack in 'Britain's Immigration Dam', as water poured in overhead, muttering 'Does anyone know another politically correct word for "swamped"?' In the first decades of the twenty-first century, just as in the first decades of the twentieth, the press portrayed Britain as an overcrowded and besieged island, whose economy and welfare systems could not withstand the strain caused by an influx of outsiders.[35]

The brief period of press positivity about the European Community in the 1970s had also long since vanished. Tony Blair's attempts to develop a more positive relationship with the Union foundered on the rock of tabloid Euroscepticism, with the *Sun* and *Mail* resolutely opposed to British entry to the euro, relentlessly suspicious of the operations of the Human Rights Act, and repeatedly scathing about the regulations governing cross-border mobility. 'Brussels' could be conveniently blamed for a range of discontents. The *Express's* accusatory headline 'Surrender to Asylum: Outrage as Blair Gives Up Our Veto on Immigration to Brussels Bureaucrats' was typical of the conflation of the different tabloid enemies. Britain's economic difficulties could also be blamed on Europe. 'Barmy EU rules cost UK firms and taxpayers £8.6billion a year', the *Sun* reported in November 2011, adding that 'slashing' the red tape would be the equivalent of producing 140,000 new jobs. The economic benefits brought by Britain's participation in the community receded further into the background.[36]

The British popular press found it difficult to adjust to Britain's changing world role. The tabloids retained a residual faith in British national greatness, insisting that Britain could be a major player on the world stage while resisting any threats to its sovereignty and keeping outsiders at bay, but by the end of the century these positions had become increasingly difficult to reconcile. There was a gradual recognition of the greater internal diversity of Britain, but a metropolitan outlook continued to dominate papers serving a multi-cultural nation with a range of devolved institutions. In a globalised media environment, moreover, appeals to the nation appeared increasingly old-fashioned, but they were so deeply ingrained in the tabloid formula that editors continued to rely on them. The opening ceremony of the London Olympics in 2012 gave a glimpse of how a modern, outward-looking form of national identity could be celebrated in popular culture, but such creativity remained rare in the tabloids. It remained easier for journalists to define the nation against external threats, just as they had done for a hundred years and more.

Conclusion: The Life and Death of the Tabloid Model

Despite the scepticism, Alfred Harmsworth had been right in January 1901: the tabloid was, indeed, the newspaper of the future. By the middle of the twentieth century, the *Daily Mirror*, which pioneered the tabloid format in Britain, had established itself as the market leader; by the end, all of its popular rivals had copied its format, language and style. If overall circulations started to decline in the final decades of the century, the *Sun* demonstrated that it was still possible for a new tabloid to rise and capture a huge readership. The tabloids also continued to wield significant political and cultural power into the 1980s and 1990s, playing a key role in supporting Thatcherism, causing endless headaches for the royal family, and setting the tone of much public conversation.

Such success could not be sustained in the changed media environment of the twenty-first century. Circulation graphs have started looking less like rolling hills and more like cliff faces. The *Sun*, still selling 3.7 million copies a day in 1998, struggled to sell 2 million in 2014. The *Daily Mirror*'s circulation, over 5 million copies in its 1960s heyday, had fallen below 1 million. Even the *Daily Mail*, which for so long bucked the trend of decline, was losing readers at a dramatic rate. The figures for the Sunday papers are even more sobering. The *News of the World*, market leader throughout the century, with the incredible sales peak of 8.44 million in 1950, declined to 2.7 million by the time of its abrupt closure in July 2011; its successor paper, the *Sun on Sunday*, sold only 1.7 million. The *Sunday Express* sold 411,000 copies, less than a tenth of its sales in 1970.[1]

The sales decline has been reinforced by a loss of reputation and influence. The drip-feed of revelations about phone-hacking, the payment of officials, and the illegal use of personal information, which culminated in the vigorous criticisms of the Leveson Report and the jailing of former *Sun* editor Andy Coulson, has severely damaged the standing of the tabloids.

Trust ratings, never high, have fallen further, and the brutal treatment of ordinary families, such as the Dowlers, who were victims of high-profile crimes, generated real shock and outrage. Politicians have been emboldened to distance themselves from, and be more critical of, major titles and their proprietors. The belief that the tabloids speak for, and represent, significant sections of the population, which had done so much to sustain their political and cultural power, is crumbling.

These problems reflect the success, rather than the failure, of the tabloid model. Other media forms – broadcasting, magazines and then the internet – took on board, and adapted themselves to, the populist priorities of the tabloid, embracing the drive for speed, brevity, accessibility, drama and controversy. Tabloid values colonised the media landscape, leaving popular newspapers less and less distinctive, and finding it difficult to match their imitators. At the same time, broader social and intellectual shifts since the 1960s have eroded class distinctions and the barriers between 'high' and 'low' culture, enabling the tabloid staples of popular entertainment, sport and celebrity to be taken up by a wider and more diverse range of media outlets. Globalisation, the liberalisation of media regulation, and the rise of international media conglomerates – exemplified by Rupert Murdoch's News Corporation – have all reinforced the trend towards providing bright, eye-catching and immediately accessible chunks of content that can be packaged and repackaged across different media forms and in different territories. By the turn of the twenty-first century, 'tabloidisation' was becoming a cliché of media commentary and academic writing.[2]

The tabloid colonisation was increasingly apparent from the 1980s. Tabloid values were increasingly imported into television as broadcasting hours were extended, channels proliferated and competition intensified. Breakfast television, launched in 1983, encouraged the adoption of a more populist, entertainment-driven, 'sofa journalism' on BBC and ITV, while the arrival of terrestrial Channels 4 and 5, satellite and cable television greatly expanded the range of news and entertainment providers, and inevitably introduced the sort of market-driven pressures that had been largely absent in the broadcasting 'duopoly' of the 1960s and 1970s. A study of ITV's *News at Ten* in 1995 revealed a 65 per cent decline in international coverage and a doubling of 'show business and entertainment' news since the late 1980s – clear evidence of the way the new commercial situation pushed news programming into tabloid territory. News producers became acutely conscious of the limited attention span of viewers. 'We live in "zapland" where the remote control is too easy to reach,' observed Steve Hewlett, the editor of BBC's flagship current affairs programme *Panorama*, in 1996: as a result, he added, it was 'absolutely incumbent upon us' to deliver material that 'people want to watch.' In 1999, ITV signalled a shift into personality-driven and human-interest focused current affairs programming by replacing the acclaimed investigative show *World in Action* with *Tonight with Trevor MacDonald*. The introduction of rolling 24-hour news channels on BBC and Sky, meanwhile, significantly reinforced the preoccupation with speed, as journalists competed with each other to provide the 'latest' on the 'breaking news'. The tabloid obsession with 'scoops' increasingly shaped the outlook of the BBC as well as its commercial rivals.[3]

With the rise of 'reality television', moreover, broadcasting pursued the traditional tabloid agenda of finding interest in the trials and tribulations of everyday life. *Changing Rooms* (1996) and *Ground Force* (1997) dwelt upon domestic issues of taste and design, while *Driving School* (1997) demonstrated the humour – and cruelty – involved in watching people struggle to master common skills. These series all highlighted the dramatic potential of providing a platform for ordinary people to star in their own televised storylines. Channel 4's *Big Brother* (2000), which allowed viewers to watch a group of housemates compete against each other in an artificially closed environment, increased the voyeuristic element and offered the prospect of sexual titillation. By the first decade of the twenty-first century, broadcasters were scrambling to find new formats to meet the seemingly insatiable demand for reality programming, with *Pop Idol*, *X-Factor*, and *The Apprentice* among the most successful shows. The tabloids themselves offered extensive coverage of all of these series, but this left them in the weakened position of commenting on, and interpreting, other media content – a role which would subsequently be undertaken more flexibly and conveniently by the internet and social media.

The tabloids also lost control of the celebrity and pin-up genres. The UK launch of *Hello!* magazine in 1988 paved the way for a flourishing celebrity magazine sector, dominated by titles such as *Ok*, *Heat* and *Closer*. These glossy, full-colour magazines not only offered greater depth and more lavish illustration, they were free of the tabloid features that alienated some female readers. On the other side of the market, 'lads' mags' such as *Loaded*, *FHM*, *Nuts* and *Zoo* provided so much naked female flesh that the *Sun's* 'Page 3 girl' was left looking decidedly old-fashioned. These magazines, in turn, were soon challenged by internet equivalents. The Drudge Report's breaking of the Monica Lewinsky scandal in 1998 offered an early indication of how online writers and bloggers would take greater risks than the print and broadcast media, and would become a rich source of revelation, accusation and commentary. The migration of endless varieties of pornography onto the internet likewise left the print and broadcast media struggling to compete in terms of sexual content. The internet could combine speed, sensation, titillation and convenience in ways that the tabloids, with their daily (or weekly) news cycle, limited space and need to remain within the bounds of mainstream respectability, could never achieve.

Elite newspapers such as *The Times*, *Guardian* and *Daily Telegraph* also adopted elements of the tabloid model. The increased pagination levels enabled by the move out of Fleet Street in the mid-1980s led to an expansion of feature content and entertainment coverage. Interviews with celebrities, popular music and television reviews, consumer advice and guidance about health and relationships became increasingly common, especially in the new tabloid sections that many broadsheets developed. Readers were often kept up-to-date with the latest scandals in columns that purported to criticise tabloid intrusiveness, although over time such alibis were no long required. The reality television star Jade Goody's problematic life and tragic death were debated as widely in the elite press as they were in the popular tabloids. Over the same period, some traditional 'heavy news' items were reduced or dropped. Detailed reporting of parliamentary debates, for example, became rare, replaced by humorous sketches written by the likes of Matthew Parris and Simon Hoggart. Most striking of all, the *Independent* and the *Times* shifted from broadsheet to tabloid size in 2003 and 2004 respectively, with the *Guardian* moving to the slightly larger 'Berliner' format in 2005. Although all three papers worked hard to maintain a more sober appearance than their popular rivals, the reduction in size encouraged a more dramatic and hard-hitting presentation of stories, especially on the front-page. The *Independent*, in particular, ran crusading front-pages reminiscent of the *Daily Mirror's* 'Shock Issues' of the 1960s.

As tabloid values colonised the mainstream media, tabloid newspapers had to work harder and harder to produce distinctive stories and features that would maintain the loyalty of their readers. The hacking of celebrities' phones, the use of private detectives to uncover personal information, the insistent surveillance of the famous, the snatching of photographs at every opportunity – all of these ultimately stemmed from the pressure in tabloid newsrooms to obtain scoops, beat competitors and stay ahead of the game. In the short term this enabled the tabloids to spring surprises and stay relevant. Many celebrities simply could not understand how journalists acquired their stories, and many innocent friends and family members were accused of leaking information. Plenty of readers were intrigued by the latest revelations, and kept coming back for more, even if they felt uncomfortable at the invasions of privacy. Yet this was a battle that the press could never win. The illegal newsgathering techniques were always likely to be exposed eventually, but even with them the newspapers could not keep outdoing the more nimble and less constrained internet providers in the race to package sex, sensation and celebrity. The intensified pursuit of gossip and salacious content damaged the trust and credibility that might have enabled to editors to find new ways of appealing to an audience. The most successful tabloid of recent decades, after all, has been the *Daily Mail*, which has thrived not by providing scoops and exclusive news, but by staying faithful to a core set of conservative beliefs and interpreting the world in a compelling way for its particular audience. The preoccupation with 'beating the opposition' has come at the expense of understanding, and building relationships with, a defined readership.

There will always be a market for news and comment delivered in the tabloid style, and a twenty-first-century Alfred Harmsworth would doubtless be looking to new technologies to find the best format for providing it. He would note with approval that the *Daily Mail* has not only adapted confidently to the changing environment with its spectacularly successful *MailOnline* website, but that its journalism still reliably generates controversy and continues to infuriate critics. The tabloid newspaper may have been the medium of the twentieth century, but its values and approaches will continue to define the twenty-first.

Notes

Introduction: The Rise of the Tabloid

1. *The World*, 1. Jan. 1901, 1; R. Pound and G. Harmsworth, *Northcliffe* (London: Cassell, 1959), 265–8.
2. L. Shepard, *The History of Street Literature* (London: David & Charles, 1973), 21.
3. W. Ong, *Orality and Literacy: The Technologizing of the Word* (London: Methuen & Co, 1982); T. Watt, *Cheap Print and Popular Piety 1550–1660* (Cambridge: Cambridge University Press, 1991); Shepard, *History of Street Literature*, 24.
4. K. Williams, *Read All About It! A History of the British Newspaper* (Abingdon: Routledge, 2010), 90–2.
5. K. Jackson, *George Newnes and the New Journalism in Britain, 1880–1910: Culture and Profit* (Aldershot: Ashgate, 2001), 13; L. Brake and M. Demoor, *Dictionary of Nineteenth-Century Journalism in Great Britain and Ireland* (Gent: Academia Press, 2009), 19–20.
6. H. Fyfe, *Northcliffe: An Intimate Biography* (London: G. Allen & Unwin, 1930), 343.
7. G. Dyer, *Advertising as Communication* (London: Methuen, 1982), 42.
8. S. Dark, *The Life of Sir Arthur Pearson* (London: Hodder & Stoughton, 1922); R. D. Blumenfeld, *The Press in my Time* (London: Rich & Cowan, 1933).
9. Eric Cheadle, 'Picture Editing' in W. W. Hadley (ed.), *The Kemsley Manual of Journalism* (London: Cassell, 1950), 79, 81; D. Griffiths, *The Encyclopedia of the British Press, 1422–1992* (London: Macmillan, 1992), 183–5, 286; H. Cudlipp, *Publish and Be Damned! The Astonishing Story of the Daily Mirror* (London: Andrew Dakers, 1953), 13.
10. H. Richards, *The Bloody Circus: The Daily Herald and the Left* (London: Pluto Press, 1997), 12; Bodleian Library, Oxford, Daily Herald Papers, X. Films 77/7, LP/DH/521, Report on Advertising, Dec. 1926.
11. Royal Commission on the Press 1947–9, *Report* (London: HMSO, 1949), Cmd. 7700, 15.

12. R. Harling, 'Newspaper Make-Up and Typography', in W. W. Hadley (ed.), *The Kemsley Book of Journalism* (London: Cassell, 1950).

13. W. Coglan, *The Readership of Newspapers and Periodicals in Great Britain, 1936* (London: ISBA, 1936), 1A; Cudlipp, *Publish and be Damned!*, 48–62; M. Edelman, *The Mirror: a Political History* (London: Hamish Hamilton, 1966), 38–41; R. Edwards, *Newspapermen: Hugh Cudlipp, Cecil Harmsworth and the Glory Days of Fleet Street* (London: Secker and Warburg, 2003).

14. Cudlipp, *Publish and be Damned!*; H. Cudlipp, *Walking on Water* (London: Bodley Head, 1976); R. Connor, *Cassandra: Reflections in a Mirror* (London: Cassell, 1969); Cardiff University, Bute Library, Hugh Cudlipp papers, HC/2/2, Hugh Cudlipp to Cecil King, 27 May 1960.

15. P. Kimble, *Newspaper Reading in the Third Year of the War* (London: George Allen and Unwin, 1942), 6; D. Butler and G. Butler, *Twentieth-Century British Political Facts 1900–2000*, 8th edn (Basingstoke: Macmillan, 2000), 538; J. Tunstall, *Newspaper Power: The New National Press in Britain* (Oxford: Clarendon Press, 1996), 13.

16. *Daily Mirror*, 30 July 1949, 1.

17. House of Lords Record Office, Beaverbrook Papers, H/227, Blackburn to Beaverbrook, 26 Mar. 1963; H/228 Blackburn to Beaverbrook, 25 Oct. 1963.

18. B. Franklin, *Newszak and News Media* (London: Hodder, 1997), 10.

19. *Sun*, 17 Nov. 1969; 22 Nov. 1969, 2; P. Chippindale and C. Horrie, *Stick It Up Your Punter! The Uncut Story of the Sun Newspaper* (revised edn, London: Pocket Books, 1999), 25–6.

20. L. Lamb, *Sunrise: The remarkable rise of the best-selling Soaraway Sun* (London: Papermac, 1989), 78–85.

21. Butler and Butler, *British Political Facts*, 536, 538.

22. *Daily Mail*, 3 May 1971, 6; Griffiths, *Encyclopedia of the British Press*, 294.

23. *UK Press Gazette*, 6 Nov. 1978, 3; *Daily Star*, 2 Nov. 1978, 1.

Chapter 1: War

1. S. J. Taylor, *The Great Outsiders: Northcliffe, Rothermere and the Daily Mail* (London: Weidenfeld & Nicolson, 1996), 143.

2. D. Edgerton, *Warfare State: Britain 1920–70* (Cambridge: Cambridge University Press, 2006).

3. K. Jones, *Fleet Street and Downing Street* (London: Hutchinson, 1920), 132, 146–7; *Daily Express*, 24 Apr. 1900, 4; House of Lords Record Office, Beaverbrook Papers, H/104, Beaverbrook to Strube, 2 May 1934; Royal Commission on the Press, *Minutes of Evidence* (London: HMSO, 1948), Day 26, Cmd. 7416, 4–5.

4. *Daily Express*, 19 May 1900, 1, 4, 6; G. Wilkinson, '"The Blessings of War": The Depiction of Military Force in Edwardian Newspapers', *Journal of Contemporary History* 33/1 (1998), 98, 101.

5. Taylor, *The Great Outsiders*, 141; S. Dark, *The Life of Sir Arthur Pearson* (London: Hodder & Stoughton, 1922), 92.

6. S. Koss, *The Rise and Fall of the Political Press, Vol. 2, The Twentieth Century* (London: Hamish Hamilton, 1984), 134.

7. *Daily Mail*, 3 Aug. 1914, 4; *Daily Express*, 5 Aug. 1914, 1; *Daily Express*, 6 Aug. 1914, 1, 4; *Daily Mirror*, 8 Aug. 1914, 5.

8. *Daily Mail*, 6 Aug. 1914, 4; *Daily Express*, 14 Aug. 1914, 4; *Daily Mail*, 8 Sep. 1914.

9. Taylor, *The Great Outsiders*, 150.

10. *Daily Chronicle*, 3 Sep. 1914, 1; J. Rose, *The Intellectual Life of the British Working Classes* (New Haven: Yale University Press, 2001), 339; M. Hampton, *Visions of the Press in Britain, 1850–1950* (Urbana: University of Illinois Press, 2004), 157.

11. R. Pound and G. Harmsworth, *Northcliffe* (London: Cassell, 1959), p. 470.

12. Taylor, *The Great Outsiders*, 157; Pound and Harmsworth, *Northcliffe*, 478.

13. Thompson, *Northcliffe*, 163; *Daily Mail*, 5 July 1915.

14. *Daily Mail*, 2 Dec. 1916, cited in Taylor, *Great Outsiders*, 178; N. Ferguson, *The Pity of War* (London: Penguin, 1999), 230.

15. Austen Chamberlain, House of Commons Debates, Vol. 103, 19 Feb. 1918, col. 656–7.

16. Taylor, *The Great Outsiders*, 176–7; *Daily Mirror*, 3 Jul. 1916, 5; *Daily Express*, 3 Jul. 1916, 1.

17. S. Hynes, S., *A War Imagined: The First World War and English Culture* (London: Bodley Head, 1990), 111, 222–3; P. Knightley, *The First Casualty* (London: Pan Books, 1989), 109.

18. *Daily Express*, 11 Nov. 1918, 4; *Daily Mail*, 2 Dec. 1918, 4; Thompson, *Northcliffe*, 325–6.

19. *Daily Express*, 11 Nov. 1918, 4; 3 May 1919, 1; 12 Nov. 1918, 2; 8 May 1919, 4; 12 Nov. 1924, 8.

20. *Daily Herald*, 11 Nov. 1919, 1; 9 May 1919, 4; 8 May 1919, 1; 17 May 1919; *Daily News*, 1 Nov. 1922, 4.

21. Beaverbrook Papers, H/64, Russell to Whelan, 8 Sep. 1929; Russell to Beaverbrook, 14 Sep. 1929.

22. *Daily Express*, 11 Feb. 1932, 8; 21 Oct. 1933, 10; 24 Oct. 1933, 9; *Daily Mirror*, 12 Jun. 1934, 13; *Parliamentary Debates*, 378 H. C. Deb, 5th ser., 26 Mar. 1942, col. 2300.

23. P. Addison, 'Lord Rothermere and British Foreign Policy', in C. Cook and G. Peele (eds), *The Politics of Reappraisal* (London: Macmillan, 1975), 200–1; Taylor, *The Great Outsiders*, 309.

24. *Daily Mirror*, 9 Mar. 1936, 13.

25. *Daily Express*, 22 Aug. 1939, 8; R. Cockett, *Twilight of Truth: Chamberlain, Appeasement and the Manipulation of the Press* (London: Weidenfeld & Nicolson, 1989); Koss, *Rise and Fall*, 546.

26. *Daily Mirror*, 24 Sep. 1938, 13; 30 Aug. 1939, 16; S. Rose, *Which People's War? National Identity and Citizenship in Britain, 1939–1945* (Oxford: Oxford University Press, 2003), ch. 5.

27. *Daily Mirror*, 28 Aug. 1939, 1; *Daily Express*, 4 Sep. 1939, 6; A. C. H. Smith, with E. Immirizi and T. Blackwell, *Paper Voices: The Popular Press and Social Change 1935–65* (London: Chatto and Windus, 1975), 64.

28. Mass-Observation File Report 1173, Mar. 1942, p. 1.

29. *Daily Mirror*, 1 June 1940, 3–7; 3 June 1940.

30. *Daily Mirror*, 5 June 1940; *Daily Mail*, 31 Dec. 1940, 1.

31. Mark Connelly, 'The British People, the Press and the Strategic Air Campaign against Germany, 1939–45', *Contemporary British History* 16/2 (2002), 39–58.

32. *Daily Express*, 27 Mar. 1942, 2; *Daily Mirror*, 4–5 June 1941, cited in Smith, *Paper Voices*, 67–9.

33. Smith, *Paper Voices*, 95–6; 378 H. C. Deb 5s., Freedom of the Press, 26 Mar. 1942, col. 2288; *Daily Mirror*, 2 Sept. 1941, 2.

34. H. Cudlipp, *Publish and be Damned! The Astonishing Story of the Daily Mirror* (London: Andrew Dakers, 1953), 142–98; Mass-Observation File Report, 1197, Apr. 1942, p. 2.

35. *Daily Express*, 7 June 1944, 2; *Daily Mirror*, 14 June 1944, cited in Smith, *Paper Voices*, 75–6.

36. *Sunday Pictorial*, 11 July 1943, 1, 4; *Daily Express*, 28 Apr. 1945, 3; 30 Apr. 1945, 3; *Daily Mirror*, 20 Apr. 1945, 2, all cited in David Patrick, 'Framing Disinterest: Anglo-American Press Responses to The Holocaust, Bosnia and Rwanda', unpublished PhD thesis (University of Sheffield, 2013).

37. *Daily Express*, 7 Aug. 1945, 1, 4; 5 Sep. 1945, 1.

38. *Daily Express*, 11 Aug. 1945, 2; 2 Aug. 1950, 4; 4 Oct. 1952, 1; *Daily Mirror*, 4 Oct. 1952, 1.

39. *Daily Express* 15 Oct. 1953, 4; 28 Mar. 1953, 1, 4; 27 Aug. 1956, 4.

40. *Daily Mail*, 27 July 1956, 1, cited in R. Greenslade, *Press Gang: How Newspapers Make Profits from Propaganda* (London: Macmillan, 2003), 132; L. Anderson, 'Get out and push!', in T. Maschler (ed.), *Declaration* (London: MacGibbon & Kee, 1957), 156–7.

41. *Daily Mirror*, 10 Aug. 1956, 2; 11 Sep. 1956, 1; 1 Nov. 1956, 1–2; see J. Tulloch, 'Tabloid Citizenship: The *Daily Mirror* and the invasions of Egypt (1956) and Iraq (2003)', *Journalism Studies* 8/1 (2007).

42. H. Cudlipp, *Walking on Water* (London: Bodley Head, 1976), 230; *Daily Express*, 10 Dec. 1962, 6; *Daily Mirror*, 18 Dec. 1964, 1.

43. *Sun*, 5 April 1982, 6; 6 April 1982, 6; *Daily Mirror*, 5 Apr. 2, 10; R. Harris, *Gotcha! The Media, the Government and the Falklands Crisis* (London: Faber and Faber, 1983), 40, 51.

44. Harris, *Gotcha*, 36, 46–8.

45. *Daily Express*, 15 Jun. 1982, 1–6; *Sun*, 16 Jun. 1982, 14–16; *Daily Mirror*, 16 Jun. 1982, 3.

46. *Sun*, 14 Jan. 1991, 4–5; 15 Jan. 1991, 2–3; 16 Jan. 1991, 1, 6; 17 Jan. 1991, 2; 18 Jan. 1991, 24–5; 19 Jan. 1991, 2–3; *Daily Mirror*, 15 Jan. 1991, 4; 18 Jan. 1991, 19.

47. *Sun*, 12 Sep. 2001, 1; *News of the World*, 16 Sep. 2001, 1.

48. Tulloch, 'Tabloid Citizenship'.

49. *Sun on Sunday*, 26 Feb. 2012, 12; *Sun*, 28 Aug. 2013, 1.

Chapter 2: Politics

1. S. J. Taylor, *The Great Outsiders: Northcliffe, Rothermere and the Daily Mail* (London: Weidenfeld & Nicolson, 1996), 32.

2. L. Lamb, *Sunrise: The Remarkable Rise of the Best-Selling Soaraway Sun* (London: Papermac, 1989), 154.

3. K. Jones, *Fleet Street and Downing Street* (London: Hutchinson, 1920), 145; British Library, Northcliffe Papers, Add MSS 62201, Northcliffe to W. G. Fish, 21 Nov. 1910; House of Lords Record Office, Beaverbrook Papers, H/81 Beaverbook to Baxter, 28 Mar. 1931; A. Christiansen, *Headlines All My Life* (London: Heinemann, 1961), 2–3, 147.

4. R. Edwards, *Newspapermen: Hugh Cudlipp, Cecil Harmsworth King and the Glory Days of Fleet Street* (London: Secker and Warburg, 2003), 225.

5. *Daily Mirror*, 21 Nov. 1923, 15; *Daily Express*, 29 Oct. 1924.

6. H. Cudlipp, *Publish and Be Damned! The Astonishing Story of the Daily Mirror* (London: Andrew Dakers, 1953), 81.

7. *Daily Mail*, 1 Oct. 1903, 5; 26 Dec. 1903, 5; *Daily Mirror*, 10 Apr. 1929, 2.

8. *Daily Mail*, 23 Dec. 1905; 4 Nov. 1909, 6; 22 Nov. 1906, 6; J. Lee Thompson, *Northcliffe, Press Baron in Politics 1865–1922* (London: John Murray, 2000), 180.

9. *Daily Mail* 17 Jan. 1906, 6; J. Thomas, *Popular Newspapers, the Labour Party and British Politics* (Abingdon: Routledge, 2005), 8.

10. *Daily Mail*, 6 Mar. 1912, 4; M. Pugh, *The March of the Women: A Revisionist Analysis of the Campaign for Women's Suffrage 1866–1914* (Oxford: Oxford University Press, 2000), 229–31; G. Lansbury, *The Miracle of Fleet Street: The Story of the Daily Herald* (London: Labour Publishing, 1925), 75–7.

11. R. Pound and G. Harmsworth, *Northcliffe* (London: Cassell, 1959), 517–18; *Daily Mail*, 26 Nov. 1918, 2.

12. Thomas, *Popular Newspapers*, 8; *Daily Mail*, 11 Oct. 1924, 9.

13. *Daily Mail*, 25 Oct. 1924, 9; *Daily Express*, 29 Oct. 1924, 6; Thomas, *Popular Newspapers*, 10.

14. *Daily Mail*, 2 May 1927, 10; 28 Mar. 1928, 10; 9 June 1931, 10; 14 Jul. 1931, 10; 1 Feb. 1932, 10.

15. *Daily Mail*, 15 Jan. 1934, 10; 14 Jul. 1934; M. Pugh, 'The British Union of Fascists and the Olympia Debate', *Historical Journal*, 41/2 (1998), 529–42.

16. A. Chisholm and M. Davie, *Beaverbrook: A Life* (London: Hutchinson, 1992), chs 14–15.

17. H. Richards, *The Bloody Circus: The Daily Herald and the Left* (London: Pluto Press, 1997).

18. F. Williams, *Dangerous Estate: The Anatomy of Newspapers* (first pub. 1957; London: Longmans Green, 1958), 198.

19. Royal Commission on the Press 1947–49, *Report* (London: HMSO, 1949), Cmd. 7700, Appendix VII, Table 4, 250; Table 14, 257–8.

20. *Daily Mirror*, 9 Feb. 1937, 12; 1 Mar. 1939, 14.

21. *Daily Mirror*, 3 Jul. 1945, 2; 5 Jul. 1945, 1; M. Pugh, 'The *Daily Mirror* and the Revival of Labour 1935–45', *Twentieth Century British History*, 9/3 (1998), 420–38.

22. *Daily Express*, 5 Jun. 1945, 1; 6 Jun. 1945, 1.

23. Beaverbrook paper H/114 LA Plummer to Robertson, 13 Jun. 1945; H/141 Arthur Christiansen to Beaverbrook, 27 Jan. 1950.

24. *Daily Express*, 19 Jan. 1950, 4.

25. Thomas, *Popular Newspapers*, 32; *Daily Mirror*, 25 Oct. 1951, 1; R. Greenslade, *Press Gang: How Newspapers Make Profits from Propaganda* (London: Macmillan, 2003), 84–5.

26. *Daily Mail*, 15 Oct. 1964, cited in Thomas, *Popular Newspapers*, 54.

27. *Daily Mirror*, 12 Oct. 1964, 16–17; 10 May 1968, 1; Greenslade, *Press Gang*, 208–11.

28. *Daily Express*, 8 Feb. 1974, 8; C. Seymour-Ure, 'The Press', in D. Butler and D. Kavanagh, *The British General Election of February 1974* (London: Macmillan, 1974), 174–5; C. Seymour-Ure, 'Fleet Street', in D. Butler and D. Kavanagh, *The British General Election of October 1974* (London: Macmillan, 1975), 164–74.

29. *Sun*, 11 Jan. 1979, 1; Thomas, *Popular Newspapers*, 79, 81; *Daily Express*, 8 Feb. 1979.

30. M. Bilton and S. Himelfarb, 'Fleet Street' in D. Butler and D. Kavanagh, *The British General Election of 1979* (London: Macmillan, 1980), 241–5; *Daily Mail*, 26 Apr. 1979, 1; *Sun*, 3 May 1979; Thomas, *Popular Newspapers*, 85.

31. C. Moore, *Margaret Thatcher, The Authorized Biography, Vol. 1: Not For Turning* (London: Penguin, 2013), 440.

32. L. Price, *Where Power Lies: Prime Ministers v The Media* (London: Simon and Schuster, 2010), 247; Greenslade, *Press Gang*, 452.

33. *Sun*, 1 Jun. 1987; Thomas, *Popular Newspapers*, 103.

34. Thomas, *Popular Newspapers*, 99; *Sun*, 9 Apr. 1992, 1; M. Scammell and M. Harrop, 'The Press', in D. Butler and D. Kavanagh, *The British General Election of 1997* (London: Macmillan, 1997), 156.

35. M. Scammell and M. Harrop, 'The Press', in D. Butler and D. Kavanagh, *The British General Election of 1997* (Basingstoke: Macmillan, 1997), 156–74; Thomas, *Popular Newspapers*, 130–1.

36. *Daily Express*, 7 June 2001, 1.

37. M. Scammell and C. Beckett, 'The Press', in D. Kavanagh and P. Cowley, The British General Election of 2010 (Basingstoke: Macmillan, 2010), 280–6.

38. *Daily Star*, 7 Jun. 2001, 1, 6; 6 May 2005, 1, 6 May 2010, 1.

Chapter 3: Monarchy and Celebrity

1. Bodleian Library, Oxford, MS.Eng.hist d.303–5, Northcliffe Bulletins, 13 Nov. 1919; British Library, Northcliffe Papers, Add MSS 62234, Northcliffe to Alexander Kenealy, 'The Ten Commandments', undated; Add MSS 62199, Memo to Marlowe 26 Dec. 1918.

2. D. Cannadine, 'The Context, Performance and Meaning of Ritual: The British Monarchy and the "Invention of Tradition", c. 1820–1977' in E. Hobsbawm and

T. Ranger (eds), *The Invention of Tradition* (Cambridge: Cambridge University Press, 1983).

3. *Daily Mail*, 23 Jun. 1897, cited in J. Thompson, *Northcliffe: Press Baron in Politics 1865–1922* (London: John Murray, 2000), 43; S. J. Taylor, *The Great Outsiders: Northcliffe, Rothermere and The Daily Mail* (London: Weidenfeld & Nicolson, 1996), 45.

4. *Daily Mirror*, 16 May 1910, 1; D. and E. Seymour (eds), *A Century of News: A Journey Through History with the Daily Mirror* (London: Contender Books, 2003), 15–16.

5. *Daily Mail*, 26 Apr. 1923, 6; House of Lords Record Office, H/ 82, Beaverbrook Papers, Beaverbrook to Baxter, 12 Dec. 1931; *Daily Mirror*, 22 Apr. 1926, 9.

6. B. Pimlott, *The Queen: A Biography of Elizabeth II* (London: Harper Collins, 1996), 34; The National Archives, PREM 1/446, Constitutional Crisis – Attitude of the British press [unsigned memo], Dec. 1936.

7. A. Chisholm and M. Davie, *Beaverbrook: A Life* (London: Hutchinson, 1992), 336–8; PREM 1/446, H. A. Gwynne to Baldwin, 12 Nov. 1936.

8. H. Cudlipp, *Publish and be Damned! The Astonishing Story of the Daily Mirror* (London: Andrew Dakers, 1953), 92; *Daily Mirror*, 5 Dec. 1936, 1, 6–7; S. Williams, *The People's King: the True Story of the Abdication* (2003).

9. *Daily Express*, 11 Dec. 1936, 12.

10. M-O, File Report 375 'The Popular Press?', *Horizon* Aug. 1940, 169.

11. H. Fyfe, *Northcliffe: An Intimate Biography* (London: G. Allen & Unwin, 1930), 93; R. McKibbin, *Classes and Cultures* (Oxford: Oxford University Press, 1998), 34; R. Wilkes, *Scandal: A Scurrilous History of Gossip* (London: Atlantic Books, 2003), 3.

12. *Daily Herald*, 17 June 1925; 25 March 1925, 4; 24 Mar. 1925, 4; P. Balfour, *Society Racket: A Critical Survey of Modern Social Life* (London: John Long Ltd., 1933), 92.

13. Beaverbrook Papers, H/97, Beaverbrook to Robertson, 13 Jun. 1932; Balfour, *Society Racket*, 97–8; S. Somerfield, *Banner Headlines* (Shoreham-by-Sea: Scan Books, 1979), 64; J. Junor, *Memoirs: Listening for a Midnight Tram* (London: Chapmans, 1990), 62–3.

14. Northcliffe Papers, Add. MS 62200, Northcliffe to Marlowe, 6 Jul. 1919; Northcliffe to Marlowe, 17 Sep. 1919.

15. *Daily Mail*, 24 Aug. 1926, 10; *Daily Express*, 11 May 1931, 9; 21 Oct. 1931, 1; 17 Aug. 1939, 3.

16. *Daily Mail*, 7 May 1935, 23; *Daily Mirror*, 27 Feb. 1927, 4; 22 Apr. 1926, 8; *Daily Express*, 13 Nov. 1935, 3.

17. *Daily Herald*, 23 Feb. 1923.

18. *Daily Express*, 18 Nov. 1935, 1; R. C. K. Ensor, 'The Press', in Sir Ernest Barker (ed.) *The Character of England* (Oxford: Clarendon Press, 1947), 419; Royal Commission on the Press 1947–9, *Report* (London: HMSO, 1949), Cmd. 7700, 131.

19. *Sunday Pictorial*, 2 Feb. 1947, 7.

20. H. Cudlipp, *Walking on Water* (London: Bodley Head, 1976), 180.

21. *Sunday Pictorial*, 5 Jan. 1947, 1; 19 Jan. 1947, 1, 3, 7; Beaverbrook papers, H/120, Arthur Christiansen to Beaverbrook, 17 Jan. 1947.

22. *Daily Mail*, 9 Jul. 1947, 1; 10 Jul. 1947, 1; *People*, 21 Mar. 1948, 1; 6 Jun. 1948, 1; Beaverbrook Papers, H/152, John Gordon to Beaverbrook, 14 Feb. 1952; H/155 Arthur Christiansen to Beaverbrook, 21 Feb. 1952; Pimlott, *The Queen*, 165.

23. *The People*, 14 Jun. 1953, 1; 12 Jul. 1953, 1; *Daily Mirror*, 3 Jul. 1953, 1, 10 Jul. 1953, 17 Jul. 1953, 1; *Tribune*, 10 Jul. 1953; *Daily Mirror*, National Archives, PREM 11/524 (Press Speculation about Princess Margaret), JRC, Note, 16 Jul. 1953.

24. *Daily Mirror*, 21 Jul. 1953, 1; Press Council, *Press and the People: First Annual Report* (London: Press Council, 1954), 22; *The Times*, 24 Jul. 1953, 9.

25. *Daily Mirror*, 19 Aug. 1955, 1, 27 Aug. 1955, 1; Press Council, *The Press and the People: Third Annual Report* (London: Press Council, 1956), 24.

26. T. Aronson, *Princess Margaret: A Biography* (London: Michael O'Mara, 1997), 142; *Daily Herald* Archives from TUC archive, Modern Record Centre, Warwick, MSS.292/790.3/5 Complaints 1956–63, HT Buckle to Chairman, TUC, 24 May 1957; *Daily Mirror*, 26 Oct. 1955, 1, 4 Nov. 1955, 6; 5 Nov. 1955, 2.

27. M. Muggeridge, 'Royal Soap Opera', *New Statesman*, 22 Oct.1955, 499–500; *Daily Sketch*, 10 Oct. 1956; Press Council, *Press and the People: Fourth Annual Report* (London: Press Council, 1957), 22; *Daily Mirror*, 11 Feb. 1957, 1.

28. H. Cudlipp, *At Your Peril* (London: Weidenfeld and Nicolson, 1962), 91–5; *Daily Mirror*, 3 Aug. 1957, 1; 21 Aug. 1957, 1; 17 Oct. 1957, 1; *The Times*, 21 Mar. 1962, 5; Beaverbrook Papers, H/223, Blackburn to Beaverbrook, 23 Mar. 1962.

29. S. Bernstein, *Mr. Confidential: The Man, the Magazine & the Movieland Massacre* (New York, Walford Press, 2006).

30. Beaverbrook Papers, H/259, Elland to Beaverbrook, 3 Jul. 1956; Elland to Beaverbrook, 30 Nov. 1956; H/185, Christiansen to Beaverbrook, 24 Jul. 1956; H/198, Harold Keeble to Beaverbrook, 21 Aug. 1958; H/208, Max Aitken to Beaverbrook, 9 Nov. 1960.

31. *People*, 25 Oct. 1959, 2–3; 15 Nov. 1959, 4; 22 Nov. 1959, 2–3; Cudlipp, *At Your Peril*, 294–5.

32. Somerfield, *Banner Headlines*, 111, 115; News of the World Archive, EDF/ 61, 61/1 Christopher Shaw, Director of London International Press Ltd, to Acting Editor of NotW, 16 Jan. 1960; *News of the World*, 17 Jan. 1960, 1; 24 Jan. 1960,

1, 4–5; 31 Jan. 1960, 4–5; 7 Feb. 1960, 4–5; 14 Feb. 1960, 4–5; *Sunday Pictorial*, 24 Jan.–21 Feb. 1960.

33. Press Council, *The Press and the People: Seventh Annual Report* (London: Press Council, 1960), 31–2; *The Press and the People: Eleventh Annual Report* (London: Press Council, 1964), 19–20; News of the World Archive, EDF/27; EDF/145/2 CJ Lear, Features Editor, to Christopher Shaw, London International Press, 11 Nov. 1960.

34. *Sun*, 17 Nov. 1969, 1; 8 Jan. 1973, 1; 22 Jan. 1973, 7.

35. *News of the World*, 22 Feb. 1976, 1; J. Rook, *Rooks Eye View: The First Lady of Fleet Street Tells the Story Behind the Stories* (London: Express Books, 1979) 9–10.

36. *Sun*, 1 Mar. 1978, 1; 5 Apr. 1978, 1; 7 Apr. 1978, 6; *Daily Star*, 6 Nov. 1978, 1, 15–17.

37. *Daily Express*, 17 Jun. 1977, 1; *Daily Mail*, 18 Jun. 1977, 1; *Sun*, 8 Sep. 1980, 1; 18 Sep. 1980, 1; *Sunday Mirror*, 23 Nov. 1980, 1; R. Greenslade, *Press Gang: How Newspapers Make Profits from Propaganda* (London: Macmillan, 2003), 353–7.

38. *Daily Express*, 28 Jul. 1981, 8; 30 Jul. 1981, 1; *Daily Mirror*, 17 Jun. 1982, 2; *Sun* 18 Feb. 1982, 1; *Star* 18 Feb. 1982, 1; Chippindale and Horrie, 123–5.

39. *Sunday Mirror*, 21 Oct. 1990, 1; 20 Aug. 1992, 1; *Sun*, 23 Dec. 1992, 1.

40. *Sun*, 1 Sep. 1997, 10; 4 Sep. 1997; 8 Sep. 1997, 8.

41. *Sun*, 26 May 1999, 1.

42. *Guardian*, 14 May 2014.

43. Greenslade, *Press Gang*, 499.

44. Greenslade, *Press Gang*, 506, 509–10, 534.

45. Charlotte Church, Evidence to Leveson enquiry, Monday 28 Nov. 2011, <http://webarchive.nationalarchives.gov.uk/20140122145147/http:/www.levesoninquiry.org.uk/>.

46. Lord Shawcross, 'Curbs on the Rights of Disclosure', *The Press and the People – The Tenth Annual Report of the Press Council* (London: Press Council, 1963), 10.

Chapter 4:   Gender and Sexuality

1. *Daily Mail*, 4 May 1896, 7.

2. *Daily Mail*, 4 May 1896, 7.

3. N. Angell, *After All: The Autobiography of Norman Angell* (London: Hamish Hamilton, 1951), 120–1; Bodleian Library. Oxford, MS Eng.hist.d. 303–5,

Northcliffe Bulletins, 11 May 1920; T. Clarke, *My Northcliffe Diary* (London: Hutchinson, 1931), 279.

4. Clarke, *Diary*, 136, 197; Northcliffe Bulletins, 10 Apr. 1916, 1 Jul. 1918, 27 Apr. 1921.

5. K. Jones, *Fleet Street and Downing Street* (London: Hutchinson, 1920), 227; *Daily Mirror*, 2 Nov. 1903, 3; H. Cudlipp, *Publish and Be Damned! The astonishing story of the Daily Mirror* (London: Andrew Dakers, 1953), 122.

6. Jones, Fleet Street, 232; T. Clarke, *Northcliffe in History: An Intimate Study of Press Power* (London: Hutchinson, 1950), 23.

7. H. Fyfe, *Northcliffe: An Intimate Biography* (London: G. Allen & Unwin, 1930), 94; British Library, Northcliffe Papers, Add MS 62234, Northcliffe to Kenealy, 20 Nov. [1912?].

8. Clarke, *My Northcliffe Diary*, 246; Northcliffe Bulletins, 1 Aug. 1920; 5 Aug. 1920; 23 Jul. 1920; Northcliffe papers, Add MSS 62229, Northcliffe to Falk, [undated, mid-1921].

9. *Manchester Guardian*, 13 Nov. 1925, cited in *The Guardian Century: The Twenties* (London: The Guardian, 1999), 5; *Daily Mail*, 14 Aug. 1920, 3; Clarke, *Northcliffe Diary*, 162–3.

10. Clarke, *Northcliffe Diary*, 163; S. Moseley, *Short Story Writing and Freelance Journalism* (London: Pitman, 1926), 96.

11. *Daily Mirror*, 3 Dec. 1935, 7; Cudlipp, *Publish and Be Damned!*, 84–5; A. Temple, *Good or Bad – It's Life* (London: Nicholson & Watson, 1944), ch. 1, quotation 7.

12. Temple, *Good or Bad*, 5; Press Council, *The Press and People: 23rd Annual Report of the Press Council, 1976* (London: Press Council, 1977), 100; Claire Rayner, *How Did I Get Here From There?* (London: Virago, 2003), 359; Michael Bromley, '"Watching the Watchdogs"? The Role of Readers' Letters in Calling the Press to Account', in Hugh Stephenson and Michael Bromley (eds), *Sex, Lies and Democracy: The Press and the Public* (London: Longman, 1998), 151; Larry Lamb, *Sunrise: The remarkable rise of the best-selling Soaraway Sun* (London: Papermac, 1989), 183.

13. *Daily Mirror*, 16 Jul. 1938, 20; Temple, *Good or Bad*, 99.

14. *Daily Mirror*, 16 Jul. 1938, 20; 7 Sept. 1938, 22; Temple, *Good or Bad*, 83, 99; *Daily Mirror*, 10 Aug. 1943, 3.

15. Mass-Observation File Report 1573, 'Public Attitudes to VD', Jan. 1943, 1–2, further notes, 3; M-O File Report 1599, 'The Public and VD', Feb. 1943, 2–3; The National Archives, Kew, RG/23/38, Wartime Social Survey Inquiry 18 Mar. to 17 Apr. 1943.

16. Liz Stanley, *Sex Surveyed: From Mass Observation's 'Little Kinsey' to the National Survey and the Hite Reports* (London, 1995), 3–4; *Sunday Pictorial*, 3 Jul. 1949,

6–7; A. Bingham, *Family Newspapers? Sex, Private Life and the Popular Press, 1918–78* (Oxford: Oxford University Press, 2009), ch. 3.

17. *Daily Mirror*, 20 Aug. 1953, 9.
18. *Daily Mirror*, 29 May 1951, 4; *News of the World*, 27 Nov. 1955, 6.
19. *Sunday Mirror*, 14 Apr. 1963, 13; 7 July 1963, 13.
20. *Daily Mirror*, 20 Jul. 1966, 24; Angela Patmore, *Marje: The Guilt and the Gingerbread: The Authorized Biography* (London: Warner, 1993), 180, 252.
21. Moira Peelo and Keith Soothill, 'Personal Power and Public Control: Sex Crimes and Problem Pages', *Howard Journal of Criminal Justice* 33/1 (1994), 10–24'; *Daily Mirror*, 8 Dec. 1960, 13; 26 Nov. 1964; *Sunday Mirror* 2 Feb. 1964; 14 July 1964; Patmore, *Marje*, 230.
22. R. Loncraine, 'Bosom of the Nation: Page Three in the 1970s and 1980s', in M. Gorji (ed.), *Rude Britannia* (Abingdon: Routledge, 2007), 104; *Daily Mirror*, 8 Nov. 1935, 19; 11 Nov. 1935, 9; *Sunday Pictorial*, 17 Apr. 1938, 19; H. Cudlipp, *At Your Peril!* (London: Weidenfeld and Nicolson, 1962), 47–8; H Cudlipp, 'Exclusive: the first nude in Fleet Street', *British Journalism Review*, 5/3, 1994, 17–19; Daily Mirror Newspapers, *Jane at War* (London: Wolfe, 1976); A. Saunders, *Jane: A Pin-up at war* (Barnsley: Leo Cooper, 2004).
23. *Daily Sketch*, 23 Jun. 1938, 2, 29; *Daily Telegraph*, 23 Jun. 1938, 21; Mass-Observation File Report A11, 'Motives and Methods of Newspaper Reading', Dec. 1938, 36.
24. R. Davenport-Hines, *An English Affair: Sex, Class and Power in the Age of Profumo* (London: Harper Press, 2013), 128–31; *Daily Mirror*, 2 Feb. 1957, 1; 15 Feb. 1957, 1; *Daily Mail*, 24 Sep. 1957, 7.
25. *Daily Mirror*, 12 Nov. 1956, 9; 13 Sep. 1957, 11; 17 Sep. 1957, 19; 1 Oct. 1957, 11.
26. R. Greenslade, *Press Gang: How Newspapers Make Profits from Propaganda* (London: Macmillan, 2003), 59; *Daily Mirror*, 12 Sep. 1957, 9; News of the World Archive, CIR/7/1, Report on the Irish Edition, 10 Sep. 1961; C. Bainbridge and R. Stockdill, *The News of the World Story: 150 Years of the World's Bestselling Newspaper* (London: HarperCollins, 1993), 213.
27. M. Houlbrook, *Queer London: Perils and Pleasures in the Sexual Metropolis* (Chicago: University of Chicago Press, 2005), 222.
28. *Sunday Express*, 19 Aug. 1928, 10.
29. *Sunday Pictorial*, 11 May 1952, 1; 18 May 1952, 3; 25 May 1952, 6.
30. *Sunday Express*, 25 Oct. 1953, 6; P. Higgins, *Heterosexual Dictatorship: Male Homosexuality in Postwar Britain* (London: Fourth Estate, 1996), 214; 'John Alcock', quoted in S. Jeffery-Poulter, *Peers, Queers and Commons: The Struggle for Gay Law Reform from 1950 to the Present* (London: Routledge, 1991), 23–4.

31. *Daily Express*, 12 Jul. 1967, 6; Jeffery-Poulter, *Peers, Queers and Commons*, 80–1; R. Davidson and G. Davis, '"A Field for Private Members": The Wolfenden Committee and Scottish Homosexual Law Reform, 1950–67', *Twentieth Century British History* 15/2 (2004), 174–201.
32. *Daily Mirror*, 26 Sep. 1956; *Sunday Mirror*, 28 Apr. 1963, 7.
33. D. Smith, *Sex, Lies and Politics: Gay Politicians in the Press* (Eastbourne: Sussex Academic Press, 76–8, 84–90; J. Rook, *Rook Eye's View* (London: 1979), 131–3.
34. *Sun*, 12 Dec. 1986; 14 May 1990; Smith, *Sex, Lies and Politics*, 68, 118.
35. Smith, *Sex, Lies and Politics*, chs 8–9.
36. *Sun*, 17 Nov. 1969, 23–6, 33; 18 Nov. 1969, 2; *Sun*, 20 Nov. 1969, 1. 22 Nov. 1969, 2; 30 Dec. 1969, 9; 6 Oct. 1970, 12.
37. *Sun*, 7–14 Oct. 1970; 15 Jan. 1973, 14–15; 23 Jan. 1973, 16–17.
38. *Sun*, 17 Nov. 1970, 1–3; Lamb, *Sunrise*, 115.
39. P. Holland, 'The Page Three Girl Speaks to Women, too: A Sun-Sational Survey', *Screen* 24/ 3 (1983), 84–102; Lamb, *Sunrise*, 111; Loncraine, 'Bosom of the nation', 102; *Daily Mirror*, 29 Dec. 1975, 1, 31 Dec. 1975, 12.
40. P. Chippindale and C. Horrie, *Stick it up your Punter: The Uncut Story of the Sun Newspaper* (London: Simon & Schuster, 1999), 83.
41. Lamb, *Sunrise*, 110; Chippindale and Horrie, *Stick it Up your Punter!*, 109; Rayner, *How did I get Here*, 397.
42. *Sun*, 17 Nov. 1969, 14; Lamb, *Sunrise*, 56.
43. S. J. Taylor, *The Reluctant Press Lord: Esmond Rothermere and the Daily Mail* (London: Weidenfeld and Nicholson, 1998), 211.
44. *Daily Mirror*, 21 Jul. 1981, 9.
45. *Daily Express*, 29 Apr., 3 May 1972.
46. *Daily Mirror*, 21 Nov. 1970, 1; *Sunday Express*, 22 Nov. 1970; K. Mendes, *Feminism in the News: Representations of the Women's Movement since the 1960s* (Basingstoke: Palgrave Macmillan, 2011), 154.
47. *Daily Mail*, 5 Mar. 2003, 24; 16 Jul. 2014; *News of the World*, 30 May 2004, 3.

Chapter 5: Class

1. R. Greenslade, *Press Gang: How Newspapers Make Profits from Propaganda* (London: Macmillan, 2003), 123.

2. Note this survey counted readership rather than purchase of newspapers: Institute of Practitioners in Advertising, *National Readership Survey* (London: IPA, 1956), 81.

3. *Daily Mail*, 4 May 1896, 4.

4. *Daily Mail*, 4 May 1896, 4, 7.

5. T. Clarke, *My Northcliffe Diary* (London: Victor Gollancz, 1931), 201; British Library, Northcliffe Papers, Add MSS 62192, Northcliffe to Burton 11 Nov. 1912.

6. Northcliffe Papers, Add MSS 62234, Northcliffe to Kenealy 11 Mar. 1911; Add MSS 62199 Northcliffe to Marlowe 20 Jan. 1914; Add MSS 62206 Northcliffe to Macleod 14 Feb. 1921; Bodleian Library, Oxford, Northcliffe Bulletins, 30 July 1920.

7. *Daily Express*, 18 Jun. 1900.

8. *Daily Mirror*, 25 Jan. 1904 7; 20 Jun. 1904, 6; 5 Feb. 1904, 3

9. *Daily Mirror*, 11 Aug. 1904, 4.

10. H. Richards, *The Bloody Circus: The Daily Herald and the Left* (London: Pluto Press, 1997), 16–17; *Daily Herald*, 1 Nov. 1912; 15. Nov. 1912, 16 Nov. 1912.

11. T. Jeffery and K. McClelland, 'A World fit to Live in: the *Daily Mail* and the Middle Classes 1918–39', in J. Curran, A. Smith and P. Wingate (eds), *Impacts and influences: Essays on Media Power in the Twentieth Century* (London: Methuen, 1987), 42–3; Northcliffe Bulletins, 18 Oct. 1919.

12. K. Morgan, *Consensus and Disunity: The Lloyd George Coalition Government 1918–1922* (Oxford: Oxford University Press, 1986), 244–6; R. McKibbin, *Parties and People: England 1914–51* (Oxford: Oxford University Press), 48–9.

13. *Daily Mail*, 3 May 1927, 16.

14. *Daily Mirror*, 3 May 3 1926, 7; 11 May 1926, 2.

15. George Orwell, *Road to Wigan Pier* (Harmondsworth: Penguin, 1978), 116–17.

16. Bodleian Library, Oxford, X. Films 77/6, Daily Herald Archives, LP/DH/490, Advertisement Manager to General Manager, 20 Jan. 1926, 6; *Daily Herald*, 17 Mar. 1930, 7; 8 Apr. 1930, 1.

17. *Daily Herald*, 17 Mar. 1930, 7; 8 Apr. 1930, 1; 5 Aug. 1931, 5; 13 Nov. 1935, 5; Modern Record Centre, University of Warwick, Daily Herald Archives, MSS.292/790.3/2, Pankhurst to Citrine, 6 Apr. 1936; Thomas Ashurst, Feb. 1937.

18. *Daily Herald*, 24 Aug. 1931, 8; 27 Oct. 1931, 1.

19. Mass-Observation File Report A11, Motives and Methods of Newspaper Reading, Dec. 1938, 13.

20. A. Christiansen, *Headlines all my life* (London: Heinemann, 1961), xi, 48; Beaverbrook Papers, C/285b, Rothermere to Beaverbrook, 14 July 1933; H/82 Beaverbrook to Baxter, 30 May 1931; H/103 Beaverbrook to Peter Aitken 24 Apr. 1934.

21. *Daily Mirror*, 5 Dec. 1936, 13; 1 June 1938, cited in A. C. H. Smith, *Paper Voices: The Popular Press and Social Change 1935–65* (London: Chatto & Windus, 1975), 94.

22. *Daily Mirror*, 17 Feb. 1939, 12; 9 Sep. 1938, 15; 10 Apr. 1939, 11.

23. *Daily Mirror*, 9 Dec. 1936, 12; N. J. Crowson (ed.), *Fleet Street, Press Barons and Politics: The Journals of Collin Brooks 1932–40* (London: Royal Historical Society, 1998), 250.

24. Smith, *Paper Voices*, ch. 3; *Daily Mirror*, 23 Jun. 1945, 2.

25. *Daily Mirror*, 24 Sep. 1955, 1; 8 Nov. 1955, 9; D. and E. Seymour, *A Century of News*, 110.

26. R. McKibbin, *Classes and Cultures: England 1918–1951* (Oxford: Oxford University Press, 1998), Conclusion.

27. Smith, *Paper Voices*, 146–9.

28. Beaverbrook Papers, H/152, John Gordon to Beaverbrook, 2 Oct. 1952; H/166, Max Aitken to Beaverbrook, 18 Nov. 1954.

29. Cudlipp, *At Your Peril*, 371.

30. M. Abrams, *The Newspaper Reading Public of Tomorrow* (London: Odhams Press, 1964), 57.

31. *Sun*, 15 Sep. 1964, 1; Greenslade, *Press Gang*, 156–8.

32. *Daily Mirror*, 13 Oct. 1959; H. Cudlipp, *At Your Peril*, 351, 368–9.

33. *Sun*, 18 Nov. 1969, 2; 22 Nov. 1969, 2; Lamb, *Sunrise*, 27.

34. P. Holland, 'The Page Three Girl Speaks to Women, too: A Sun-Sational Survey', *Screen*, 24/3 (1983), 101–2; P. Chippindale and C. Horrie, *Stick it up your Punter: The Uncut Story of the Sun Newspaper* (London: Simon & Schuster, 1999), 47–9.

35. S. Hall, 'The Great Moving Right Show', *Marxism Today*, Jan. 1979, 17.

36. Chippindale and Horrie, *Stick it Up Your Punter*, 147–8.

37. *Sun*, 21 Jan. 1982.

38. *Sun*, 21 Jan. 1982, 2; 22 Jan. 1982, 15; 23 Jan. 1982, 1; 29 Jan. 1982, 9; Holland, 'Page 3 Girl', 101.

39. *Sun*, 10 Jan. 1984; 19 Mar. 1984, 6.

40. *Sun*, 21 Mar. 1986, 6; 24 Mar. 1984, 2; 15 May 1984, 1; 11 Apr. 1984, 6.

41. *Daily Mirror*, 17 Mar. 1984, 2; 2 Feb. 1984, 2.

42. *Daily Mirror*, 8 Mar. 1984, 2.

43. M. Pursehouse, 'Looking at *The Sun*: Into the Nineties with a Tabloid and Its Readers', in A. Biressi and H. Nunn, *The Tabloid Culture Reader* (Maidenhead: Open University Press, 2008), 298.

44. *Sun*, 13 Aug. 2010, 12–13.

45. <http://www.theguardian.com/media/2013/dec/06/daily-mail-overtakes-sun-sales>, [accessed 24.09.2014].

46. L. Collins, 'Mail Supremacy', *New Yorker*, 2 Apr. 2012; *Daily Mail*, 17 Feb. 2011, 1; 7 Feb. 2013.

47. *Daily Mail*, 5 Feb. 2011; 24 May 2012; 26 Dec. 2012, 1; 10 May 2013.

Chapter 6: Race and Nation

1. B. Anderson, *Imagined Communities: Reflections on the Origin and Spread of Nationalism* (revised edn, London: Verso, 1991). In this book, the term 'race' is understood to have no fixed meaning, but is used to denote changing historical ideas about perceived biological differences between groups of people, especially as related to skin colour; racial language is a way of marking out power.

2. G. Wilkinson, '"The Blessings of War": The Depiction of Military Force in Edwardian Newspapers', *Journal of Contemporary History* 33/1 (1998), 98; *Daily Mirror*, 6 Oct. 1904, 3.

3. C. Kaul, 'Popular Press and Empire: Northcliffe, India and the *Daily Mail*, 1896–1922', in P. Catterall, C. Seymour-Ure and A. Smith (eds), *Northcliffe's Legacy: Aspects of the British Popular Press, 1896–1996* (Basingstoke: Macmillan, 2000), 50–3; British Library, Northcliffe Papers, Add. MS 62222, Fos. 91–2, circulars from Evelyn Wrench, 27 Aug. 1910, Nov. 1910.

4. Kaul, 'Popular Press and Empire', 52–3.

5. *Daily Express*, 26 Apr. 1900; 21 Jun. 1900.

6. D. Feldman, 'The importance of being English: Jewish immigration and the decay of liberal England', from D. Feldman and G. Stedman Jones (eds), *Metropolis London: Histories and Representations since 1800* (London: Routledge, 1989), 56; *Daily Express*, 25 Nov. 1901, cited in J. Simpson, *Unreliable Sources: How the 20th Century was Reported* (London: Macmillan, 2010), 50–1.

7. *Daily Mirror*, 4 May 1904, 4; 20 Dec. 1904, 11; Simpson, *Unreliable Sources*, 53.

8. *Daily Express*, 6 Aug. 1914, 4; British Library, Northcliffe Papers, Add MSS 62193, Northcliffe to Burton, 6 Jan. 1915; *Daily Mail*, 13 May 1915.

9. Northcliffe Papers, Marlowe to Northcliffe, 27 Nov. 1918; Northcliffe to Marlowe, 22 Apr. 1919; *Daily Mail*, 2 Dec. 1918, 4, 6.

10. L. Bland, 'White Women and Men of Colour: Miscegenation Fears in Britain after the Great War' *Gender & History* 17/1 (2005), 36; *Sunday Chronicle*, 23 Mar. 1919, 3.

11. S. Nicholas, 'From John Bull to John Citizen: Images of National Identity and Citizenship on the Wartime BBC', in R. Weight and A. Beach (eds), *The Right to Belong: Citizenship and National Identity in Britain 1930–1960* (London: I. B. Tauris, 1998).

12. *Daily Express*, 24 May 1929, 10; 25 May 1937, 11.

13. *Daily Express*, 7 Aug. 1939, 1; Gerald Barry Papers, File 9, George Buchanan to Gerald Barry, 27 Aug. 1939; *Daily Herald*, 8 May 1939, 10; Trinity College, Cambridge, Walter Layton Papers, Box 89, Fo. 37, Notes on Policy Conference No. 31, 21 Jul. 1939.

14. *Daily Express*, 4 Aug. 1939, 8; 25 Aug. 1939, 11; 30 Aug. 1939, 8; 29 Aug. 1939, 6; *Daily Mirror*, 25 Aug. 1939, 16–17; *News Chronicle*, 9 Aug. 1939, 3.

15. *Daily Mirror*, 11 May 1940, 6.

16. *Daily Mirror*, 11 Mar. 1942, 1, 5; 12 Mar. 1942, 1.

17. *Sunday Pictorial*, 11 Jul. 1943, 1, 4.

18. *Daily Express*, 23 Jun. 1948; M. Young, 'Racism, Tolerance and Identity: Responses to Black and Asian Migration into Britain in the National and Local Press, 1948–72', unpublished thesis (University of Liverpool, 2012), 167.

19. *Daily Record*, 13 Aug. 1954, 4; *Picture Post*, 30 Oct. 1954, cited in W. Webster, *Englishness and Empire: 1939–1965* (Oxford: Oxford University Press, 2005); Young, 'Racism, Tolerance and Identity', 189–93.

20. *Daily Mirror*, 3 Sep. 1958; Young, 'Racism, Tolerance and Identity', 167, 197–8;

21. Young, 'Racism, Tolerance and Identity', ch. 3.

22. Young, 'Racism, Tolerance and Identity', ch. 4; *Daily Mirror* 3 Sep. 1958.

23. Young, 'Racism, Tolerance and Identity', ch. 5; *Daily Express*, 12 Oct. 1966, 10.

24. *Daily Mirror*, 24 Apr. 1968, 17; 25 Apr. 1968, 14; C. Seymour-Ure, 'Enoch Powell's "earthquake"' in C. Seymour-Ure, *The Political Impact of Mass Media* (London, 1974); *News of the World*, 21 Apr. 1968; Young, 'Racism, Tolerance and Identity', ch. 5;

25. *Sun*, 25 Sep. 1985, 2; 15 Jan. 1982, 2; 2 Sep. 1987, 2; P. Gordon, D. Rosenberg, *Daily Racism: The Press and Black people in Britain* (London: Runnymede Trust, 1989), 3–4.

26. *Sun*, 17 Jan. 1986, 3; 7 Apr. 1988, 1; 3 Apr. 1987, 6; 10 Apr. 1987, 6; 22 Jun. 1990, 6.

27. *Sun*, 14 Jun. 1982, 2; 16 Jan. 1990, 1; 18 Jan. 1991; 19 Jan 1991, 6.

28. Beaverbrook Papers, H/ 197, Blackburn to Beaverbrook, 24 Mar. 1958; H/198, A Christiansen to Beav, 30 Jan. 1958.

29. R. Dewey, Jr., *British National Identity and Opposition to Membership of Europe 1961–3* (Manchester: Manchester University Press, 2009), 2, 41; *Daily Express*, 30 Jan. 1963, 1.

30. R. Greenslade, *Press Gang: How Newspapers Make Profits from Propaganda* (London, Macmillan: 2002), 298.
31. *Sun*, 1 Nov. 1990, 1; 24 Jun. 1996, 11; J. Tunstall, *Newspaper Power: The New National Press in Britain* (Oxford: Oxford University Press, 1996), 353.
32. *Sun*, 11 Apr. 1987, 1, 4.
33. *Sun*, 19 Jun. 1996, 34; *Daily Mirror*, 24 Jun. 1996, 1.
34. *Guardian*, 19 Jul. 2004, 7. *Sun*, 8 Oct. 2014, 1.
35. *Guardian*, 11 Aug. 2001, 10; 15 Mar. 2008, 7; R. Greenslade, *Seeking Scapegoats: The coverage of asylum in the UK press* (London: IPPR, 2005), 21; *Daily Mail*, 29 Oct. 2014, 1, 19.
36. Greenslade, *Seeking Scapegoats*, 21; *Sun*, 7 Nov. 2011, 2.

Conclusion:
The Life and Death of the Tabloid Model

1. ABC figures <http://www.theguardian.com/media/table/2014/oct/10/abcs-national-newspapers>; <http://www.theguardian.com/news/datablog/2011/jul/08/news-of-the-world-circulation-data>.
2. C. Sparks and J. Tulloch, *Tabloid Tales: Global Debates over Media Standards* (Lanham: Rowman & Littlefield, 2000).
3. B. Franklin, *Newzak and News Media* (London: Arnold, 1997), 11–12; N. Davies, *Flat Earth News* (London: Chatto & Windus, 2008), ch. 3.

Index